NATCHITOCHES COLONIALS

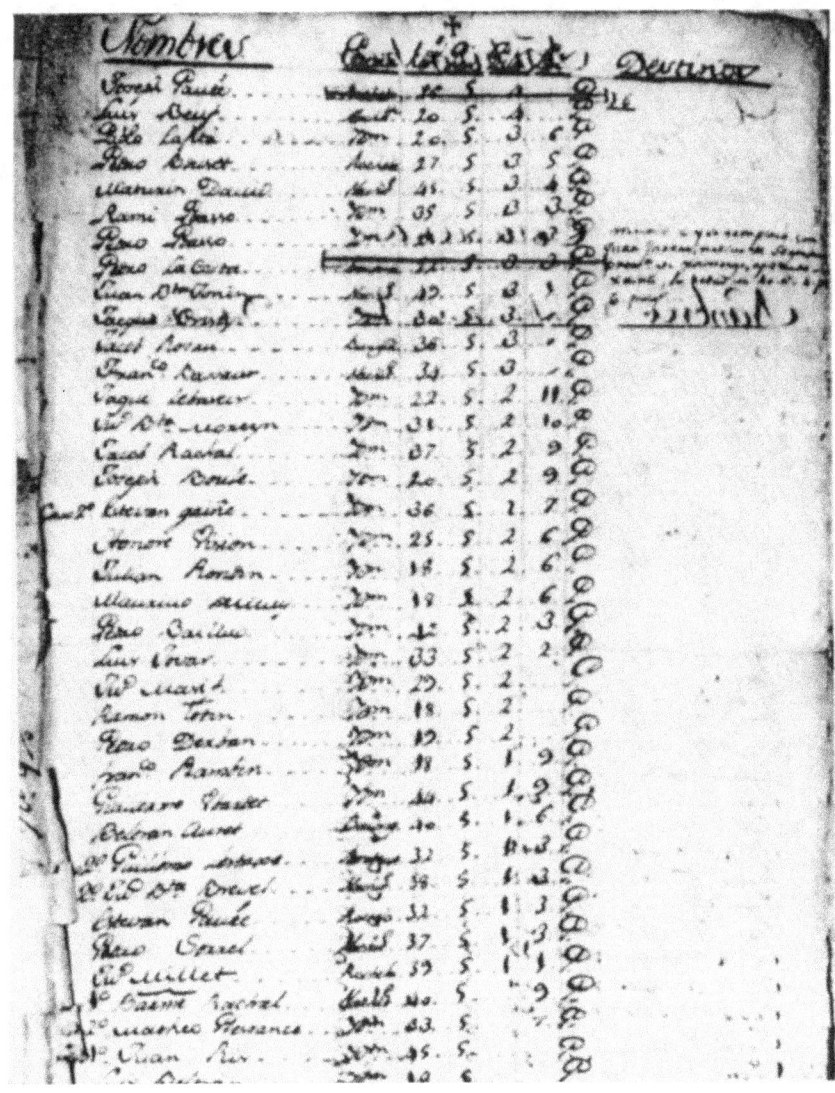

1772 Militia Roll, Natchitoches

This document, the only locally preserved roll of militiamen (civilian troops) for colonial Natchitoches, lists soldiers by height as well as by rank, age, birthplace, and term of service.

— Doc. 741, Colonial Notarial Records, Office of the Clerk of Court, Natchitoches.

NATCHITOCHES COLONIALS

A Source Book:
Censuses, Military Rolls, and Tax Lists
1722–1803

Elizabeth Shown Mills
&
Ellie Lennon

Volume 5
Cane River Creole Series

Tricentennial edition
Revised & greatly expanded
2017

Copyright 1981, 2017
Elizabeth Shown Mills
All rights reserved

ISBN 9780806320656

Published by
Genealogical Publishing Co.
Baltimore, Maryland

Cover design by Ruth Brossette Lennon
Depicting the replicated Fort St. Jean Baptiste des Natchitoches
as erected in the winter of 1717–18 by soldiers of France
Photo: compliments of Fort St. Jean Baptiste des Natchitoches

In Memory of

François (Guyon) Dion Despres Derbanne
Natchitoches' first known settler
of European extraction
&
Jeanne de la Grande Terre
his Chitimachas wife

Other volumes in this series ...

All are available from Amazon.

Vol. 1
Chauvin dit Charleville
(1976)

Vol. 2
Natchitoches, 1729–1803: Abstracts of the Catholic Church Registers of the French and Spanish Post of St. Jean Baptiste des Natchitoches in Louisiana
(1977, 2016)

Vol. 3
Tales of Old Natchitoches
(1978, 2016)

Vol. 4
Natchitoches, 1800–1826: Translated Abstracts of Register Number Five of the Catholic Church Parish of St. François des Natchitoches in Louisiana
(1980, 2016)

Vol. 6
Natchitoches Church Marriages, 1818–1850: Translated Abstracts from the Registers of St. François des Natchitoches, Louisiana
(1985, 2016)

Table of Contents

Page

Foreword	9
1722 Census of Natchitoches	14
1726 Census of Natchitoches	16
1737 Statistical Summary: Population of Natchitoches	18
1745 Troop List : Natchitoches Post	19
1752 Illinois Troop List Identifying Soldiers Detached to Natchitoches	21
1755 Muster Rolls: Garrison of Natchitoches	22
1756 Muster Rolls: Garrison of Natchitoches	28
1757 Muster Rolls: Garrison of Natchitoches	32
1758 Muster Rolls: Garrison of Natchitoches	36
1759 Muster Rolls: Garrison of Natchitoches	42
1766 French Census of Natchitoches	46
1766 Spanish Census of Natchitoches	54
1766 Census: Indian Tribes under Jurisdiction of Natchitoches	62
1769 Statistical Summary: Population of Natchitoches	63
1769 Statistical Summary: Natchitoches & Rapides	64
1772 Militia Roll of Natchitoches	66
1774 Census of Natchitoches Slaveowners	70
1774 Tax List of Natchitoches Slaveowners	76
1776 Statistical Summary: Natchitoches Post	78
1779 Roll of Militiamen Dispatched to San Antonio	79
1780 Militia Roll of Natchitoches (Revolutionary War Rosters)	80
1780 Census of Indian Allies: Natchitoches Jurisdiction	84
1782 Militia Roll of Natchitoches (Revolutionary War Rosters)	86

1783 Militia Roll of Natchitoches	89
1785 Militia Roll of Natchitoches	94
1787 Census of Natchitoches	99
1787 Militia Roll of Natchitoches	120
1788 Infantry Roll of Natchitoches: Regular Troops	125
1789 Militia Roll of Natchitoches	126
1790 Church Tax Roll of Natchitoches	132
1790 Delinquent Tax Roll of Natchitoches	141
1791 Militia Roll of Natchitoches	142
1793 Delinquent Tax Roll of Natchitoches	146
1793 Militia Roll of Natchitoches	149
1793 Tax Roll of Natchitoches Post	155
1794 Old Debts: Quarter of Isle Brevelle & Rivière aux Cannes	164
1794 Public Works Roster	165
1795 Delinquent Tax Roll: Bayou Plat through Lac Noir	173
1795 Delinquent Tax Roll: Isle Brevelle & Rivière aux Cannes	175
1795 Delinquent Tax Roll: Bayou Portage to Bayou Brevelle	177
1795 Census of Slaveholders	178
1795 Church Census (Statistical)	183
1796 Tax Roll: Grand Coast & the Town	185
1796 Church Census (Statistical)	187
1798 Church Census (Statistical)	188
1799 Church Census (Statistical)	189
1800 Church Census (Statistical)	191
1801 Church Census (Statistical; with Burials & Marriages)	192
1802 Church Census (Statistical)	196
Appendix A: Name Conversion Table	197
Appendix B: Nicknames & *Dit* Names in Colonial Natchitoches	199
Source List	202
Further Study	203
Index	206

Foreword

Historical researchers who work in the colonial period of Louisiana's history are both blessed and bedeviled. Even the most enthusiastic of them seldom anticipate the wealth of raw information that awaits the inquisitive and persistent explorer of Louisiana's past. No settlement was so remote, no family so humble, that its fortunes cannot be traced through a network of archives from Canada to Mobile, from New Orleans to Washington, from Mexico City to Seville to Paris, and in hundreds of depositories in between. Still, research into colonial Louisiana has vexations that are almost as considerable as its rewards — and too few Americans, raised as we are in an Anglo-oriented environment, are culturally prepared for the challenges inherent in any study of Latin Louisiana. Simply put, original research on colonial Louisiana requires a working knowledge of at least two foreign languages, an understanding of a unique legal system, and a familiarity with the customs and practices of an established religion that, as often as not, is different from that of the researcher.

Early in the twentieth century, scholars of the New Orleans area began the tremendous task of preparing translations, English abstracts, calendars, and indices to the various colonial archives of that region. In the decades since, others have extended this work into the hinterlands of the colony; and their tremendous efforts are making historical resources easily digestible by researchers everywhere who seek to analyze Louisiana society and to compare it with America at large.

Regrettably, the colonial outpost of St. Jean Baptiste or San Juan Bautista (as it was variously called by the French and Spanish) still remains a neglected stepchild of Louisiana history. Four years older than New Orleans itself, this northwest Louisiana settlement was not merely the first continuous settlement in all the Louisiana Purchase (as it likes to boast today), but also one of the most strategic and overburdened.

For half a century — from its inception to the day that France relinquished Louisiana to Spain — the little post of Natchitoches was woefully ill-equipped, lamentably unfortified, and manned by a motley crew of marines detached from various companies. Still, it stood as the bulwark against Spanish aggression into French Louisiana. For more than a century its jurisdiction embraced over ten thousand square miles of present Louisiana, and its power extended across modern Arkansas,

Oklahoma, and Texas. Natchitoches commandants played political chess with many of the Western Indian nations—checkmating tribal hostilities and earning almost perpetual peace for Louisiana's colonial frontier.

A study of colonial Natchitoches is also a study in international relations, not so much as it was played in the great chamber halls of Europe, and not so much as it is seen in history's famous battles, as in the day-to-day lives of those common folk whom international politics often victimized. Just fifteen miles or so from Natchitoches, well within the present bounds of Louisiana, there stood the capital of Spanish Texas, the small presidio of Nuestra Señora del Pilar de los Adaïs. For half a century, while relations between France and Spain blew hot and cold, while myriad colonial regulations forbade and restricted intercourse between the two nations, the settlers of Natchitoches and Los Adaïs coexisted in harmony, cooperated in hardship, and courted both licitly and illicitly. The dispersion and loss of so many of the colonial records generated at Los Adaïs have made the Natchitoches archives an even more valuable source for a study of the Spanish in North Louisiana.

Yet these resources have been scarcely tapped.

Our Cane River series has attemped to fill this void to some degree—translating, abstracting, and capsulizing the colonial records into convenient reference works for those who lack the time, facilities, or language skills to study the original documents. Other volumes have offered glimpses into the activities of the plain folk of Natchitoches or focused upon the intrinsically valuable registers of the Catholic Church where the lives of the rich and poor—black, red, and white—have been chronicled from baptism to burial in often barely legible French, Spanish, and Latin. This present volume embraces both civil and ecclesiastical (diocesan-level) records. The 34 documents presented in the original 1981 edition have expanded to 104. They represent every census, military roll, or tax list known to exist on colonial Natchitoches and have been gleaned from a number of archives in the United States and abroad.

The value of censuses, military rolls, and tax lists have long been recognized by researchers. However, those accustomed to working early Anglo-American records are often astounded at the degree of detail provided by comparable records in the Latin colonies. Only rarely did a colonial census of the English colonies enumerate every individual in a household by name, but a number of such detailed censuses exist for colonial Louisiana. One such census of Natchitoches is included in this volume—a priceless 1787 enumeration that identifies numerous children born during the January 1763–April 1765 and January 1770–June 1776 periods for which no baptismal records survive. Other rare items in this present collection include a five-year run of monthly military rosters for enlisted soldiers serving the frontier; a pair of militia rolls taken 1780 and 1782 that document the service of citizen-soldiers in the Gàlvez Campaigns of the American Revolution; and a 1772 militia roll that provides not only ages and birthplaces of colonial Natchitoches militiamen, but their *heights* as well!

Since its original publication in 1981 as a much smaller compilation, *Natchitoches Colonials* has served two generations of researchers: demographers, genealogists, historians, sociologists, and other students of the social sciences. Some two dozen of the documents provide excellent economic data on the ownership of land and slaves, while eight present statistics on the colony's livestock and crop production. The material added to this new edition fills significant gaps in the identification of the military and settler populations at mid-century—silently attesting the troubles of the 1750s that caused more than a few desertions. It speaks to the perseverance of the frontier fortication after French troops pulled out in the 1760s and the village of Natchitoches lost almost all its population. The numerous delinquent tax rolls of the 1790s starkly evidence the economic hardships suffered by all but a few elite, as the Spanish era drew to a close.

A few words of caution are warranted for those who are just beginning their own research. Census data of colonial Louisiana is no more (and no less) reliable then the nineteenth-century data recorded in the American states. Even within a community as small as Natchitoches, even when most of the settlers were clustered within a few miles of the post, and even when many of the settlers were interrelated and presumably most knew each other, mistakes occurred in every record.

Our detailed comparisons of each of these documents with a wealth of other existing data on every single family at the post shows a checkered record of reliabilty. Some families were omitted completely, even when their presence at the post can be documented in the same month that the census was taken. Some children were left out of the family unit to which they belonged. Some individuals were listed in more than one household in the same year. More positively, in cases involving the native-born population for whom baptismal records are available, census ages are remarkably correct.

Researchers should keep in mind that *not one of these records, nor any other any where, should be considered an absolute authority in itself.* To reliably reconstruct a human life—or a family—researchers are urged to gather as much data on each individual from as many different sources as possible; to verify published accounts against the unprocessed original records; and to form their own conclusions about identity and kinship, based on the weight of the best existing evidence that still survives.

Natchitoches researchers who are interested in families living north and west of present Natchitoches Parish should be aware that, in the colonial period, this region lay within the jurisdiction of Spanish Texas—not in Louisiana. The numerous censuses of colonial Nacogdoches, which begin in 1792 and continue until 1835, regularly enumerated French and Anglo families living east of the Sabine in present northwest Louisiana. These censuses should also be consulted by students of colonial Natchitoches.

The presentation of such a volume as this would not be possible without the assistance of many different archivists who generously shared their time and their expertise as well as their holdings. The first edition of this volume recognized the debt owed then to a number of archivists and librarians—particuarly, Carolyn M. Wells of the Northwestern State University Archives at Natchitoches and Donald MacKenzie, Director of the university's Eugene P. Watson Memorial Library; Dr. Carl A. Brasseux, Director of the Colonial Records Collection, Center for Louisiana Studies, University of Louisiana at Lafayette; Rosario Parra, Directora, Archivo General de Indias, Seville, Spain; Gary D. Jensen, Head, Thomas Jefferson Reading Room, Library of Congress, Washington, D.C.; Dr. L. Stone Miller, Director, Department of Archives, Louisiana State University, Baton Rouge; Richard M. Cochran, Assistant Archivist, The Archives of the University of Notre Dame, Indiana; Winston DeVille, FASG, the dean of Louisiana genealogy; and the Natchitoches Parish Clerk of Court, Irby L. Knotts Jr. and his efficient deputies Douglas Knotts, Eddie Gallien, and Elaine Smith—all of whom generously gave me years of assistance. To that number, we should add our gratitude to three subsequent archivists and researchers: Mary Lynn Wernet, who succeeded Carol Wells as director of the NSU Archives, and Robert de Berardinis and Mike Hilton, researchers extraordinaire, who have located for us or pointed us to some of the new documents in this volume.

—Elizabeth Shown Mills & Ellie Lennon
2017

NATCHITOCHES COLONIALS

1722 Census of Natchitoches
1 May 1722

Census of inhabitants of the Fort St. Jean Baptiste des Natchitoches, situated on Red River, by Sir. Diron, Inspector-General of the troops of the province of Louisiana, taken on the voyage that he has just made there as part of this tour, together with the number of women, children, slaves, horned cattle, and horses that are found there.

	Men	Women	Children	Negro Slaves	Indian Slaves	Horned Cattle	Horses
Monsieur de ST. DENIS, Commandant / A Frenchman in his service [Chs. Dumont]	2	0	2	5	4	0	33
Sr. DE RECLOT, Lieutenant of the Company	0	0	0	0	1	0	0
Sr. DUPUY, Ensign	0	0	0	4	0	0	0
Sr. CLAUSSEN, Half-pay Lieutenant	0	0	0	0	0	0	0
A German servant	1	0	0	0	0	0	0
Sr. DERBANE, Warehouse Keeper	1	0	3	4	3	0	8
Sr. JALLOT	1	0	0	0	0	0	1
Pierre COTOLLEAU	1	0	0	0	0	0	0
Pierre FAUSSE	1	0	0	0	0	0	0
Ives LEON	1	0	0	0	0	0	0
Fran BERRY	1	0	0	0	0	0	0
Fran LEMOINE	1	0	1	0	0	0	0
Estienne LE ROY	1	0	0	0	0	0	0
Pierre DUBOIS	1	0	0	0	0	0	0
Marianna BENOIST, wife of a soldier	0	1	0	0	0	0	0
Louise Françoise GILLOT, ditto	0	1	0	0	0	0	0

Colonies, G[1] 464, Archives Nationales d'Outre Mer, Aix-en-Provence, France; microfilmed images, Colonial Records Collection, Center for Louisiana Studies, University of Louisiana at Lafayette.

1722 Census of Natchitoches

	Men	Women	Children	Negro Slaves	Indian Slaves	Horned Cattle	Horses
Jeanne LONGUEVILLE, ditto	0	1	0	0	0	0	0
Pierre DUPUY *dit* GOUPILLON	1	1	0	0	0	0	0
Jeanne GRENOT, wife of a soldier	0	1	0	0	0	0	0
Marie Catherine DE POUTRE, ditto	0	1	0	0	0	0	0
Martine BONNET, ditto	0	1	1	0	0	0	0
Antoinette AUDEBRANDE, ditto	0	1	0	0	0	0	0
Pierre MARIONNEAU	1	0	0	3	0	0	0
Widow of deceased PIERRIER	0	1	4	3	0	12	0
Sr. DE CHAMPIGNOLE, Sergeant	0	0	0	1	0	0	0
The Natchitoches Indians have about twenty or twenty-five horses							25
	14	10	10	20	8	12	74*

All of the inhabitants contained in this enumeration, except Sr. Derbanne, Warehouse Keeper, and the one called Jallot, are former soldiers who have been discharged and who have established themselves here.

[Signed] DIRON

---

*The document apparently contains an error in the addition of this column.

1726 Census of Natchitoches
1 January 1726

General Census of the inhabitants & concessions of the colony of Louisiana ... on the first of January 1726 ... The Natchitoches [Post].

	Masters	Hired Hands	Negro Slaves	Indian Slaves	Horned Cattle	Horses	Cleared Land
M. de S^T DENIS, commandant, his wife and three children	5	2	10	0	11	50	15
Mons. de S^T DENIS, in possession of the lands of deceased Charles DUMONT on which St. Denis has ...	0	2	0	0	20	2	5
MULER and three children	4	0	2	0	2	3	5
S^T FRANCOIS & his wife, MARION & his wife, associates	4	1	0	0	0	0	5
CHAGNAU, his wife, and one child	3	1	0	0	0	0	10
LA VERGNE and his wife	2	0	0	0	0	0	6
S^T PIERRE [PRIX], soldier, his wife and two children	4	0	0	0	0	0	6
Guillaume BARBOT	1	0	0	0	0	0	2
ALORGE, PRUD'HOMME, his wife and 1 child	4	0	0	0	0	0	0
DAUPHINE and ACCAUX, Associates	2	0	0	0	0	0	4
[RACHAL *dit*] S^T DENIS, his wife and three children	5	0	0	0	0	0	3
ROLLAND	1	0	0	0	0	0	2
PREVOSTIERE, his wife and 1 child	3	0	0	0	0	0	2

Colonies G[1] 464:17–18, Archives Nationales d'Outre Mer; [transcript], Louisiana Miscellany Collection, 1724–1837, Manuscripts Division, Library of Congress, Washington, DC. "Domestics" included "Hired Hands." Land is expressed in *arpents* of frontage along the river. A French *arpent* was the equivalent of about .84 of an English acre.

1726 Census of Natchitoches

	Masters	Hired Hands	Negro Slaves	Indian Slaves	Horned Cattle	Horses	Cleared Land
MAUBEUGE	1	0	0	0	0	0	3
LA TULIPE	1	0	0	0	0	0	2
DUPIN & his wife, 2 children	4	0	0	0	0	0	2
NANTAIS, his wife & associate	3	0	0	0	0	0	5
JOLYBOIS and DUBOIS, associates	2	0	0	0	0	0	5
Nicolas PREVOST & his wife & 1 child	3	0	0	0	0	0	4
MARECHAL, his wife & 3 children	5	0	1	0	0	1	5
CHARDON and another with his wife, associates	3	0	0	0	0	0	4
CROMIR & his wife	2	0	0	0	0	0	4
DROUILLON, his wife & 1 child	3	0	0	0	0	0	6
CUSSON, POUSSET & his wife, associates	3	0	0	0	0	0	4
Jean DESANCE	1	0	0	0	0	0	6
BOQUET	1	0	0	0	0	0	8
VERGER & LA BOUCHERIE, associates	2	0	0	0	0	0	6
PIEDFERME, his wife; MEUNIER & his wife, associates	4	0	0	0	0	0	10
LE BRUN and his wife	2	0	3	0	0	0	10
ST LOUIS *dit* BLARD and his wife	2	0	0	0	0	0	6
TOTAINE, LA FONTAINE & his wife, associates	3	0	0	0	0	0	12
DUPLESSIS and TOURANGEOT, associates	2	0	1	1	0	0	15
DERBANNE, his wife & 4 children	6	0	15	2	5	16	40
People without establishments at this said place	4						
	96	6	32	3	38	72	230

1737 Statistical Summary: Population of Natchitoches
Undated

Recapitulation of the General Census of Louisiana in 1737 ...Natchitoches.

Men Capable of Bearing Arms	33
Women	27
Boys	27
Girls	25
Negro Men	50
Negro Women	24
Negro Boys	14
Negro Girls	19
Indian Males	1
Indian Females	13
Horses	225
Sheep	0
Goats	0
Horned Cattle	460
Hogs	250
Firearms	33

Colonies, C[13] C.4:197, Archives Nationales d'Outre Mer; [transcript], Library of Congress, Washington.

1745 Troop List: Natchitoches Post
Undated

Recapitulation of French Troops Stationed in Louisiana with List of the Deceased for 1744 by company.

Company of Chavois, Natchitoches

Rank	Names of Officers & Soldiers
Captain	Mr. de CHAVOIS
Lieutenant	Mr. de la HOUSSAYE
Half-pay lieutenant	Mr. de TAILLEFER
Ensign 1st class	Mr. DU CODER
Ensign 2nd class	Mr. BALLÉ (in France)
Sergeants	Claude BERTRAND *dit* Dauphine
	Pierre ALORGE *dit* St. Pierre
Corporals	Jean HORÉ *dit* Horé
	Alexis GRAPPE *dit* St. Alexis
Enspassades	Pierre HERAULT *dit* Herault
	Guillaume CHEVER *dit* Duffresne
Cadet a'*laig*te*	Le Sr. JUSSIAU
Cadet	Le Sr. ST. DENIS
	Le Sr. DE COUR [Louis Mathias LE COURT de Presle]
Drummer	Pierre RACHAL *dit* St. Denis
Riflemen	Étienne LE ROY *dit* Framboise
	Pierre OBREVILLE *dit* Rencontre
	Jean Bte BIBO *dit* La Joye
	Pierre BERNARDIN *dit* La Boute
	Joseph DUC *dit* VilleFranche
	Pierre DORÉ *dit* Sans Quartier
	Jean RACHAL *dit* St. Denis

Extracted from the colony-wide list titled "Recapitulation of French Troops Stationed in Louisiana with List of the Deceased for 1744; by Company," Doc. LO 299 (1745), Vaudreuil Papers, The Huntington Library, San Marino, California.

*Enspassade and *cadet a l'eguillette* are now defunct French military ranks for which there are no modern English equivalent.

1745 Troop List

Rank	Names of Officers & Soldiers
Riflemen (cont'd.)	Jean B^{te} DAVION *dit* St. Pierre [St. Prix]
	Dominique MONTECHE *dit* St. Dominique
	René GAUTIER *dit* La Fleur
	Pierre PRUDHOMME *dit* Sanspeur [Sampeur?]
	Jean PRUDHOMME *dit* La Jeunesse
	François DOUCET *dit* St. Eustache
	Charles TOUTIN *dit* Villeneuve
	Charles D'ARDENNE *dit* Bellerose
	Jacques Daniel MARMILLON *dit* St. Mailae
	Louis RACHAL *dit* St. Denis
	Julien DAVION *dit* L'Eveille
	François HERVÉ *dit* Hervé
	Jean? FRILLARD *dit* La Lancette

1752 Illinois Troop List
(Identifying Soldiers Detached to Natchitoches & Other Locales)
2 September 1752

Company or Unit	Names of Soldiers
Monsieurs:	
DE LA MAZILLIER, Capt.	45 officers & soldiers at Illinois 3 male habitants at Illinois 5 soldiers detached at Tunica and Natchez **1 soldier detached at Natchitoches:** Pierre RACHAL dit St. Denis, married man
DE NOYON, Capt.	35 officers & soldiers at Illinois 3 male habitants at Illinois 17 soldiers at Peoria, Ouyas & Natchez **1 soldier detached at Natchitoches:** Pierre DORE [DOLÉ] *dit* Sans Quartier, married man

DE REGIO, Capt.	38 officers & soldiers at Illinois
	2 male habitants at Illinois
	4 soldiers detached at Missouri and Natchez
	2 soldiers detached at Natchitoches:
	    Barthelemie RACHAL dit Tulippe
	    Jean Baptiste BOUTIERE dit La Rose

The full list is not being transcribed here—only the references to Natchitoches. For the full roster, which also includes the companies of Moncharveaux, de Varenne, and de la Gauvray, see Macarty to Vaudreuil, "Report on Actual Status of the Six Companies [at Illinois]," 2 September 1752; Manuscript LO 377, Vaudreuil Papers.

1755 Muster Rolls: Garrison of Natchitoches
Monsieur Deblanc, Commandant
Monthly from 1 January 1755

Company or Unit	Names of Officers & Soldiers
	Officers
	Messieurs ...
POPULUS	DE GRANDMAISON, 1st Lieutenant
"	DE MÉZIÈRES, Half-pay Lieutenant
PERRIER	Le Chr DE LA RONDE, Ensign, 1st class
No. 34	JUCHEREAU de St Denis, ditto
PERRIER	LE COURT de Prelle, Ensign, 2nd class
	Sergeants
BENOIST	Claude BERTRANT *dit* Dauphine
DUTILLET	Pierre ALORGE *dit* St Pierre
	Corporals
PERRIER	Antoine MAIGROS *dit* Bourbon
36th	Pierre HARAUD
37th	Jean HORÊ
	Alexy GRAPPE *dit* Laverdure
	Cadet a l'eguillette
DUTILLET	Le Sr MONGIN
	Drummer
CHAVOY	François LANGLOIS *dit* Sans Regret
	Riflemen
DE LA GAUVRAY	François BEAUTEMPS

Colonies D2c 51:256*ff.*, Archives Nationales d'Outre Mer; documents located and supplied by Robert D. Berardinis. The 1755 rolls were compiled monthly. The above list presents the January 1755 roll, followed by an addenda with monthly alterations.

1755 Muster Rolls

Company or Unit	Names of Soldiers
BENOIST	François DOUCET ____rgon
	Jean ROUBLET
DERNEVILLE	Henry DUBOIS *dit* Jolybois
"	Marin GRILLET
"	Claude François LA POULE
CHAVOYE	Paul BOURDELLE *dit* St Nicolas
"	Jean Bap^{te} RENAUD *dit* de Rosiers
GRANDCHAMP	Pierre DE MORTIER
PERRIER	Jean MAGNY *dit* St Jean
LATOUR	René GOUTIER *dit* La Fleur
HAZEUR	Jean SAMÜEL *dit* Lionnois
MONCHARVAUX	Pierre Sebastien PRUDHOMME *dit* La Douceur
"	Jacques TURPEAUX *dit* La France
PONTALBA	Jacques BONNEAUX
"	Jean Bap^{te} BIBO *dit* La Joye
DE MONBERAULT	Jean FAUPIED
"	Pierre CHARLY
"	Louis RACHAL *dit* Blondin
DE LA MAZILLIERE	Pierre RACHAL *dit* St Denis
DE REGGIO	Barthelemy RACHAL *dit* La Tulippe
"	Jean Bap^{te} BOUTIÉRE *dit* La Rose
DE NOYON	Pierre DORÊ *dit* Sans Quartier
DE MURAT	Guillaume CHEVERT *dit* Duffresne
"	Claude ROÜENLE *dit* Picard
"	Jean RISSE
DE VARENNES	Jean PRUDHOMME *dit* La Jeunesse
DUTILLET	Jean Bap^{te} BOULET *dit* Brindamour
"	Claude DUVERGER *dit* Joly Coeur
"	Jean DUPART *dit* Le Maigre
DE LARRÉ	Simon MANGUIN
"	Pierre MERCIER *dit* Navare
No. 35	Charle LAUNAY *dit* La Forest
No. 35	Antoine DESPREZ *dit* Pretaboire
"	Jean Bap^{te} MALBERT *dit* Sans Façon

1755 Muster Rolls

Company or Unit	Names of Soldiers
No. 36	Philippe MOUTON
"	Jean Bap^{te} Le COMPTE
No. 37	René THOMAS *dit* La Croix

I have ended the present review in presence of Monsieur Commandant, showing the quantity of two sergeants, four corporals, one cadet a l'eguillette, one drummer, and thirty-eight riflemen. This copy signed [*illegible*] at Natchitoches, the first of January 1755.

By me, PAIN

Alterations

Editor's comment:

These muster rolls were drawn up on the first of each month. Throughout the year, each monthly roll duplicated the January list, with some alterations. Soldiers were dropped and added, they changed ranks, and their names were sometimes rendered in a different way. The following list itemizes each of the changes, by month.

February:

Dit added:	François DOUCET, now *dit* St Eustache
Dit added:	Jean ROUBELET, now *dit* La Rivière
Dit added:	Marin GRILLET, now *dit* Sautrelle
Dropped:	Claude François LA POULE, "left 9 January"
Name alteration:	Jean Bap^{te} SAMÜEL *dit* Lionnois
Name alteration:	Sebastien PRUDHOMME *dit* La Douceur
Company change:	Guillaume CHEVERT *dit* Duffresne, assigned to Du Tillet's company
Company change:	Claude ROÜENLE [ROÜENLE?] *dit* Picard, ditto
Company change:	RISSE

1755 Muster Rolls: Alterations

March:
Dropped: Jean HORÉ, "Died 1st March"
Promoted: Jean Bapte RENAUD *dit* De Rosiers, promoted to corporal, 1 March, now in Chavoye's Co.
Rank change: François LANGLOIS *dit* Sans Regret, rank change from drummer to soldier
Added: Jean Christophe BÂTON, "arrived 17 Feb."

April:
Added: Jean RAISON dit Joly Cöuer, "arrived 17 March," De la Houssaye's Company

May:
Company change: Jean Bapte RENAUD *dit* Rosiers, now in Company 37
Place change: François BEAUTEMPS, sent to New Orleans, 20 April, still there 1 June; arrived Natchitoches 13 June
Place change: François LANGLOIS *dit* Sans Regret, also sent to New Orleans on 20 April, still there 1 June; arrived Natchitoches 13 June
Place change: Pierre DE MORTIER, also to New Orleans on 20 April, still there 1 June; arrived Natchitoches 13 June
Added: Philippe MOUTON, Company 36

June:
Added: Pierre Emanüel Victor DU PAIN, arrived 8 May, Derneville's Company
Added: Cesar De MAGNY, arrived 8 May, Murat's Company
Dropped: Jean Christophe BÂTON, died 31 May
Dit added: Philippe MOUTON, now *dit* Belle Fleur

July:
Rank change: DE MÉZIÈRES, half pay captain, from 1 Feb. 1754

1755 Muster Rolls: Alterations

July (cont'd)

Company change:	Le Ch^r DE LA RONDE, Ensign, 1st class, now in De Sommes' Company
Company change:	LE COURT de Prelle, ensign 2nd class, now in De Sommes' Company
Company change:	Antoine MAIGROS *dit* Bourbon, now in De Sommes' Company
Company change:	Jean MAGNY *dit* St Jean, transferred to De Sommes' Company
Company change:	Simon MONGUIN, now in De Villiers' Company
Company change:	Pierre MERCIER *dit* Maigre, now in De Villiers' Company
Dropped:	Cesar DE MAGNY, deserted 15 June
Added:	The Sieur FAZENDE, arrived 25 June, Murat's Company
Added:	Etienne GUINCHARD, arrived 25 June, De La Mazilliere's Company
Company change:	René THOMAS *dit* La Croix, transferred to De Gourdon's Company

August:

Company change:	JUCHERAUD de St Denis, 1st Lieutenant
Company change:	Jean Bap^{te} RENAUD *dit* Rosiers, now in Company 36
Rank change:	LE COURTE de Prelle, "Ensign 1st Class, since 1 February 1754"

September:

Company change:	LE COURTE de Prelle, now in Macarty's Company
Added:	Le Ch^r St DENIS, Ensign 2nd class, Marantin's Company, "at post [illegible]"
Rank Change:	FAZENDE, Ensign 2nd class, "from 1 February 1754"

1755 Muster Rolls: Alterations

September (cont.)
Rank Change: MONGIN, Ensign 2nd class, "from 1 February 1754," Mazola's Company

October:
Rank change: François LANGLOIS *dit* Sans Regret, now a rifleman

Added: Gabriel PERRON, Drummer, Company 35, arrived at the post, 12 September

December:
Dit added: Gabriel PERRON, now *dit* Sans Chagrin

1756 Muster Rolls: Garrison of Natchitoches
Monsieur Deblanc, Commandant
Monthly from 1 January 1756

Company or Unit	Names of Officers & Soldiers
	Officers
	Messieurs ...
	DE MÉZIÉRES, Captain, Half-pay
DE SOMMES	Le Che^v DE LA RONDE, Ensign 1st class
GRANDMAISON	JUCHERAUD de St. Denis, Ditto [Lt.?]
DE SOMMES	LE COURT de Prelle, Ditto
MARANTIN	Le Chevalier de ST. DENIS, Ensign 2d class
MURAT	FAZENDE, Ditto
DUTILLET	MONGIN, Ditto
	Sergeants
BENOIST	Claude BERTRANT *dit* Dauphine
DUTILLET	Pierre ALORGE *dit* St. Pierre
	Corporals
DERNEVILLE	Pierre Emanüel Victor DU PAIN
DE SOMMES	Antoine MAIGROS *dit* Bourbon
No. 36	Pierre HARAUD
"	Jean Bap^{te} RENAUD *dit* De Rosiers
No. 35	Alexy GRAPPE *dit* La Verdure
	Drummer
No. 35	Gabriel PERON *dit* La Guerre*
	Riflemen
DE MACARTY	François BEAUTEMPS

Colonies D^{2c} 51: 270 *ff.*, Archives Nationales d'Outre Mer; documents located and supplied by Robert D. Berardinis.

* In 1755 and 1757 the drummer Gabriel Perron (*var.* Peron) is clearly called *"dit* Sans Chagrin." In this one year 1756, he is just as clearly called *"dit* La Guerre."

1756 Muster Rolls

Company or Unit	Names of Officers & Soldiers
BENOIST	François DOUCET *dit* St. Eustache
DE NOYON	Jean ROUBELET *dit* La Rivière
DERNEVILLE	Henry DUBOIS *dit* Jolyboïs
"	Marin GRILLET *dit* Sautrelle
SAVOYE [CHAVOYE]	Paul BOURDELLE *dit* St. Nicolas
SAVOYE [CHAVOYE]	François LANGLOIS *dit* Sansregret
GRANDCHAMP	Pierre DE MORTIER
PERRIER	Jean MAGNY *dit* St. Jean
DE LA TOUR	René GAUTIER *dit* La Fleur
HAZEUR	Jean SAMÜEL *dit* Lionnois
DE MONCHARVAUX	Pierre Sebastien PRUDHOMME *dit* La Douceur
"	Jacques TURPEAUX *dit* La France
DE PONTALBA	Jacques BONNEAUX
"	Jean Bap^{te} BIBO *dit* La Joye
DE MONBERAULT	Jean FAUPIED
"	Pierre CHARLY
"	Louis RACHAL *dit* Blondin
LA MAZILLIERE	Pierre RACHAL *dit* St. Denis
DE REGGIO	Barthelemy RACHAL *dit* La Tulippe
"	Jean Bap^{te} BOUTIERE *dit* La Rose
DE NOYON	Pierre DORÊ *dit* Sans Quartier
DE MURAT	Guillaume CHEVERT *dit* Duffresne
"	Claude ROÜENLE *dit* Picard
"	Jean RISSE *dit* Lallemand
DE VARENNES	Jean PRUDHOMME *dit* La Jeunesse
DUTILLET	Jean Bap^{te} BOULET *dit* Brindamour
"	Claude DU VERGER *dit* Joly Coeur
"	Jean DUPART *dit* La Maigre
DE LA HOUSSAYE	Jean RASSON *dit* Joly Coeur
DE VILLIERS	Simon MANGUIN
"	Pierre MERCIER *dit* Navarre
No. 35	Charle LAUNNAY *dit* La Forest
"	Antoine DESPRES *dit* Pret a boire
"	Jean Bap^{te} MALBERT *dit* Sans facon

1756 Muster Rolls

Company or Unit	Names of Officers & Soldiers
No. 36	Philippe MOUTON *dit* Belle fleur
"	Jean Bapt^e LE COMPT
DE GOURDON	René THOMAS *dit* La Croix

I have ended the present review in the presence of Monsieur DE BLANC, Commandant, showing the quantity of two sergeants, five corporals, one drummer, thirty-eight riflemen, at Natchitoches, the 1st of January 1756.

PAIN

Alterations

Editor's comment:

These muster rolls were drawn up on the first of each month. Throughout the year, each monthly roll duplicated the January list, with some alterations. Soldiers were dropped and added, they changed ranks, and their names were sometimes rendered in a different way. The following list itemizes each of the changes, by month.

February:
Company change:	LE COURT de Prelle, now in Macarty's Co.
Dropped:	François BEAUTEMPS
Company change:	Jean MAGNY, now in Desomme's Co.

March:
Company change:	FAZENDE, now in Mazola's Co.
Company change:	MONGIN, now in Murat's Co.
Place change:	Gabriel PERRON *dit* La Guerre, "sent to New Orleans, sick, on 20 February"
Place change:	Jean Bapt^e BIBO *dit* La Joye, "sent, sick, to the city [New Orleans] on 20 February"
Name variant:	Jean RASSON, now spelled RAISON

1756 Muster Rolls: Alterations

April (cont.)
Dropped: René THOMAS dit La Croix
Company change: Alexy GRAPPE, now in De Chabert's Co. [De Chabert has apparently been put in charge of the old Co. 35]

Dropped: Antoine MAIGROS, reduced to rifleman 1 April

Name variant: Pierre DORE *dit* Sans Quartier, now spelled Sans Cartier

Name variant: Charle LAUNNAY, now spelled LAUNAY

May:
Company change: MONGIN, now in Mazola's [d'Arrazola] Co.
Place change: Pierre DE MORTIER, sent to New Orleans on 25 April

Place change: Jean Bap^{te} BOUTIERE, sent to New Orleans
Died: Pierre RACHAL *dit* St. Denis, died 19 April
Company change: Charle LAUNAY, Antoine DESPRES, and Jean Bap^{te} MALBERT, now in De Chabert's Co.

June: No changes

July:
Company change: Pierre HARAUD and Jean Baptiste RENAUD now in D'AUTRIVES' Co. [d'Autrive has apparently taken command of Co. 36]

August:
Added: Gabriel PERRON *dit* La Guerre, arrived 17 July from [New Orleans?]

Added: Jean Bap^{te} BIBO *dit* La Joye, arrived 17 July from New Orleans

September:
Added: "Le Sr. Hugues OLIVIER, Cadet Soldier, effective 1 July, arrived 18 June," De Villemont's Co.

October: No changes

November-December: Rolls not found

1757 Muster Rolls: Garrison of Natchitoches
Monsieur Deblanc, Commandant
Monthly from 1 January 1757

Company or Unit	Names of Officers & Soldiers
	Officers
	Messieurs ...
	DE MÉZIÉRES, Captain, Half-pay
DE SOMMES	Le Che^v DE LA RONDE, Ensign 1st class
GRANDMAISON	JUCHERAUD de St. Denis, Ditto
DE MACARTY	LE COURT de Prelle, Ditto
DE MARENTIN	Le Che^v [JUCHEREAU] de St. Denis, Ensign 2d
DE MURAT	FAZENDE, Ditto
DARRAZOLA	MONGIN, Ditto
	Sergeants
DUTILLET	Pierre ALORGE *dit* St. Pierre
	Corporals
DERNEVILLE	Pierre Emanüel Victor DU PAIN
DE CHABERT	Alexy GRAPPE *dit* La Verdure
D'AUTRIVES	Pierre HARAUD
"	Jean Bap^{te} RENAUD *dit* De Rosiers
	Drummer
DE CHABERT	Gabriel PERRON *dit* Sans Chagrin
	Cadet Soldiers
[Unassigned]	Le Sr. Athanaze DE MÉZIÉRES, *fils* [the son]
DE VILLEMONT	Le Sr. Hugues OLIVIER
	Riflemen
BENOIST	François DOUCET *dit* St. Eustache

Colonies D^{2c} 5: 432 *ff.*, Archives Nationales d'Outre Mer; documents located and supplied by Robert D. Berardinis.

1757 Muster Rolls

Company or Unit	Names of Officers & Soldiers
DE NOYON	Jean ROUBELET *dit* La Rivière
DERNEVILLE	Henry DUBOÏS *dit* Jolyboïs
"	Marin GRILLET *dit* Sautrelle
CHAVOYE	Paul BOURDELLE *dit* St. Nicolas
"	François LANGLOIS *dit* Sansregret
DE LA TOUR	René GAUTIER *dit* La Fleur
HAZEUR	Jean SAMÜEL *dit* Lionnois
DE MONCHARVAUX	Pierre Sebastien PRUDHOMME *dit* La Douceur
"	Jacques TURPEAUX *dit* La France
DE PONTALBA	Jacques BONNEAUX
"	Jean Bap^te BIBO *dit* La Joye
DE MONBERAULT	Jean FAUPIED
"	Pierre CHARLY
"	Louis RACHAL *dit* Blondin
DE LA HOUSSAYE	Jean RAISON *dit* Joly Coeur
DE REGGIO	Barthelemy RACHAL *dit* La Tulippe
"	Jean Bap^te BOUTIERE *dit* La Rose
DE NOYON	Pierre DORÊ *dit* Sans Quartier
DE MURAT	Guillaume CHEVERT *dit* Duffresne
"	Claude ROÜENLE *dit* Picard
"	Jean RISSE
DE VARENNES	Jean PRUDHOMME *dit* La Jeunesse
DUTILLET	Claude DU VERGER *dit* Joly Coeur
"	Jean DUPART *dit* La Maigre
"	Jean Bap^te BOULET *dit* Brindamour
DE SOMMES	Antoine MAIGROS *dit* Bourbon
"	Jean MAGNY *dit* St. Jean
DE MACARTY	François BEAUTEMPS
DE VILLIERS	Simon MANGUIN
"	Pierre MERCIER *dit* Navarre
DE CHABERT	Charle LAUNAY *dit* La Forest
"	Antoine DESPRES *dit* Pretaboire
"	Jean Bap^te MALBERT *dit* Sans facon
D'AUTRIVES	Philippe MOUTON *dit* Belle fleur
"	Jean Bap^te LE COMPTE

1757 Muster Rolls

I have ended the present review in the presence of Monsieur DE BLANC, showing the quantity of one sergeant, four corporals, one drummer, two cadet soldiers, and thirty-five riflemen, at Natchitoches, the 1st of January 1757.

PAIN

Alterations

Editor's comment:
These muster rolls were drawn up on the first of each month. Throughout the year, each monthly roll duplicated the January list, with some alterations. Soldiers were dropped and added, they changed ranks, and their names were sometimes rendered in a different way. The following list itemizes each of the changes, by month.

February:
Dropped: Jean Bap^{te} BOUTIERE *dit* La Rose
Name variant: Pierre DORE *dit* Sans Quartier now *dit* San Cartier

Name variant: Jean RISSE now *dit* L'Allemand

March: No changes

April:
Deserted: François BEAUTEMPS, "deserted to the Spaniards"

May:
Name variant: Pierre ALORGE now ALLORGE
Name variant: Alexy GRAPPE now Alexis GRAPPE
Name variant: Gabriel PERRON now PERON

June:
Company change: FAZENDE now assigned to DeSommes

1757 Muster Rolls: Alterations

July:
Dropped: Le Chev DE LA RONDE
Added: Claude CHARROIS, Sgt., Artaud's Co., arrived 21 June 1757
Rank change: Alexis GRAPPE promoted 22? Juin
Rank change: Jean PRUDHOMME *dit* La Jeunesse, Corporal as of 1 April
Company assignment: Le Sieur Athanaze DE MÉZIÉRES, *fils*, cadet, assigned to De Gourdon
Added: Le Sieur Louis DE BLANC, Cadet soldier, effective 1 January 1757
Name variant: Jean SAMÜEL *dit* Lionnois now Jean Baptiste SAMÜEL *dit* Lyonnois

August:
Name variant: Claude CHARROIS now Claude CHAROYE

September:
Added: François NEVEU, Dartaud's Co.

October:
No changes

November:
Name variant: Gabriel PERRON again called *dit* La Guerre
Added: Jean RACHAL *dit* St. Denis, Dartaud's Co.

December:
Death: Pierre ALORGE *dit* St. Pierre, died 19 Nov.

1758 Muster Rolls: Garrison of Natchitoches
Monsieur Deblanc, Commandant
Monthly from 1 January 1758*

Company or Unit	Names of Officers & Soldiers
	Officers
	Messieurs ...
	DE MÉZIÉRES, Captain, Half-pay
DE GRANDMAISON	JUCHERAUD de St. Denis, Ensign 1st class
DE MACARTY	LE COURT de Prelle, Ditto
DE MARENTIN	Le Chev de ST. DENY, Ensign 2d class
DE MURAT	FAZENDE, Ditto
DARRAZOLA	MONGIN, Ditto
	Sergeants
ARTAUD	Claude CHARROY
POPULUS	Alexis GRAPPE *dt* La Verdure
DERNEVILLE	Pierre Emanüel Victor DU PAIN "Corporal"
	Corporals
DE TRANT	Jean PRUDHOMME *dt* La Jeunesse
D'AUTRIVES	Pierre HARAUD
"	Jean Bapte RENAUD *dt* De Rosiers
DE NOYON	Jean ROUBELET *dt* La Rivière "Soldier"
	Drummer
DE CHABERT	Gabriel PERON *dt* Sans Chagrin
	Cadet Soldiers
DE GOURDON	Le Sr. Athanaze DE MÉZIÉRES
DE VILLEMONT	Hugues OLIVIER
LA TOUR	Louis DE BLANC

Colonies D2c 51:8 *ff.*, Archives Nationales d'Outre Mer; documents located and supplied by Robert D. Berardinis.

1758 Muster Rolls

Company or Unit	Names of Officers & Soldiers
	Riflemen
BENOIST	François DOUCET *d^t* St. Eustache
DERNEVILLE	Henry DUBOÏS *d^t* Jolyboïs
"	Marin GRILLET *d^t* Sautrelle
CHAVOYE	Paul BOURDELLE *d^t* St. Nicolas
LA TOUR	René GAUTIER *d^t* La Fleur
HAZEUR	Jean B^{te} SAMÜEL *d^t* Lionnois
DE MONCHARVAUX	Pierre Sebastien PRUDHOMME *d^t* La Douceur
"	Jacques TURPEAUX *d^t* La France
DE PONTALBA	Jacques BONNEAUX
"	Jean Bap^{te} BIBO *d^t* La Joye
DE MONBERAULT	Jean FAUPIED
"	Pierre CHARLY
"	Louis RACHAL *d^t* Blondin
LA HOUSSAYE	Jean RAISON *d^t* Joly Coeur
DE MAZILLIERS	Estienne GUINCHARD, "arrived at the post 4[?] December 1757
REGGIO	Barthelemy RACHAL *d^t* La Tulippe
NOYON	Pierre DORÊ *d^t* Sans Quartier
DE MURAT	Guillaume CHEVERT *d^t* Duffresne
"	Claude ROÜENLE *d^t* Picard
"	Jean RISSE *d^t* L'ALLEMAND
DUTILLET	Claude DU VERGER *d^t* Joly Coeur
"	Jean DUPART *d^t* La Maigre
"	Jean Bap^{te} BOULET *d^t* Brindamour
DE SOMMES	Antoine MAIGROS *d^t* Bourbon
"	Jean MAGNY *d^t* St. Jean
DE VILLIERS	Simon MANGUIN
"	Pierre MERCIER *d^t* Navarre
CHABERT	Charle LAUNAY *d^t* La Forest
"	Antoine DESPRES *d^t* Pretaboire
"	Jean Bap^{te} MALBERT *d^t* Sans facon
D'AUTRIVES	Philippe MOUTON *d^t* Bellefleur
"	Jean Bap^{te} LE COMPTE

1758 Muster Rolls

Company or Unit	Names of Officers & Soldiers
ARTAUD	François NEVEU
"	Jean RACHAL d^t St. Denis

I have ended the present review in the presence of Monsieur DE BLANC, Commandant, showing the quantity of three sergeants, four corporals, one drummer, three cadet soldiers, and thirty-five riflemen, at Natchitoches, the 1st of January 1758. A copy has been signed by PAIN and Mons. DE BLANC.

PAIN

Alterations

Editor's comment:
These muster rolls were drawn up on the first of each month. Throughout the year, each monthly roll duplicated the January list, with some alterations. Soldiers were dropped and added, they changed ranks, and their names were sometimes rendered in a different way. The following list itemizes each of the changes, by month.

February:
Company change: Jean ROUBELET *dit* Larivière, now in Dorgon's Co.

March:
Death: Jacques BONNEAUX, died 13 February

April:
Dropped: Claude CHARROY, Sergt.
Company change: Pierre Emanüel Victor DU PAIN, now assigned to Dutillet

1758 Muster Rolls: Alterations

May:
Dropped: Hugues OLIVIER, Cadet soldier

June:
Rank change: Jean ROUBELET d^t La Rivière, "received Sergeant on 25 May"
Rank change: Jean Bapt^e LE COMPTE, "received Corporal, 25 May"

July:
Company change: Jean Bapt^e LE COMPTE, now assigned to Detrant
Dropped: René GAUTIER d^t La Fleur
Deserted: Jean FAUPIED, "deserted 19 June"
Deserted: Jean RACHAL d^t St. Denis, "deserted 24 June"

August:
Added: Le Sieur Caesaire Marie DE MÉZIÉRES, "effective 1 May last," assigned to Grandpres' Co.
Added: Le Sieur Jacques FAZENDE, "arrived at the post, 25 July," De Varennes' Co.
Added: Le Sieur François Daniel Pain, "effective 1 May[?]," no company assigned
Deserted: Jean Bapt^{te} BIBO d^t La Joye, "deserted 1 Aug."
Deserted: Pierre CHARLY, "deserted 1 August"
Added: Antoine VACOCÛ, De la Mazilliere's Co.
Deserted: Claude DU VERGER *dit* Joly Coeur, "deserted 1 August"
Deserted: Antoine DESPRES d^t Pretaboire, "deserted 1 August"
Added: Jean Bapt^{te} EGARD, "enlisted 1 August"

September:
Died: Jean DUPART *dit* Le Maigre, "died 7 Aug."

1758 Muster Rolls: Alterations

October:
Company change:	Jean ROUBELET *dit* Larivière, now in Artaud's Co.
Dropped:	Jean RAISON *d^t* Joly Coeur

November:
Name variant:	Le Sieur Caesaire Marie DE MÉZIÉRES is called "the younger"
Name variant:	Le Sieur Jacques Fazende is called "the younger"
Dropped:	Simon MANGUIN

December:
Name variant:	Ensign FAZENDE is called "the elder"
Note added:	Le Sieur Athanaze DE MÉZIÉRES, the older [son], cadet soldier "by memoir"
Note added:	"Le Sieur Louis DEBLANC, cadet soldier "by memoir"
Note added:	Le Sieur Cesaire Marie DE MÉZIÉRES, the younger, cadet soldier "by memoir"
Note added:	Le Sieur Jacques FAZENDE, the younger, cadet soldier "by service"
Note added:	Le Sieur François Daniel Pain, cadet soldier "by memoire"
Added:	François FLAMIER, "arrived at the post, 4 December, coming from *La Ville* [New Orleans], Dorgon's Co.
Added:	Antoine GERARD *dit* Printems, De Grandpre's Co., "Deserted at Illinois [returned by] Spaniards, 1 December"
Added:	Jean JAMBERT *dit* Champagne, De Reggio's Co., "Deserted at Illinois, returned by Spaniards, 1 December"
Added:	Pierre ST. AIGNE, De MaCarty's Co., "deserted at Illinois, returned by Spaniards, 1 December"

1758 Muster Rolls: Alterations

Added: Jacques BUNEL, [de] Trant's Co., "arrived at this post 4 December, coming from [edge of paper not filmed]

1759 Muster Rolls: Garrison of Natchitoches
Monsieur Deblanc, Commandant
Monthly from 1 January 1759

Company or Unit	Names of Officers & Soldiers
	Officers
	Messieurs ...
	DE MÉZIÉRES, Captain, Half-pay
DE GRANDMAISON	JUCHERAUD de St. Denis, Ensign 1st class
DE MACARTY	LE COURT de Prelle, Ditto
DE MARENTIN	Le Ch^{vr} de ST. DENIS, Ensign 2d class
DE MURAT	FAZENDE, the elder, Ditto
	Sergeants
POPULUS	Alexy GRAPPE *dit* Laverdure
DUTILLET	Pierre Emanüel Victor DU PAIN
DARTAUD	Jean B^{te} ROUBLET
	Corporals
D'AUTRIVES	Pierre HARAUD
"	Jean Bap^{te} RENAUD *dit* Derosiers
DE TRANT	Jean PRUDHOMME *dit* La Jeunesse
[no company assigned]	Jean Bap^{te} LE COMPTE
	Drummer
DE CHABERT	Gabriel PERRON *dit* Sans Chagrin
	Cadet Soldiers
DE GOURDON	Le Sieur Athanaze DE MÉZIÉRES, the elder
DE LA TOUR	Le Sieur Louis DE BLANC
DE GRANDPRES	Le Sieur Cesaire Marie DE MÉZIÉRES, the younger
DES VARENNES	Le Sieur Jacques FAZENDE, the younger

Colonies D^{2c} 52:113 *ff.*, Archives Nationales d'Outre Mer; documents located and supplied by Robert D. Berardinis.

1759 Muster Rolls

Company or Unit	Names of Officers & Soldiers
[no company assigned]	Le Sr François Daniel PAIN
" " "	Le Sr Louis PAIN "to commence this 1 Jan."
	Riflemen
DE BENOIST	François DOUCET *dit* St Eustache
DERNEVILLE	Henry DUBOÏS *dit* Jolyboïs
"	Marin GRILLET *dit* Sautrelle
DORGON	François FLAMIER
DE CHAVOYE	Paul BOURDELLE *dit* St. Nicolas
"	François LANGLOIS *dit* Sansregret
D'HAZEUR	Jean B^{te} SAMÜEL *dit* Lionnois
DE GRANDPRES	Antoine GIRARD *dit* Printemps
DE MONCHARVAUX	Pierre Sebastien PRUDHOMME *dit* La Douceur
"	Jacques TURPEAUX *dit* La France
DE MONBERAULT	Louis RACHAL *dit* Blondin
DE MAZILLIERS	Etienne GUISCHARD
"	Antoine VACOCÛ
DE REGGIO	Barthelemy RACHAL *dit* La Tulippe
"	Jean JAMBART *dit* Champagne
DE NOYON	Pierre DORÊ *dit* Sans Cartier
DE MURAT	Guillaume CHEVERT *dit* Duffresne
"	Claude ROÜENLE [ROÜENCE?] *dit* Picard
"	Jean RISSE *dit* L'Allemand
DE MACARTY	Pierre ST. AIGNE
DE TRANT	Jacques BUNEL
DUTILLET	Jean Bap^{te} BOULET *dit* Brindamour
DE SOMMES	Antoine MAIGROS *dit* Bourbon
"	Jean MAGNY *dit* St. Jean
DE VILLIERS	Pierre MERCIER *dit* Navarre
CHABERT	Charle LAUNAY *dit* La Forest
"	Jean Bap^{te} MALBERT *dit* Sans façon
D'AUTRIVES	Philippe MOUTON *dit* Bellefleur
DARTAUD	François NEVEU
"	Nicolas BRAGNARD
"	Jean Bap^{te} EGARD

1759 Muster Rolls: Alterations

I have ended the present review in the presence of Monsieur De Blanc, Commandant, showing the quantity of three sergeants, four corporals, one drummer, six cadet soldiers, and thirty riflemen, at Natchitoches, the 1st of January 1759. This copy conforms to the original.

PAIN

Alterations

Editor's comment:
These muster rolls were drawn up on the first of each month. Throughout the year, each monthly roll duplicated the January list, with some alterations. Soldiers were dropped and added, they changed ranks, and their names were sometimes rendered in a different way. The following list itemizes each of the changes, by month.

January-February
Name alteration: The name of sergeant "Jean ROUBELET *dit* Larivière" is lined through and replaced by "Jean B^{te} Roublet"

February:
Name alteration: Le Sieur François Daniel PAIN is called "the elder"

Name alteration: Le Sieur Louis PAIN is called "the younger"

March:
Name alteration: "Jean B^{te} Roublet" is again "Jean ROUBELET *dit* Larivière"

Dit added: Jacques BUNEL, *dit* Normand
Added: Pierre DUBOÏS *dit* St. Pierre, "Returned from Adays 11[?] February"

April:
Dropped François FLAMIER

1759 Muster Rolls: Alterations

May:
Rank change: Gabriel PERRON *dit* Sans Chagrin is reduced to rifleman as of 1 April
Added: François LANGLOIS *dit* Sansregret, drummer, beginning 1 April
Dropped: Antoine GIRARD *dit* Printemps
Dropped: Pierre DUBOÏS *dit* St. Pierre, "deserted 17 April"

June:
Company assignment: Jean Bap^te LE COMPTE, assigned to Derneville's Company

July:
Company assignment: Le Sr François Daniel PAIN, assigned to Des Varennes

September:
Note under "cadets" Le S^r Le Doux "to arrive 16 October"?
Dropped: Paul BOURDELLE *dit* St. Nicolas
Note under "riflemen" Jacques LECOUR "from 1 October"

October:
Added: Le Sr LEDOUX, Cadet "arrived 16th of the month at this post," De Reggio's Company
Added "Jacques LACOUR frater" arrived 1 October, De La Gautrie's Company

December:
Added: "LE DOUX, Lieutenant, 1st class," De Reggio's Company (Le Sieur LE DOUX" still appears as a "cadet soldier," also in De Reggio's Company

1766 French Census of Natchitoches
27 January 1766

	Married Men & Widowers	Married Women & Widows	Boys	Girls	Free Male Halfbreeds	Free Female Halfbreeds	Free Female Indians	Free Male Mulattoes
Monsieur de la PERRIER, Commandant	0	0	0	0	3	3	1	0
Sr. Daniel PAIN, Subdelegate	1	1	2	4	0	0	0	1
Mr. DEMÉZIÈRES, Half-pay Captain	1	1	5	1	1	0	0	0
Mr. LECOURT DE PRELLE, Half-pay Ensign	1	0	1	0	0	0	0	0
Mrs FAZENDE, brothers, Half-pay Ensigns	0	0	2	0	0	0	0	0
Mr. BORME, Captain of the Militia	1	1	2	1	0	0	0	0
Mr. POISSOT, Lieutenant of the Militia	1	1	1	0	0	0	0	0
Sr. DUPAIN, Ensign & Aide-Major "	1	1	0	1	0	0	0	0
Srs St. DENIS, brothers, inhabitants	1	1	1	0	1	0	0	0
Jean Bapte DUBOIS	1	1	4	3	0	0	0	0
Jean Bapte DUPRES	1	1	1	0	0	0	0	0
Remis POISOT, bachelor	0	0	1	0	0	0	0	0
Joseph DUPRES	1	1	3	2	0	0	0	0
Joseph LATTIER	1	1	1	3	0	0	0	0
JEANNOT, free mulatto, trader	0	0	0	0	0	0	0	1
Charles LEMOINE	1	1	2	1	0	0	0	0
Mathurin DAVID, bachelor, hunter	0	0	1	0	0	0	0	0
Marin GRILLET	1	1	1	4	0	0	0	0
Bapte BREVEL	1	1	0	2	0	0	0	0

Vol. 91, Ramo de Historia, Archivo General de la Nación, Mexico City; imaged as part of Archivo General de la Nacion, microfilm collection, reel 57, University of Texas Archives, Austin.

1766 French Census of Natchitoches

Negro Men Slaves	Negro Women Slaves	Negro Boy Slaves	Negro Girl Slaves	Mulatto Male Slaves	Mulatto Female Slaves	Indian Male Slaves	Indian Female Slaves	Firearms	Sidearms	Horned Cattle	Horses, Mares, etc	Pigs	Sheep	Pounds of Tobacco (in twists)	Barrels of Corn (on the ear)	Barrels of Beans of Different Kinds
1	0	0	0	0	0	0	0	2	2	0	0	0	0	0	0	0
7	7	3	3	1	0	2	3	10	5	50	25	18	60	6000	180	18
14	9	1	5	1	1	2	2	4	3	100	30	50	60	10000	400	50
4	1	2	0	0	0	2	2	4	2	30	12	15	0	3000	80	15
3	1	0	2	0	1	0	0	3	2	6	4	10	0	1000	50	8
1	2	0	0	0	0	0	2	4	2	50	50	8	0	0	0	0
7	5	2	3	1	0	0	0	3	1	35	12	12	0	4000	100	20
2	0	0	0	0	0	0	0	2	1	15	2	10	0	1000	50	6
7	2	0	0	1	1	0	0	4	2	150	100	60	30	2500	100	10
4	1	0	0	0	0	0	0	5	0	30	10	20	0	2860	60	8
2	2	0	0	0	0	0	0	2	0	8	10	6	0	2000	35	2
1	1	0	0	0	0	0	0	2	0	6	5	4	0	1000	30	2
1	1	0	0	0	0	0	0	2	0	5	6	5	0	1000	28	2
0	0	0	0	0	0	0	0	1	0	1	2	4	0	600	25	2
0	1	0	0	0	0	0	0	1	0	0	2	3	0	0	0	0
1	0	0	0	0	0	0	0	1	0	0	0	0	0	600	25	2
0	0	0	0	0	0	0	0	2	0	0	6	0	0	0	0	0
2	1	0	0	0	0	0	0	1	0	15	4	10	0	1500	45	4
0	0	0	0	0	0	0	0	2	0	10	12	6	0	800	30	0

1766 French Census of Natchitoches

	Married Men & Widowers	Married Women & Widows	Boys	Girls	Free Male Halfbreeds	Free Female Halfbreeds	Free Female Indians	Free Male Mulattoes
Jean Bap^{te} MALBERT	1	1	1	3	0	0	0	0
Robert DUPRES	1	1	0	0	0	0	0	0
Widow LE DUC	0	1	1	2	0	0	0	1
Gabriel BUARD	1	1	2	7	0	0	0	0
Pierre BADIN	1	1	0	0	0	0	0	0
Barthelemy RACHAL	1	1	2	1	0	0	0	0
Jacques RACHAL	1	1	0	1	0	0	0	0
Ignace ANTY, shoemaker	1	1	2	0	0	0	0	0
François CARLES, widower	1	0	0	0	0	0	0	0
Jean Bap^{te} LABERRY	1	1	3	4	0	0	0	0
Rev. Father STANISLAS, curate of post								
Gaspard DERBANNE, widower & his sister-in-law	1	0	0	0	0	0	0	0
Joseph & Etienne VERGER, brothers, bachelors	1	1	3	0	0	0	0	0
Jean LAMBRE	0	0	2	0	0	0	0	0
Dominique MONTECHE	1	1	1	2	0	0	0	0
Widow of Pierre DOLE	1	1	1	0	0	0	0	0
Jean RISSE	0	1	1	0	0	0	1	1
Jean Bap^{te} LECOMTE	1	1	1	2	0	0	0	0
Louis RACHAL	1	1	4	1	0	0	0	0
Pierre VALENTIN, bachelor & servant	0	0	1	0	0	0	0	0
PRETABOIRE, bachelor & servant	0	0	1	0	0	0	0	0
Manuel SOTTO	1	1	3	3	0	0	0	0
François LANGLOIS, bailiff	1	1	1	1	0	0	0	0

1766 French Census of Natchitoches

Negro Men Slaves	Negro Women Slaves	Negro Boy Slaves	Negro Girl Slaves	Mulatto Male Slaves	Mulatto Female Slaves	Indian Male Slaves	Indian Female Slaves	Firearms	Sidearms	Horned Cattle	Horses, Mares, etc	Pigs	Sheep	Pounds of Tobacco (in twists)	Barrels of Corn (on the ear)	Barrels of Beans of Different Kinds
0	0	0	0	0	0	0	0	1	0	2	1	4	0	600	24	4
1	1	0	0	0	0	0	0	1	0	6	4	4	0	1000	36	2
0	0	0	0	0	0	0	0	1	0	0	0	0	0	0	0	0
3	3	3	5	0	0	0	0	2	1	40	12	10	0	3500	50	6
1	0	0	0	0	0	1	0	2	0	3	1	8	0	900	30	2
0	0	0	0	0	0	0	0	1	0	6	3	8	0	800	26	?
0	0	0	0	0	0	0	0	1	0	0	2	4	0	700	20	?
1	1	0	0	0	0	0	0	1	0	10	6	8	0	0	60	?
0	0	0	0	0	0	0	0	1	0	4	0	4	0	400	15	?
1	2	0	1	0	1	1	0	1	0	8	6	8	0	1500	30	?
1	0	0	0	0	0	0	0	0	0	0	0	0	0	0	0	?
2	0	0	0	0	0	0	0	2	0	6	6	8	0	2000	30	30
0	0	0	0	0	0	0	0	2	0	4	6	0	0	1000	20	1
1	0	0	0	0	0	0	1	1	0	20	3	10	0	1600	35	3
1	1	2	0	0	0	0	1	1	1	12	2	12	7	1500	30	1
0	0	0	0	0	0	0	0	1	0	0	0	0	0	0	0	0
0	0	0	0	0	0	0	0	1	0	5	3	6	0	500	15	2
0	1	0	2	0	0	0	0	1	0	8	4	8	0	2000	35	0
0	1	1	0	0	0	0	2	2	0	6	4	10	0	1000	40	6
0	0	0	0	0	0	0	0	1	0	0	0	6	0	2000	30	0
0	0	0	0	0	0	0	0	1	0	0	0	4	0	1000	15	0
1	4	2	4	0	0	0	0	1	0	10	2	6	0	0	0	0
0	0	0	0	0	0	0	0	1	0	0	0	2	0	0	0	0

1766 French Census of Natchitoches

	Married Men & Widowers	Married Women & Widows	Boys	Girls	Free Male Halfbreeds	Free Female Halfbreeds	Free Female Indians	Free Male Mulattoes
Widow BOURDELLE	0	1	1	0	0	0	0	0
M. de SAINTALETTE, merchant	0	0	2	0	1	0	0	0
M. MESNARD, merchant	0	0	1	0	0	0	0	0
André RAMBIN	1	1	2	2	0	0	0	0
Sr CHARBONNET, merchant	0	0	1	0	0	0	0	0
Widow ALORGE	0	1	3	0	0	0	0	0
Sr SURRIRAY, merchant	0	0	1	0	0	0	0	0
S^r DE LA BARRIERE, merchant	0	0	1	0	0	0	0	0
Sr PAVIE, merchant	0	0	1	0	0	0	0	0
Charles LARENAUDIERE	1	1	2	3	0	0	0	0
Jacques NAIGLE, blacksmith	1	1	0	0	0	0	0	0
Joseph LAURENT, gunsmith & bachelor	0	0	1	0	0	0	0	0
Pierre SAURELLE, blacksmith	1	1	2	1	0	0	0	0
Pierre BAILLIO	1	1	0	1	0	0	0	0
Louis LAMALATIE, Widower	1	0	1	1	0	0	0	0
Jacques LAMBRE	1	1	1	1	0	0	0	0
François LEVASSEUR	1	1	0	0	0	0	0	0
Henry TRICHEL, Widower	1	0	3	0	0	0	0	0
Widow RONDIN	0	1	2	2	0	0	0	0
Louis RONDIN	1	1	1	0	0	0	0	0
Louis LE CLERC	1	1	0	0	0	0	0	0
Pierre DERBANNE	1	1	4	2	0	0	0	0
Jean Bap^{te} DAVION	1	1	3	2	0	0	0	0

1766 French Census of Natchitoches

Negro Men Slaves	Negro Women Slaves	Negro Boy Slaves	Negro Girl Slaves	Mulatto Male Slaves	Mulatto Female Slaves	Indian Male Slaves	Indian Female Slaves	Firearms	Sidearms	Horned Cattle	Horses, Mares, etc	Pigs	Sheep	Pounds of Tobacco (in twists)	Barrels of Corn (on the ear)	Barrels of Beans of Different Kinds
0	0	0	0	0	0	0	0	2	1	15	6	2	0	0	0	0
0	1	0	0	0	0	0	0	2	1	0	1	6	0	0	0	0
1	0	0	0	0	0	0	0	1	0	35	100	5	0	0	0	0
0	0	0	0	0	0	1	1	2	0	2	3	6	0	0	0	0
2	1	0	0	0	0	0	0	1	1	0	0	0	0	0	0	0
0	0	0	0	0	0	0	0	3	0	12	6	15	0	1000	25	2
0	0	0	0	0	0	0	0	1	1	0	0	0	0	0	0	0
0	0	0	0	0	0	0	0	1	1	0	0	0	0	0	0	0
0	0	0	0	0	0	0	0	1	0	0	0	0	0	0	0	0
0	0	0	0	0	0	0	0	3	0	6	3	10	0	600	26	2
0	0	0	0	0	0	0	0	1	0	0	0	4	0	0	0	0
1	0	0	0	0	0	1	2	2	1	0	1	4	0	0	0	0
1	0	0	0	0	0	0	0	1	0	4	1	4	0	0	0	0
0	0	0	0	0	0	0	0	1	0	0	0	5	0	400	12	?
0	0	0	0	0	0	0	0	2	1	6	8	6	0	700	?	?
3	2	1	0	1	0	0	1	1	0	6	1	8	0	3000	50	?
0	0	0	0	0	0	0	0	1	0	4	1	4	0	600	20	?
5	5	2	1	0	0	0	0	4	1	35	20	12	0	4000	100	?
0	0	0	0	0	0	0	0	1	0	0	3	2	0	0	0	0
0	0	0	0	0	0	0	0	1	0	0	1	0	0	0	0	0
2	2	0	0	0	0	0	0	1	0	0	0	4	0	1000	30	2
3	4	4	5	2	1	0	0	2	0	18	12	8	0	2000	45	6
2	0	0	0	0	0	0	0	2	0	20	4	8	0	2000	30	2

1766 French Census of Natchitoches

	Married Men & Widowers	Married Women & Widows	Boys	Girls	Free Male Halfbreeds	Free Female Halfbreeds	Free Female Indians	Free Male Mulattoes
Jean PREVAU, carpenter	1	1	1	1	0	0	0	0
Jean MORIN, wheelwright	1	1	1	0	0	0	0	0
François CHAIGNEAU	1	1	2	3	0	0	0	0
Pierre VILLEDEQUE *dit* Perrau	1	1	3	3	0	0	0	0
Jean CHAIGNEAU & associate	1	1	1	0	0	0	0	0
Alexis GRAPPE	1	1	4	5	0	0	0	0
Pierre PRUDHOMME, wid'r & LALANDE	1	0	1	0	0	0	0	0
Sebastien PRUDHOMME	1	1	2	3	0	0	0	0
Pierre GOUTIERE	1	1	3	2	0	0	0	0
Antoine VASTCOCU	1	1	2	2	0	0	0	0
ANDRE and NAVARRE, bachelors	0	0	2	0	0	0	0	0
Guillaume CHEVER, wid'r & LIONNOIS	1	0	1	0	0	0	0	0
Total	55	54	[115] 125	84	6	3	2	4

Note:
Subtotals on the original document indicate that errors were made while tallying

1766 French Census of Natchitoches

Negro Men Slaves	Negro Women Slaves	Negro Boy Slaves	Negro Girl Slaves	Mulatto Male Slaves	Mulatto Female Slaves	Indian Male Slaves	Indian Female Slaves	Firearms	Sidearms	Horned Cattle	Horses, Mares, etc.	Pigs	Sheep	Pounds of Tobacco (in twists)	Barrels of Corn (on the ear)	Barrels of Beans of Different Kinds
1	1	1	1	0	0	0	1	1	0	10	4	6	0	0	0	0
0	0	0	0	0	0	0	0	1	0	6	2	4	0	0	0	0
0	0	0	0	0	0	0	0	2	0	10	4	10	0	700	20	6
0	0	0	0	0	0	0	0	1	0	6	2	8	0	0	0	0
0	0	0	0	0	0	0	0	2	0	0	0	0	0	0	0	0
3	3	3	4	2	1	0	1	5	0	15	15	14	0	3000	60	6
0	0	0	0	0	0	0	0	2	0	30	12	20	0	1000	40	2
0	0	0	0	0	0	1	0	2	0	10	6	12	0	800	28	3
0	0	0	0	0	0	0	0	2	0	0	4	0	0	0	0	0
0	0	0	0	0	0	0	0	1	0	0	2	8	0	400	12	?
0	0	0	0	0	0	0	0	2	0	0	2	10	0	1500	25	4
0	0	0	0	0	0	0	0	2	0	0	0	12	0	1800	40	3
										[911]				[84360]		
94	67	27	36	9	6	11	19	142	30	914	581	597	157	83360	2359	258

three columns. The correct totals of these columns are shown in brackets.

1766 Spanish Census of Natchitoches
6 May 1766

Census and List of Militiamen and Inhabitants of the Post of Natchitoches, according to the Review made on 5 May 1766 — Borme's Company

	Men Bearing Arms	Women	Older Boys	Older Girls	Boys	Girls
Mr de la PERRIERE, Commandant	0	0	0	0	0	0
PAIN, Warehouse Keeper & Subdelegate	1	1	0	0	2	4
Juan Luis BORME, Militia Captain	1	1	0	1	2	0
POISSOT, Lieutenant of the Militia	2	1	1	0	1	0
PAIN, Ensign and Aide-Major of Militia	1	1	0	0	0	1
Rev. Father STANISLAS, Capucin	1	0	0	0	0	0
DE MESSIERES, Captain of the Infantry	2	2	0	0	5	1
LE COURT DE PRELLE, Ensign of Infantry	1	0	0	0	0	0
DE SN. DENIS, the elder	1	1	0	0	0	0
DE SN. DENIS, the bachelor	1	0	0	0	0	0
The two brothers FAZENDE	2	0	0	0	0	0
J^{no} Bapt^a PRUDHOMME, Captain of Militia	1	1	0	0	2	1
BONNAFONS, Physician	1	0	0	0	0	0
MONTECHE, 1st Lieut. of Militia	2	1	1	0	0	0
TRICHELE, Churchwarden	4	0	3	0	0	0
SAINTELETTE, bachelor and merchant	1	0	0	0	0	0
The brothers CHARBONNET	2	0	0	0	0	0
MESNARD	1	0	0	0	0	0
PISSARAU, merchant	1	1	0	0	1	1
Estevan PAVIA	1	0	0	0	0	0

Legajo (bundle) 2585, Audencia de Santo Domingo, Archivo General de Indias, Seville (hereinafter ASD-AGI); microfilmed images, Colonial Records Collection, Center for Louisiana Studies, University of Louisiana at Lafayette.

1766 Spanish Census of Natchitoches

	Slaves	Land (Arpents of Frontage)	Horses	Cattle	Hogs and Sheep	Guns
PERRIERE	1	0	0	0	0	0
PAIN, Warehouse Keeper	21	40	30	60	75	12
BORME	3	30	60	70	10	3
POISSOT	17	50	8	30	20	5
PAIN, Ensign	2	12	2	14	10	2
Rev. Father STANISLAS	3	0	0	100	2	1
De MESSIERES	37	150	50	30	60	14
LE COURT	5	30	15	200	20	5
DE SN. DENIS, elder	11	40	50	0	90	6
DE SN. DENIS, bachelor	1	0	0	15	0	0
FAZENDE	6	0	6	15	12	4
J.B. PRUDHOMME	2	9	6	0	10	2
BONNAFONS	4	0	0	13	0	2
MONTECHE	5	20	3	36	8	3
TRICHELE	10	25	6	0	12	6
SAINTELETTE	1	0	0	0	15	2
CHARBONNET	4	0	0	20	0	2
MESNARD	0	0	20	9	19	3
PISSARAU	3	0	10	0	14	?
PAVIA	0	0	3	0	2	?

1766 Spanish Census of Natchitoches

	Men Bearing Arms	Women	Older Boys	Older Girls	Boys	Girls
Partners POEYFARRE & JURINNY [Jougny]	2	0	0	0	0	0
[Denis] MELMIES & MOTAR (?), partners	2	0	0	0	0	0
BRUMEAUX & RENAUD, partners	2	0	0	0	0	?0
BOSQUE[?] & Gaspard FIOLE	2	0	0	0	0	0
Pedro [Pierre] BAILLIO	1	1	0	0	0	1
Juan Baptista DUBOIS	2	1	1	0	2	2
Juan Baptista DUPRES	1	1	0	0	1	0
Jph. DUPRES	1	1	0	0	2	2
Juan Baptista BREVEL	1	1	0	0	0	3
Carlos [Charles] LEMOINE	1	1	0	0	2	1
Remigio [Remy] POISSOT	1	0	0	0	0	0
Gabriel BUARD	2	1	1	3	1	4
Marin GRILLET	1	1	0	0	0	5
Mathurin DAVID	1	0	0	0	0	0
Joseph LATTIER, Corporal of the Troops	1	1	0	0	1	3
Robert DUPRES	1	1	0	0	0	1
Widow LE DUC	1	1	1	0	1	0
Pedro BADIN	1	1	0	0	0	0
Bartholome RACHAL	1	1	0	0	2	0
Santhiago [Jacques] RACHAL	1	1	0	0	0	1
Juan Baptista LECONTE	1	1	0	0	1	2
Widow BARRANCO	0	1	0	1	0	1
Vincent POIRIER	1	1	0	0	1	0
Luis RACHAL	1	1	0	0	4	1
Miguel [Michel] ROBIN	1	0	0	0	0	0
Juan CHEDHOME	1	0	0	0	0	0
Franco VALENTIN	1	0	0	0	0	0
Carlos CRESPES, English	1	1	0	0	0	1
Pedro GOUTIERREZ, Spanish	1	1	1	3	1	0

1766 Spanish Census of Natchitoches

	Slaves	Land (Arpents of Frontage)	Horses	Cattle	Hogs and Sheep	Guns
POEYFARRE & JURINNY	0	0	0	0	0	?
MELMIES & MOTAR [?]	0	0	0	0	0	?
BRUMEAUX & RENAUD	0	0	0	0	0	?
BOSQUE [?] & FIOL	0	0	0	0	0	?
BAILLIO	0	4	0	0	0	?
DUBOIS	4	17	17	0	0	?
J. B. DUPRES	4	12	10	0	0	?
Jph. DUPRES	2	8	0	0	0	?
BREVEL	0	3	0	0	0	?
LEMOINE	1	6	0	2	10	1
POISSOT	2	5	3	2	2	1
BUARD	13	34	10	50	10	4
GRILLET	3	12	1	6	12	1
DAVID	0	4	2	0	0	2
LATTIER	0	6	2	5	10	1
R. DUPRE	1	6	15	4	3	1
LE DUC	2	6	2	0	6	1
BADIN	1	6	1	4	7	2
B. RACHAL	0	8	1	11	7	2
Santhiago RACHAL	0	0	1	2	5	1
LECONTE	0	8	2	5	12	1
BARRANCO	0	0	3	6	12	1
POIRIER	0	6	4	10	10	1
L. RACHAL	0	8	4	6	10	2
ROBIN	0	6	0	0	6	1
CHEDHOMME	0	8	0	0	6	2
VALENTIN	2	6	0	0	3	2
CRESEPES	19	2	0	0	6	1
GOUTIERREZ	5	0	6	4	10	1

1766 Spanish Census of Natchitoches

	Men Bearing Arms	Women	Older Boys	Older Girls	Boys	Girls
Widow BOURDELLE	1	1	1	0	0	0
Franco EL ANGoz [L'ANGLOIS], Drummer & bailiff	1	1	0	0	1	1
Joseph CASTRO, Spanish	1	1	0	0	1	0
Franco CASTRO, ditto	1	1	0	1	1	2
Luisetta, free Indian [Marie Jeanne Elisabeth "Lisette" de L'ISLE, former slave companion of Claude BERTRAND]	3	6	0	0	3	3
Pierre TRISTANT	1	6	0	0	0	0
Franco CLAUSAUX, Sergt of the Garrison	1	1	0	0	1	0
Juan Baptista DAVION	1	1	0	1	4	1
Alexis GRAPPE, Interpreter to the Indians	1	1	3	2	1	3
Juan Bapta LA BERRY, his brother [in-law]	1	2	1	0	3	4
Santhiago [Jacques] LAMBRE	1	1	0	0	1	1
Juan [Jean] LAMBRE	1	1	0	0	1	2
Gaspar DERBANNE and his two sisters [in law?]	2	2	1	0	2	1
Pedro [Pierre] DERBANNE	1	1	0	0	4	3
Manuel SOTO	1	1	0	0	2	4
Franco CARLES and OLLIVIER, his brother	2	0	0	0	0	0
Franco CHAIGNEAU and his brother	2	2	1	1	3	3
Juan Baptista MORIN	1	1	0	0	0	0
Jno Bapte GONIN and JEANNEAU, a free mulatto	2	1	0	0	0	0
Luis LECLERC	0	1	0	0	0	0
Luis LAMALATIE	1	0	1	1	0	0
Pedro SAURELLE, blacksmith	1	1	0	0	2	2
Franco LEVASSER and Jno Bapta Samuels [dit LIONNOIS]	2	1	0	0	0	0

1766 Spanish Census of Natchitoches

	Slaves	Land (Arpents of Frontage)	Horses	Cattle	Hogs and Sheep	Guns
BOURDELLE	6	2	6	13	4	1
LANGLOIS	2	0	0	0	0	0
J. CASTRO	2	0	0	0	0	0
F. CASTRO	0	0	0	2	0	0
Luisetta, Indian	3	0	0	0	2	1
TRISTANT	0	6	0	0	1	1
CLAUSAUX	0	0	0	1	0	1
DAVION	2	20	3	17	12	1
GRAPPE	0	22	22[?]	13	8	4
LA BERRY	0	25	7	20	20	5
Santiago LAMBRE	0	20	1	6	11	2
Juan LAMBRE	0	12	2	17	3	1
G. DERBANNE	0	20	13	7	16	4
P. DERBANNE	16	20	8	10	2	1
SOTO	13	0	12	6	0	1
CARLES and OLLIVIER	0	8	2	4	4	2
CHAIGNEAU	0	6	6	8	13	3
MORIN	1	0	1	2	3	1
GONIN and JEANNEAU	1	6	1	8[?]	7	2
LECLERC	4	6	0	0	6	1[?]
LAMALATIE	0	4	15	1	60	1[?]
SAURELLE	1	0	0	6[?]	1	1[?]
LEVASSER and LIONNOIS	1	8	2	8	17	2[?]

1766 Spanish Census of Natchitoches

	Men Bearing Arms	Women	Older Boys	Older Girls	Boys	Girls
Ignacio HANTT [ANTY] and Lorenzo [Laurent] CALVENNE	2	1	0	0	0	2
Carlos LARENAUDIERE and Widow NAIGLE	2	2	1	0	2	3
Widow ALORGE and her widowered son	4	1	3	1	0	0
Sebastian PRUDHOMME & Guil[e] CHEVER	3	1	1	1	2	2
Andre and Pedro [Pierre] BORRANGER	2	0	0	0	0	0
Antonio VASCOCU, ropemaker	1	1	0	0	3	1
Joseph PERRAU and his associates	3	1	0	1	3	2
Andres RAMBIN, tailor	2	1	1	0	2	2
Jn[o] Bap[ta] MALBER, former artilleryman	[1]	1	0	0	1	3
Jph y Lorenzo [Joseph LAURENT], smithy	[1]	0	0	0	0	0
The Widow of RONDIN	0	1	0	0	2	2
Luis RONDIN	[1]	1	0	0	0	0
	127	75	23	17	81	250

These 15 individuals are bachelors who are newly established and do not yet own anything:

Joseph VERGER
Estevan VERGER
Juan DUVIVIER
Fran[co] PROVENSAL
Juan BONNET
Pedro Fran[co] DUDOIGT
Antoine DORVAL
Pedro TRUDAU
Nicolas LAGNON
Honorato FABRE
Matheo PLAISANCE
Pedro CHAUVIN
Fran[co] DOUCET
Fran[co] BLAN
Juan LALANDE

1766 Spanish Census of Natchitoches

	Slaves	Land (Arpents of Frontage)	Horses	Cattle	Hogs and Sheep	Guns
HANTT [ANTY] and CALVENNE	2	4	10	4	4	2
LARENAUDIERE and NAIGLE	0	4	5	4	3	2
ALORGE	0	8	6	22	14	4
PRUDHOME and CHEVER	0	6	6	8	8	3
BORRANGER	0	8	0	0	6	2
VASCOCU	0	3	3	0	8	1
PERRAU	0	4	6	25	12	4
RAMBIN	0	0	4	6	8	3
MALBER	0	6	0	0	4	1
LAURENT	1	0	1	0	7	2
Widow of RONDIN	0	0	0	0	2	0
RONDIN	0	0	0	0	0	0
	815		[illegible]			

1766 Census: Indian Tribes under Jurisdiction of Natchitoches
Right Bank of Rio Colorado [Red River]
[Undated]

Tribe	Population		Distance from Fort
NATCHITOCHES	10		Next to the Fort
APALACHES	20		At the Great Rapids of Rio Colorado [Red River], 30 leagues [South] from Fort
YATAZEES	30	*	30 leagues W-NW
PEQUENOS NAKODOCHES	40	*	40 leagues from the preceeding tribe W-NW
PEQUENOS NADACOS or NESATES	30	*	65 leagues to the S
PEQUENOS CADOX	33	*	50 leagues N-NW
GRANDES CADOX	155	*	83 leagues NW
KIDESINGUES	35	*	80 leagues W
KUAKANAS, CHEKANICHES, & KAUNION, united	400	*	95 leagues W
KUAYACHES & L' UACHITAS, united	700	*	135 leagues N
KANKAGUAYES	100		Extends from the Pridos [*presidios?*] 200 leagues to the Fort of [−?−]
LAITANOS	1400		"The same." Extends from the NW toward the West and toward the Rio Missuri until the Kingdom of Santa Fe is reached.

Legajo 2585, ASD-AGI; Colonial Records Collection, Center for Louisiana Studies, University of Louisiana at Lafayette. All data for the tribes marked (*) carries the additional notation "more or less."

1769 Statistical Summary: Population of Natchitoches
14 January 1770

Statement that shows the number of inhabitants at the fort and town of Natchitoches, with distinctions between classes, sexes, and ages.

WHITES	14 and Under	Over 14 & Under 50	50 Years or Above	General Total
Men	98	152	5	255
Women	94	102	2	198

SLAVES	Useful for Work	Useless for Work*	Total Slaves
Men	98	152	5
Women	94	102	2

Carts for Oxen	Horses, Mares	Mules/ Donkeys	Oxen, Cattle, Yearlings	Sheep/ Goats	Pigs	Total
8	815	30/4	1,752	150/50	1,268	4,069

[Signed] Eduardo Nugent
Juan Kelly

Legajo 81, Papeles Procedentes de Cuba, Archivo General de Indias, Seville, Spain [hereinafter cited as PPC-AGI].

* Slaves in the category "useless" are those under the age or 12 years.

1769 Statistical Summary: Natchitoches & Rapides
April 1777

Statistical Summary, Census of all the Individuals of the Province of Louisiana, April 1777 – District of the Natchitoches [sic] and Rapides, immense in size & distant from New Orleans 160 leagues.

White Males		236
Age Group 1*	99	
Age Group 2	127	
Age Group 3	10	
White Females		178
Age Group 1	90	
Age Group 2	80	
Age Group 3	8	
Free Mulatto Males		1
Age Group 1	0	
Age Group 2	1	
Age Group 3	0	
Free Mulatto Females	0	0
Free Negro Males	0	0
Free Negro Females	0	0
Mulatto Slave Males		6
Age Group 1	5	
Age Group 2	1	
Age Group 3	0	

Extracted from "Padron general de todos los individuos de la Provincia de la Luisiana," legajo 2351, PPC-AGI, Seville, Spain. The figures for Natchitoches are said to represent the year 1769 and were the latest figures available when the 1777 summary of the colony was compiled.

* The years represented by the age groups are not indicated. Typically, the youngest group were those under puberty. The middle group ranged between puberty and the point at which the men could do longer do militia service and women no longer bore children. The oldest group would be those past militia or childbearing age.

1769 Statistical Summary: Natchitoches & Rapides

Mulatto Slave Females		8
Age Group 1	6	
Age Group 2	2	
Age Group 3	0	
Negro Slaves Males		174
Age Group 1	40	
Age Group 2	130	
Age Group 3	4	
Negro Slave Females		136
Age Group 1	38	
Age Group 2	94	
Age Group 3	4	
Heads of households who are planters		57
Men in the Army of His Majesty		3
Militia officers in actual service		3
French officials at half-pay		1
Traders & merchants		18
Artisans		7
Herdsmen, travelers, hunters, mariners, and people without permanent abode		50
Total Individuals		**740**

1772 Militia Roll of Natchitoches
8 June 1772

A list by height of the militia company at the said post.

Rank	Name	Native Country	Age	Height	Term	Present/Absent
Capt.	Dn. Luis BORME					
Lt.	Dn. Rami POASSO					
2nd Lt.	Dn. Pedro DUPEYN					
1st Sgt.	Bta. TRICHEL	Natchit.[1]	33	5'8"	3	P
2nd Sgt.	Pedro ALORGE	"	27	5'6"	3	P
3rd Sgt.	Jacque LAMBRE	"	41	5'4"	6	P
Drummer	Franco LANGLOIS	"	42	5'3"	2	P
	Luis BUAR	"	28	5'7"	3	P
	Estevan BERGER [VERGER]	"	28	5'7"	3	P
	Bta VILLFRANCE	"	27	5'7"	1?	P
	Pedro METOYE	Rochela[2]	28	5'7"	3	P
	Franco TRUDEL	Canada	28	5'6"	9	P
	Luis VERGER [VERCHER]	"	26	5'6"	6	P
	Lorenzo REBEQIY	Provenza[3]	28	5'6"	6	P
	Pedro GAÑIER	Nachit.	35	5'6"	3	P
	Marin GRILLET	"	46	5'6"	3	P
	Anto RAMBIN	"	22	5'6	3	P
	Franco PRUDHOME	"	33	5'6"	3	P
	Gasparito DERBAN	"	22	5'6"	9	P
	Juan LAMBRE	Nachit.	33	5'5"	7	P
	Luis VERGER	"	20	5'5"	6	P
	Jno Bta DUPREST	"	42	5'5"	6	P

Doc. 741, Colonial Notarial Records, Office of the Clerk of Court, Natchitoches. Heights are expressed in Spanish inches and feet. By English measurement, each soldier would be three to five inches taller. "Term" of service is expressed in years.

1772 Militia Roll of Natchitoches

Rank	Name	Native Country	Age	Height	Term	Present/Absent
	Manuel TRICHELE	"	35	5'5"	3	P
	Juan CHAIGNAU	"	28	5'5"	3	P
	Pedro VILAR	Provence	38	5'5"	3	P
	Jⁿ Bᵗᵃ ANTY	Nachit.	19	5'5"	2	P
	Franᶜᵒ HUGUES	Gascon	24	5'5"	2	P
	Jacque LA ROCHE	Normandie	30	5'4"	10	P
	Franco. PERO	Nachit.	20	5'4"	10	P
	Pedro LACOUR	"	37	5'4"	3	P
	Guillermo CHEVERT	"	22	5'4"	3	P
	Thomas CHAIGNAU	"	22	5'4"	3	P
	Antonio RICHE	"	26	5'4"	3	P
	Jph. CHARBONAU	Canada	25	5'4"	2	P
	Jⁿ Bᵗᵃ DERBAN	Nachit.	20	5'4"	7	P
	Julian BESON	"	24	5'4"	7	P
	Joseph PAVIE	Rochela²	26	5'4"	-	P
	Luis [LE] BEUF	Natchit.	20	5'4"	-	P
	Pablo LAFITA	"	20	5'3"	6	P
	Pedro BOUSET [BROSSET]	Rochela²	27	5'3"	5	P
	Maturin DAVID	Natchit.	45	5'3"	4	P
	Rami POASSO	"	35	5'3"	3	P
	Pedro POASSO	"	22	5'3"	3	P
	Pedro LACOSTE⁴	Bacona[?]	22	5'3"	3	P
	Juan Bᵗᵃ GONIN	Natchit.	49	5'3"	?	P
	Jacque CRISTY	"	30	5'3"	"	P
	Jacob ROSAU	Burgin.⁵	36	5'3"	"	P
	Franᶜᵒ BOSSAUR	Natchit.	34	5'3"	-	P
	Jaque LEBASEUR	"	22	5'2"	11	P
	Jⁿ Bᵗᵃ MOREYN	"	31	5'2"	10	P
	Jacob RACHAL	"	37	5'2"	9	P
	Joseph BOULE	"	20	5'2"	9	P
2d Corp.	Etevan GAIÑE	"	36	5'2"	7	P
	Honore VIVIER	"	25	5'2"	6	P
	Julian RONDIN	"	18	5'2"	6	P

1772 Militia Roll of Natchitoches

Rank	Name	Native Country	Age	Height	Term	Present/Absent
	Mauricio DE MOUY	"	18	5'2"	6	P
	Pedro BAILLUO	"	42	5'2"	3	P
	Luis [LAMALATHIE dit] Jovar	"	33	5'2"	2	P
	Jⁿ MASIP	"	29	5'2"	-	P
	Ramon TOTIN	"	18	5'2"	-	P
	Pedro DERBAN	"	19	5'2"	-	P
	Fran^{co} RAMBIN	"	18	5'1"	9	P
	Guilllermo VARDET [WARDEN]	"	44	5'1"	9	P
	Beltran AURET	Baiony⁶	40	5'1"	6	P
2d Corp.	Guillermo LESTAGE	Bortguio⁷	32	5'1"	3	P
2d Corp.	Jⁿ B^{ta} BREVEL	Nachit.	38	5'1"	3	P
	Estevan PAVIE	Rochela²	32	5'1"	3	P
	Pedro SORREL	Nachit.	37	5'1"	3	P
	Jⁿ MILLET	Rochela²	39	5'1"	1	P
1st Corp.	Bar^{me}. RACHAL⁸	Nachit.	40	5'0"	9	P
2d Corp.	Matheo PLASANCE	"	33	5'0"	7	P
1st Corp.	Juan RIS	"	45	5'0"	-	P
	Luis BELTRAN	"	18	5'0"	-	P

Absent

Luis RONDIN	At the Tuacanas
Atanaz POISAU	With Mr. DE MEZIERES
Joseph VERGER	At the Ca___ [illegible]
Luis TOTIN	With Mr. DE MEZIERES
Pedro BESSON	With Mr. DE MEZIERES
Pierrite DERBAN	At the Rapids
Juan B^{te} PIEDFERME	Sick at Black Lake
Fran^{co} PERAU⁹	" " "
Mauricio DE MOUY	N'Adais [?]
Gaspard FIOL	With Mr. MEZIERES
DARTIGO	In New Orleans
Pedro LUNAU	" " "

1772 Militia Roll of Natchitoches

Major Officials
Actual Commandant   Dⁿ Athanasio MEZIERES   At San Antonio   —
Interim Commandant   Dⁿ Joseph DE LA PEÑA   P

Chaplain
Reverend Father F. STANISLAS, Parish Priest   P

Surgeon
Mr. MERCIER   P

Keeper of Arms
LA LIME

[Signed] At Natchitoches, 8 June 1772
Joseph de la PEÑA

---

    1. Many of the men identified as natives of Natchitoches actually were not.
    2. La Rochelle.
    3. The French province of Provence.
    4. Beside the name LA COSTE there appears the notation "died and replaced with Juan JONNAU, native of Segonvau, province of Xaintonge, bishopric of Xaintes, his age 40 years, his height 4 feet 6 inches."
    5. Burgundy.
    6. Probably Bayonne.
    7. Bordeaux.
    8. A tilde appears above the "rm" in Rachal's given name, indicating that letters have been omitted. The name is *Barthelemie*, variously spelled as *Barthelemy*.
    9. Beside his name a marginal notation states: Natchitoches, single, 20, 5'4".

1774 Census of Natchitoches Slaveowners
25 February 1774

General Statement of the Black and Red Slaves of the Post of Natchitoches.

Name of Inhabitants	Negro/Mulatto Males	Negresses or Mulattresses	Negro/Mulatto Children under Twelve
Monsr DE VILLIERS	2	4	2
Madme DE MEZIERES	3	3	5
Reverend Father STANISLAS	2	1	0
Monsr L. BORME	1	1	0
Monsr Remis POISSEAU	10	6	8
Mr. Pre DU PAIN	0	1	0
Monsr Dn Louis de ST. DENIS	9	2	1
Dme Dn Manuel SOTO	2	3	8
Monsr L. DEBLANC	0	0	2
Madme LE DOUX	1	1	1
Monsr DE LA CHAISE St. Denis	2	1	1
Monsr Ant. CHARBONNET	2	2	3
Mr Chevalier DE VILLIERS	0	1	0
Monsr J. Bte ROUGOT	0	1	1
Mr Pre DARTIGAUX	2	1	0
Mr Bte PRUDHOME	5	2	4
Etienne GAGÑE	2	1	0
En. [Henri] TRICHELE	4	2	9
Manuel TRICHELLE	1	1	1
Pre SORELLE	2	1	0
Monsr PISEROS	1	2	1
J. Pre VILLARD	0	1	0
Alexis GRAPPE	6	5	12
MARMILLION	0	0	1

Legajo 189-1, PPC-AGI, Seville

1774 Census of Natchitoches Slaveowners

Name of Inhabitants	Indian Males	Indian Females	Indian Children Under Twelve
DE VILLIERS	1	0	0
DE MEZIERES	2	2	1
STANISLAS	0	0	2
BORME	0	0	0
POISSEAU	0	0	2
DU PAIN	0	0	0
ST. DENIS	0	0	2
SOTO	0	0	0
L. DEBLANC	0	0	0
LE DOUX	0	0	0
DE LA CHAISE	0	0	0
CHARBONNET	0	0	0
DE VILLIERS	0	0	0
ROUGOT	0	1	0
DARTIGAUX	0	0	0
PRUDHOME	0	1	0
GAGÑE	0	0	0
E. TRICHELE	0	0	0
M. TRICHELLE	0	0	0
SORELLE	0	0	0
PISEROS	1	1	0
VILLARD	0	0	0
GRAPPE	0	1	1
MARMILLION	0	0	1

1774 Census of Natchitoches Slaveowners

Name of Inhabitants	Negro/Mulatto Males	Negresses or Mulattresses	Negro/Mulatto Children under Twelve
MERCIER	2	1	0
Boëte LAFITTE	0	1	0
Bastien PRUDHOMME	0	0	0
B^{te} TRICHELE			
Pre VALANTIN	2	0	0
Jⁿ B^{te} DAVION	2	1	1
Dominique MONTECHE	3	2	5
J. B^{te} MORAIN	0	0	0
Jean LAMBRE	5	3	5
Gaspar DERBANNE	1	0	0
François LE VASSEUR	2	0	0
J. B^{te} LABERY	4	4	7
Jacob LAMBRE	6	6	7
Barthelemy RACHAL	1	1	0
Pierre BADIN	2	2	1
Dame BUARE	4	8	9
L. BUARE	1	0	0
Louis [LAMALATHIE *dit*] Jobare	1	0	0
Marin GRILLET	2	1	0
Baptiste BREVELLE	1	1	0
P^{re} BAILLO	1	2	0
Jean B^{te} DUBOIS	2	1	0
Joseph DUPRE	4	3	1
Baptiste DUPRE	4	3	2
Athanas POISSOT	1	1	0
Remis POISSOT	1	1	2
Pierre DARBANNE	6	8	4
George LE CLAIR	1	1	0
LE COURE DE PRELLE	2	0	0
Louis RACHAL	0	1	3
Jean B^{te} LE COMPTE	0	3	2

1774 Census of Natchitoches Slaveowners

Name of Inhabitants	Indian Males	Indian Females	Indian Children Under Twelve
MERCIER	0	2	0
LAFITTE	0	0	0
PRUDHOMME	0	0	1
TRICHELE	0	0	0
VALANTIN	0	0	0
DAVION	0	0	0
MONTECHE	0	0	0
MORAIN	0	1	0
LAMBRE	0	0	0
DERBANNE	0	0	0
LE VASSEUR	0	0	0
LAMBERY	0	0	0
LAMBRE	0	0	0
RACHAL	0	0	0
BADIN	1	0	0
D. BUARE	0	0	0
L. BUARE	0	0	0
[LAMALATHIE *dit*] Jobare	0	0	0
GRILLET	0	0	0
BREVELLE	0	0	0
BAILLO	0	0	0
DUBOIS	0	0	0
J. DUPRE	0	0	0
B. DUPRE	0	1	0
A. POISSOT	0	0	0
R. POISSOT	0	0	0
DERBANNE	0	0	0
LE COMPTE	0	0	0
LE COURE DE PRELLE	1	2	4
RACHAL	0	0	0
LE COMPTE	0	0	2

1774 Census of Natchitoches Slaveowners

Name of Inhabitants	Negro/Mulatto Males	Negresses or Mulattresses	Negro/Mulatto Children under Twelve
Jacques FAZENDE	2	1	0
Mons\" ARMANT	0	0	1
Jacques HUBERT	0	1	0
POËLFERRÉ [POËYFARRÉ]	2	0	0
François REMONT	0	0	0
SAMUEL *dit* Lionnois	0	0	0
Jacques RIDE	0	0	0
N. C. THIBAULT	0	0	0
François MORVAN	0	0	0
Jacques CUREAU	0	0	0
Pierre GIRARD *dt* Leveille	0	0	0
	130	102	113

66 Masters
387 Red & Black Slaves

1774 Census of Natchitoches Slaveowners

Name of Inhabitants	Indian Males	Indian Females	Indian Children Under Twelve
FAZENDE	0	0	0
ARMANT	0	0	1
HUBERT	0	1	0
POËLFERRÉ	0	0	0
REMONT	0	1	1
SAMUEL *dit* Lionnois	0	1	0
RIDE	0	1	0
THIBAULT	0	1	1
MORVAN	0	1	0
CUREAU	0	1	1
GIRARD *d^t* Leveille	0	1	0
	6	20	15

[Signed] Balthazard DE VILLIERS

1774 Tax List of Natchitoches Slaveowners
25 February 1774

1774 Tax Roll of Slaveowners, Post of Natchitoches. Number of Negroes and Mulattoes of all sexes and ages on 26 September in the cited post, for which we have taxed the residents at the rate of 8 reales for each of the slaves they possess, in accordance with the ordinance sent by the Governor-general to his lieutenant in this said jurisdiction, dated 17th June of this year.

Names of Masters Who Have Paid —	Negro Males	Negro Females	Mulatto Males	Mulatto Females	Total Number	Reales Taxed
Dn Luis BORME	1	1	0	0	2	16
Dn Pedro DUPAIN	0	1	0	0	0	8
Dn Jn Bapta TRICHELE	8	3	1	0	12	96
Dn Remigio POISOT	13	9	2	1	25	200
Dn Luis de Sn DENIS	3	4	1	1	9	72
Dna Maria de Sn DENIS	3	4	1	1	9	72
Mada LE DOUX	1	2	0	0	3	24
Dn Anto CHARBONET	3	3	0	0	6	48
Dn Jn Bapta ROUJOT	0	1	0	0	1	8
Dn Sn Iago DE LA CHAISE	1	2	1	0	4	32
Pedro DARTIGAUX	2	1	0	0	3	24
Jn Bapta PRUDHOMME	8	3	0	0	11	88
Estevan GAGNIER	2	1	0	0	3	24
Henriqe TRICHELE	6	4	2	4	16	128
Manuel TRICHELE	1	2	0	0	3	24
Pedro SOREL	2	1	0	0	3	24
Juan PISEROS	2	3	0	0	5	40
Claudio MERCIER	3	1	1	0	5	40
Pedro VILLARD	0	1	0	0	1	8
Alexis GRAPPE	13	7	2	0	22	176
Pablo LAFFITE	0	1	0	0	1	8

Legajo 189-1, PPC-AGI, Seville.

1774 Tax List of Natchitoches Slaveowners

Names of Masters Who Have Paid —	Negro Males	Negro Females	Mulatto Males	Mulatto Females	Total Number	Reales Taxed
Franco [LE] VASSEUR	2	0	0	0	2	16
Pedro VALENTIN	2	1	0	0	3	24
Jn Bapta DAVION	2	2	0	0	4	32
Domingo MONTECHE	5	5	0	0	10	80
Juan LAMBRE	8	5	1	0	14	112
Gaspard DERBANNE	1	0	0	0	1	8
Jn Bapta LA BERRY	6	3	3	3	15	120
Diego LAMBRE	10	7	0	2	19	152
Bartholomeo RACHAL	1	1	0	0	2	16
Pedro BADIN	2	3	0	0	5	40
Widow BUART	8	13	0	1	22	176
Pedro BAILLIOT	3	3	0	0	6	48
Luis JOBART	1	0	0	0	1	8
Marin GRILLET	2	1	0	0	3	24
Jn Bapta BREVEL	1	1	0	0	2	16
Jn Bapta DUBOIS	2	1	0	0	3	24
Joseph DUPRES	4	3	1	0	8	64
Jn Bapta DUPRES	5	3	1	0	9	72
Athanasio POISOT	1	1	0	0	2	16
Remigio POISOT, the son	1	2	0	0	4	32
Pedro DERBANNE	6	10	1	1	18	144
George LE CLER	1	1	0	0	2	16
Luis BUART	1	0	0	0	1	8
JOANNIS	1	0	0	0	1	8
Pedro METOYER	0	0	3	1	4	32
Dn Sn Iago FAZENDE	2	1	1	0	4	32
Dn Luis LE COURT	2	0	0	0	2	16
Luis RACHAL	1	3	0	0	4	32
Jn Bapta LECONTE	3	0	0	2	5	40
Total	162	124	21	16	323	2,584

1776 Statistical Summary: Natchitoches Post
February 1776

Dwellings		113
Heads of Families		105
Women	86	
Youths capable of bearing arms	77	
Infants and children	106	
Unmarried young women	34	
Bachelors & nonresidents dispersed in hunting & trade with the villages, or in the pay of the citizens	84	
Free Negroes & Mulattoes		7
Male free negroes	2	
Female free negroes	2	
Male free mulattoes	2	
Female free mulattoes	1	
Slaves		422
[Male] negro slaves	134	
Working negro women	105	
Negro boys	51	
Negro girls	39	
Male mulattoes	26	
Female mulattoes	23	
Male Indians	16	
Female Indians	28	
Stock		
Horses	1,258	
Cattle	1,842	
Sheep & goats	"over 300"	
Hogs	782	

Exports: "more than 1000 horses, about 100 mules, 9 *quintals* of indigo, 15 *fanegas* of indigo seed, 30,000 packs of tobacco, 120 dressed buffalo skins, 36,000 deer skins, 5,000 *azumbres* bear oil, 5,000 pounds tallow, and some bacon and other meats salted and dried." Revenue: 400 pounds (all contributed by brandy-sellers "to secure the closing of wine shops") and 400 pounds collected from the game of trucks (half of which pays the salary of the drummer of the militia company).

Doc. 402, legajo 112, PPC-AGI, Seville, Spain.

1779 Roll of Militiamen Dispatched to San Antonio
27 September 1779

Rank and names of the Natchitoches militiamen who accompanied Don Atanacio de Mézières [to San Antonio de Bexar where de Mézières was to assume the governorship of Texas].

Don Antonio Maria DE MÉZIÈRES, Lieutenant
Don Bernardo DORTOLAN, Sublieutenant
Nicolas FOURNIER, Sergeant
Juan Manuel PADILLA, Sergeant of Bucarely
Antonio LE NOIR, Corporal from Bucarely

Riflemen

Francisco HUGUE
Crisostomo PERAULT
Joseph TRICHELLE
Luis MONET
Pedro RENAUDIERE
Joseph DUPREE
Remigio TOTIN
Mauricio de MOUY
Domingo SANT PRIMO [PRIX]
Pedro DERVANE [DERBANNE]

Nicolas PENT [PONT]
Bartolo MONPIERRE
Julian RONDIN
Andres COUPIERE
Bartolo RACHAL
Gaspar FIOL
Juan Bauptista [LE] DUC
Antonio SANT DENIS
Luis BERTRANT
Juan Bauptista BERNABANE [DERBANNE]

Ramo de Historia, vol. 299, Archivo General y Público, Mexico City.

1780 Militia Roll of Natchitoches
(Revolutionary War Rosters)
1 September 1780

Roll of the Infantry Company of Militia taken in Review, 1 September 1780.

Officers
Louis BORME, Captain
Antoine STE. ANNE, Lieutenant
Joseph PAVIE, Ensign

Sergeants
Pierre LA COUR
Antoine RAMBIN
Paul MARCOLAY

Corporals
Guilhaume LESTAGE
Mathieu PLAISANCE
François RAMBIN

Drummer
Antoine LEFEVRE

Jack D. L. Holmes Collection, microfilm roll 9, Northwestern State University Archives, Natchitoches; citing legajo 193-A, PPC-AGI, Seville. The roster above enumerates the same Natchitoches militia referred to in "S.A.R. Spanish Revolutionary Records," *Louisiana Genealogical Register* 9 (December 1962): 54–55. Descendants of the militiamen on this roster are eligible for membership in Daughters of the American Revolution, Sons of the American Revolution, and Children of the American Revolution. For an account of the Revolutionary activities of the Natchitoches militia see Elizabeth Shown Mills and Gary B. Mills, *Tales of Old Natchitoches* (Natchitoches: Association for the Preservation of Historic Natchitoches, 1978), 34–36.

1780 Revolutionary War Rosters

Riflemen

Louis VIGE
Ignace MAILLOUX
Paul Bouet LAFITTIE
Jean Baptiste MORIN
Jacob [Jacques] RACHAL [dit] St. Denys
André DAVID
François LECOMTE [dit] Clavier [?]
Bernard PIPES
Louis FORTIN
Jean ALDELT
André Phelipe [FREDERIC]
Joseph JANSOM [JEANSON]
Antoine FRENIERE
Jean Baptiste ANTY
Gil MORINO
François MORVANT
Jean Baptiste AILHAUD
Etiene PAVIE
Louis ANTY
Joseph JAN RICH [RIS, aka JEAN RIS]
François MOREAU
Jean Baptiste DENYS
Pierre BROQUEDIS
Joseph SAUVAGE
Samuel LYONAIS [SAMÜEL dit Lionnois]
Gaspard HIDALGO
Michel SANCHEZ
Mathieu LABORDE

Louis VERCHERE
Elie BERNARD
Pierre BROSSET
Joseph MARTIN
Jean LAMBRE
Pierre GANIER
François SOREL
Jean MASSIP
Jacques FORT
Pierre LABRIE
Phelipe FREDERIQ
Barnabé CHELETRE
Guilhaume BARBAROUX

Jean JARNAC
Julien RACHAL
Jean Baptiste GRAPE
Jean PAPA (POYRA?)
Louis JOBAR
Jean Baptiste ARMANT
Jacques CHRISTIL
Nicolas GALLIEN
DUBOIS, the son
Nicolas THIBAULT
Jean POMIER
PACHEQUE
Louis RACHAL, the son
TURGEON

[Signed] VAUGINE

1780 Revolutionary War Rosters

Roll of the Calvary Company of Natchitoches Militia, taken at review 1 September 1780.

Officers

Louis Charles DE BLANC, Captain
Bernard D'ORTOLAN, Lieutenant
Jean Jacques DAVID, Cornet

Lower Officers

Pierre, METOYER, Marechal de Logis
Prançois GRAPPE, Brigadier
Louis ARMANT, Under-Brigadier

Cavalrymen

Gaspard DERBANE, the son
Sebastien PRUDHOMME, the son
Emanuel PRUDHOMME
Athanaze POISSOT
Antoine LE NOIR
François PRUDHOMME
Remy TOUTIN
Louis LEBOEUF
Louis TOUTIN
Gaspard FIOLE
Jean Baptiste DAVION
Jean Baptiste LA RENAUDIERE
Barthelemy RACHAL, son of Louis
Dominique DAVION
Julien BESSON
Antoine ST. DENIS
Remy LAMBRE
Jean Baptiste DUBOIS
Antoine VASTCOCU, the son
Jean Baptiste DERBANE

Pierre SOREL, the son
André VASTCOCU
Baptiste BUART
Louis BUART
Etienne VERGER
Louis BERTRAND
Joseph DUPRE, the son
Remy POISSOT
Pierre DERBANE, the son
Pierre LA RENAUDIERE
Louis RACHAL, son of Bmy.
Ambroise LE COMTE
Louis MONET
Chrisostome PERRAULT
Joseph des NOYER
Gilbert CLOZEAU
Pierre DOLÉ
Michel CHAIGNOT
Guilhaume CHEVERT
François TOUTIN

1780 Revolutionary War Roster

Cannoniers

Guilhaume LE BRUN, Sergeant — he well knows his business

Antoine VASTCOCU, the son	Guilheaume CHEVERT
Jean Baptiste DERBANE	François TOUTIN
Joseph MARTIN	Joseph JAN RICH [Jean RIS]
Pierre BROQUEDIS	DU BOIS, the son

~~Free~~ People of Color Used as Couriers*

Jean VARANGUE	Nicolas DU PONT
Pierrot DE BLANC	Jeanote MEULON
CHIQ	Zacharie RAYMOND

[Signed] VAUGINE

---

*The word "Free" was lined through after it was written. Most of the men on this were free; Chiq apparently was not. Note that Varangue, born free of Gypsy descent, was considered by Vaugine to be "of color"; other records do not designate him as such.

1780 Census of Indian Allies: Natchitoches Jurisdiction
September 1780

Census of the Indian Nations according to the order in which they came to chant the peace pipe after my arrival, according to reports of their chiefs.

Sept. 1	The nation Nadaque, distant 60 leagues from the post of Natchitoches, having as its medal chief KYAAVA-DOUCHE. There are, including those in the cradle:

            Warriors   74
            Women   84
            Young boys 23
            Young girls 46

Sept. 5	The nation Yatasse, at 25 leagues from this post. Medal chief is COCAILLE, according to the majority vote of his nation and with my consent; brother-in-law of the deceased [of the deceased *medal chief?*].

            Warriors   16
            Women   20
            Young boys 22
            Girls of all ages 16

Sept. 6	The nation Natchitoches, situated along the Bayou of the Isle à Vaches at 2 leagues from this post. Medal chief is YAMOH.

            Warriors   13
            Women   21
            Young boys 6
            Young girls 8

Sept. 8	The nation Adaÿes at 15 leagues from the post, chief is QUENSY.

            Warriors   16
            Women   10
            Children of both sexes 7

Roll 9, Jack D. L. Holmes Collection; citing leg. 193-A, PPC-AGI.

1780 Census of Indian Allies

Sept. 13   A party from the nation Bydaye, forming a village at Rivière aux Cannes, distant 10 leagues from the post. CAPOT, chief.

Warriors	7
Women	9
Young boys	10
Girls of different ages	7

Sept. 24   The nation of the grand Cadoe Dakiou. Grand medal chief is the one called TYNIKOUAN. 100 leagues.

Warriors	77
Young boys	42
Women	87
Girls	40

Sept. 24   The nation of the Petite Cados Dakiou. The medal chief is dead. Distant 70 leagues.

Warriors	58
Young boys	31
Women	74
Girls	47

Sept. 26   The nation Quy de Singes. Medal chief is NICOTAQUE-NANAN, who has replaced his father.

Warriors	54
Young boys	37
Women	55
Girls	34

[Signed] VAUGINE

1782 Militia Roll of Natchitoches
(Revolutionary War Roster)
1 January 1782

Register of the Company of Infantry of the Natchitoches Militia, inspected 1 January 1782

Major Officers
Louis BORME, Captain
Antoine STE. ANNE, Lieut. Aide-Major
Joseph PAVIE, Ensign

Sergeants
Pierre LACOURT [LA COUR]
François RAMBIN
Jean ADLET
Pierre BROQUEDIS

Corporals
Guillaume LESTAGE
Mathieu PLAISANCE
Guillaume BARBEROUX
MAILLOUX

Riflemen

Louis VIGE	Louis VERCHER
Ellie BERNARD	Paul Bouet LAFFITTE
Pierre BROSSET	J^n B^{te} MORIN
J^{qe} RACHAL, la St. Denis	J^n LAMBRE
André FREDERIC	p^{re} GAGNIER

Roll 5, Jack D. L. Holmes Collection, citing leg. 195, PPC-AGI. The above roster, like the previous 1780 one, enumerates the same Natchitoches militia companies authenticated in 1921 by the late C. Robert Churchill, president of the Louisiana Society, Sons of the American Revolution, in the course of his search for Revolutionary records in Archivo General de Indias, Seville. See also note accompanying the 1780 roll.

1782 Revolutionary War Rosters

F^s LECOMPTE [*dit*] Saydeck
Bernard PIPES
Louis FORTIN
Jacques FORT
Philipe FREDERIC
Bernabé CHELETRE
Louis ANTY
F^s MORVAN, the father
J^n B^{te} AILHAUT [STE.ANNE]
Louis FONTENEAU
J^n B^{te} ARMAND
J^n B^{te} DENIS
Jean POMMIER
Pascal TURJON
Joseph J^n RIS
J^n TESSIER *dit* La Vigne
  (at Bayou a Pierre)
Joseph SAINT PIERRE
Pierre CHELETRE
Pierre METOYER
Estienne VERJER
J^h DERBANNE, *fils*
Augustin BUART, *fils*
Julien RACHAL
Remi PERAUX
Antoinne VASTCOCU
Niny, *fils de* Pierre DERBANNE
Michel RAMBINT
Jean DESAULES

COUTIN, resident at
  Rivière aux Cannes
François LA FOREST
Gime [Jim] the Englishman
  [likely James YOUNG]

F^s SOREL *dit* MARLY
Jean MASSIP
FORTIN, *le petit*
Pierre LABRIE
Joseph JAMSON [JEANSON]
Antoine FRENIERE
Jean JARNAC
Michel SENCHE
Zackarie [RAYMOND]
Louis JOBAR
Jacque CRISTIL
J^h SAUVAGE
Mathieu LABORDE
Joseph MARTIN
François ROUQUIER
Estienne GOGUET [DUGUET]
Pierre BELANJER
Noel DAUBLIN
François PRUDHOMME
Manuel PRUDHOMME
Michel CHAIGNOT
Charle LEMOINNE, *fils*
Pierre INGLE
Nicolas GALIEN
Louis DAVIONT
J^n B^{te} Bastien [PRUD'HOMME]
Antoinne PRUD'HOMME
Antoinne F^s MORVAN, *fils*
Nicolas LALEMAND,
  shoemaker
Baptiste LE DUC
  dit Ville Franche
Jorge STIMAT, shoemaker
Antoinne PLAUCHER
J^n B^{te} ANTY

[Signed] VAUGINE

1782 Revolutionary War Rosters

Register of the Company of Light Calvary of the Militia of the Post of Natchitoches, in the order according to inspection, on 1 January 1782.

Messieurs, the Officers
Louis Charles, DEBLANC, Captain
Bernard D'ORTOLAND, Lieutenant
Jean Jacques DAVID, Cornet
Maurice DE MOUY, Sergeant
François GRAPPE, Corporal
Louis ARMAND [no rank given]

The Troops

Gaspard FIOLLE
Pierre DOLÉ
Nicolas PONT
Antoine STE. DENIS
Pierre LARENODIERE
Crisosthomé PERAUT
Julien BESSON
André VASCOCUE
Guillaume CHEVERT
Jean B^{te} DAVION
Louis TOTIN
Jean B^{te} DERBANNE [fils de Gaspard]*
François TOTIN
Louis RACHAL, fils de Bmy.
Jean B^{te} DUBOIS
Joseph DUPRES, fils
Pierrit DARBANNE
Berthelemy RACHAL [fils de Louis]
Joseph TRICHELLE
Andres LEBOEUF

Pierre SOREL
Jean VARANGUE
Louis LEBOUGH
Jean B^{te} LARENODIERE
Jean B^{te} GRAPPE
Louis BERTRAND
Antoine LENOIR
Bastien PRUDHOMME, fils
Gilbert CLAUSAUT
Dominique DAVION
Gasparit DERBANNE
Remy TOTIN
Remy LAMBRE
Jean B^{te} BUARD
Louis BUARD
Louis MONET
Remy POISSOT
Embroise LECOINTE
Louis RACHAL dit Rat

[Signed] VAUGINE, Commandant

---

* Two Jean Baptiste Derbannes existed at Natchitoches in this generation. For an identification of this Jean Baptiste as son of Gaspard, see Elizabeth Shown Mills, "Identifying Jean Baptise Derbanne of ... the Gálvez Campaigns ... Revolutionary War," *The American Genealogist* 68 (January 1993): 33–45.

1783 Militia Roll of Natchitoches
1 June 1783

Statement of the Light Cavalry Company of the Militia at the Post of Natchitoches, in the order according to that passed in review.

Rank	Names of Officers & Soldiers
Messieurs, the officers	Louis Charles DE BLANC, Captain Bernard DORTOLAND, Lieutenant Jean Jacques DAVID, Cornet
Messieurs, the sergeants	Maurice DE MOUY, Billeting marshal François GRAPPE, Brigadier Jean B^{te} LARENODIERE, Sub-brigadier
Cavalrymen	Jean B^{te} BUARD Louis BUARD Etienne VERGÉ Gasparit DERBANNE SOREL [dit] Marly DAVION DOLÉ Joseph DUPRÉ Jean B^{te} DERBANNE [fils Gaspard] Louis MONET Remy TOTIN Jean B^{te} DUBOIS François DUBOIS Jean VARANGUE Crisosthomé PERAUT Bastien PRUD'HOME François [illegible; possibly TOTIN] Jean B^{te} GRAPPE Guillaume CHEVERT

Legajo 196, folio 448-49 *verso*, PPC-AGI, Seville.

1783 Militia Roll

Rank	Names of Officers & Soldiers
Cavalrymen	Dominique DAVION
	Cilbert [Gilbert] CLAUSEAU
	Remy LAMBRE
	Louis BOEUFS
	Remy POISSOT
	Louis TOTIN
	Nicolas PONT
	Loüis RACHAL, son of Loüis
	Embroise LECOMTE
	Julien BESSON
	Berthelemy RACHAL
	Gaspard FIOLLE
	Pierit DERBANNE
	Loüis BERTRAND
	Loüis Rat Berthelemy [Louis Barthelemy RACHAL *dit* Rat]
	André VASCOCU
	Pierre LARENODIERE

At Natchitoches, the 1st of June 1783   [Signed] Loüis DE BLANC

I certify under my word of honor that the militiamen enumerated in this statement are the same as those presenting themselves at the review passed today, at the royal fort of Natchitoches, 1 June 1783.

[Signed] VAUGINE, Commandant

Statement of the Infantry Company of Militia at the Post of Natchitoches, in the present month of June 1783

Messieurs	Loüis BORME, Captain
	Antoine STE ANNE, Lieutenant, Aide-de-camp
	Joseph PAVIE, Ensign
	Baptiste DARTIGAUX, Adjutant

1783 Militia Roll

Rank	Names of Officers & Soldiers
Sergeants	Paul MARCOLLAY, Sergeant-major
	Pierre LACOUR
	François RAMBIN
	Jean ADLÉ
	Pierre BROQUEDIS
Corporals	Guillaume LESTAGE
	Mathieu PLAISANCE
	Guillaume BARBARROUX
	Ignace MAILLIOUX
Riflemen	Loüis DURAND [*dit*] Viger
	Loüis VERCHAIRE
	Hely BERNARD
	Paul Boüet LAFFITTE
	Jean B^te MORIN
	Jacques RACHAL *d^t* St. Denis
	Jean LAMBRE
	André FREDERIC
	Pierre GANIER
	François LECONTE
	François SOREL *d^t* Marly
	Bernard PIPE
	Jean MASSIP
	Loüis FORTIN
	Loüis "Le Petit" FORTIN
	Jacques FORT
	Jean Pierre LABRIE
	Philippe FREDERIC
	Joseph JEANSON
	Barnabé CHELÊTRE
	Louis ANTY
	François MORVAN, the father
	Jean JARNAC
	Jean B^te AILHAUD
	Zacharie RAYMOND
	Loüis FONTENOT

1783 Militia Roll

Rank	Names of Officers & Soldiers

Riflemen (con'td) Loüis JOBART
Jean B^te ARMANT
Jacques CHRISTILL
Jean B^te DENIS
Jean POMMIER
Mathieu LA BORDE
Paschal TURGEON
Joseph MARTIN
Joseph JEAN RIS
François ROUQUIER
Joseph TESSIER
Etienne GOGUET [DUGUET]
Pierre BELLANGER
Joseph S^T PIERRE
Pierre CHELÊTRE
François PRUD'HOMME
Pierre METTOYER
Manuel PRUD'HOMME
Etienne VERGER
Michel CHAIGNEAU
Joseph DERBANNE, the son
Charles LEMOYNE, the son
Augustin BUARD
Pierre INGLE
Julien RACHAL
Nicolas GALIEN
Antoine VASTCOQUE

Supplement added 1 September 1781 [sic]
Remy PERAUX
Loüis DAVION
Jean B^te Bastien PRUD'HOMME
Nini, son of Pierre DERBANNE
Antoine PRUD'HOMME
Michel RAMBIN
Ant^e François MORVAN, the son
Jean DE SAULLES
Nicolas L'ALLEMAND, cobbler

1783 Militia Roll

Rank	Names of Officers & Soldiers
Riflemen (con'td)	Pierre COUTANT
	Baptiste LE DUC d^t Villefranche
	Gium L'ANGLAIS [Jim (Young), the Englishman]
	Paul François BOSSIER
	Jacques LEVASSEUR
	François CALLE
	Antoine LA GRENADE
	MURPHY

At Natchitoches, the 1st of June 1783
[Signed] BORME

I certify under my word of honor that the militiamen enumerated in this statement are the same as those presenting themselves at the review passed today, at the royal fort of Natchitoches, 1 June 1783.

[Signed] VAUGINE, Commandant

1785 Militia Roll of Natchitoches
October–November 1785

Statement of the Infantry of Militia of Natchitoches, Passed in Review, 4 October 1785.

Rank	Names of Officers & Soldiers
Messieurs, the officers	Louis BORME, Lieut. of the Army, Capt. [of militia]
	Jean B^te AILHAUT S^TE ANNE, Lieutenant, aide-de-camp of the company for the interim
	Joseph CAPURAN, Sub-lieutenant for the interim
	Baptiste DARTIGAUX, Flag-bearer, for the interim
Sergeants	Paul MARCOLLAY, Sergeant-major
	F^çois RAMBINT
	Jean ADLET
	F^çois BOSSIER
Corporals	Guillaume BARBAROUX
	Ignasse MAILLOUX
Riflemen	Louis VIGÊ
	Louis VERCHAIR
	Ellie [Elie] BERNARD
	Jean B^te MORIN
	Andre FREDERIC
	Pierre GAGNIE
	Jean MASSIP
	Louis FORTIN
	FORTIN, *le petit* [FORTIN, the smaller]
	Jacques FORT
	Philipe FREDERIC
	Joseph JAMSON
	Bernabé CHELÊTRE
	Louis ANTY
	Louis FONTENEAU
	Jean B^te DENIS

Legajo 198-A, folios 804–808, PPC-AGI, Seville.

1785 Militia Roll

Rank	Names of Officers & Soldiers
Riflemen (cont'd)	Jean POMMIER
	Mathieu LABORDE
	Pascal TUJON
	Josephe MARTIN
	Josephe JEAN RIS
	Josephe TESSIER d^t La Vigne
	Pierre CHELÊTRE
	F^{çois} PRUDHOMME
	Manuel PRUDHOMME
	Michel CHAIGNOT
	Josephe DERBANNE, the son
	Charles LEMOINE, the son
	Augustin BUART
	Julien RACHAL
	Antoine VASTCOCU, the elder son
	Jean B^{te} ANTY
	Remy PERAULT
	Louis DAVIONT
	Jean B^{te} Bastien [PRUDHOMME]
	Niny, son of Pierre DERBANNE
	Antoine PRUDHOMME
	Michel RAMBINT
	COUTANT at Rivière aux Cannes
	Gimes Irlanday [Jim the Irishman aka James Young]
	⟨illegible⟩ [RACHAL]
	Morphille Irlanday [MURPHY, the Irishman]
	Gaspar [FIOL], *cadet* [the younger]

Supplement dated 4 August 1785

MAÈS
Dominique PRUDHOMME
Luc [SOREL *dit*] Marly
B^{te} Barthelemy RACHAL
Antoine DUBOIS
Jean B^{te} LEMOINE
Antoine Remy POISSOT
Antoine RACHAL
Jean [LE]VASSEUR, the son

1785 Militia Roll

Rank	Names of Officers & Soldiers
Riflemen (con'td)	Jean B^te^ LATTIER

Jean B^{te} LATTIER
Joseph LATTIER
Athanase LECOURT
Berthelemy LECOURT
Jean VERSAILLES
F^{çois} HYMEL
Pierre CHARPENTIER
Antoine LE MOINE
Pierre GAGNON
Pierre DUPRÉ
Louis MERCIER
F^{çois} CHELÊTRE
Mathieu PAILLET
Pierre BAUDOUIN
Pierre LaCOURT [LaCOUR], the son
Alexis CLOUTIER
Berthelemy RACHAL
Jacques Bastien [PRUDHOMME]
Jean LA LANDE
Crisosthome JONKA
Jean DELOUCHE
Antoine HYMEL
Antoine GUICHARD
F^{çois} CALLÉ
Nicolas LAUVE
Josephe MARTIN, *trafiquant* [unlicensed trader]
Jean PHILISPATRI [FITZPATRICK?]
    Irlanday [Irishman] at Lac Noir

[Signed] Louis BORME

Statement of the Infantry Company of Militia at the Post of Natchitoches, in the present month of June 1783

Messieurs the officers	Loüis Charles DE BLANC, Captain
	Bernard DORTOLAND, Lieutenant
	M^{cie} DE MOUY, Billeting marshall doing duty as Sub-lieutenant

1785 Militia Roll

Rank	Names of Officers & Soldiers
Messieurs the sergeants	François GRAPPE, Brigadier Jean B^{te} LARENODIERE, Sub-brigadier
Cavalrymen	Jean B^{te} BUARD Loüis BUARD Etienne VERGER Gasparit DERBANNE DAVION Pierre DOLÉ Jean B^{te} DERBANNE Loüis MONET Remy TOTIN Jean B^{te} DUBOIS François DUBOIS Jean VARANGUE Crisostome PERAULT Bastien PRUD'HOMME François TOTIN Jean B^{te} GRAPPE Guillaume CHEVERT Dominique DAVION Manuel DAVION Loüis RACHAL, son of Louis Gilbert CLAUSEAUX Remy LAMBRE Remy POISSOT Loüis TOTIN Nicolas PONT Loüis Berthelemy RACHAL Loüis LAMBRE Gaspard FIOLLE Embroise LECOMTE Julien BESSON Pierit DERBANNE Loüis BERTRAND Antoine LE NOIR André VASCOCU

1785 Militia Roll

Rank	Names of Officers & Soldiers
Cavalrymen (cont'd)	Pierre LARENODIERE
	Berthelemy RACHAL
	Dominique PRUD'HOMME
	Loüis VACOCU
	Loüis CLAUSEAUX
	Antoine LEMOINE

[No signature]

Cover Letter:

To Colonel Don Estevan Miro

Monsieur, I have conducted the review on the 4th of this October, of all the militiamen at this post. I have the honor to send you the attached, a detailed list. It is composed only of younger men. I have removed all the men above the age of fifty years. The prayer I now have is that you will want to send me commissions for the interim officers. These are becoming very necessary, considering that by this means their rank will have more power and will produce a better effect upon the spirit of their subordinates.

I have the honor of forwarding a packet that was sent to me by the General of the Province of Texas.

The waters [here] have been as low as they have ever been. I do not have anything else to communicate that would merit your attention.

I have the honor of saluting you and do so with my deepest respect.

Your very humble and obedient servant,
[Signed] Pierre ROUSSEAU

At Natchitoches 11 November 1785

1787 Census of Natchitoches
17 August 1787

General Census of the Residents and Sieurs at the Post of Natchitoches and its dependencies.

Names	Age	Tracts	Arpents	Slaves	Cows	Horses
Mr. Louis DE BLANC	34	2	16¾	19	20	12
Dame Elisabeth Pompone DERNEVILLE, his wife	29					
Joseph Marie Charles	11					
Marie Louise Marthe	9½					
L. Chevalier	8					
Jn Bte Dorsinaux	6½					
Celeste Mathilde	5					
Jn Bte d'Espagnet	3½					
Cesaire	2					
Ailhaud STE. ANNE & his wife	35	4	43	6	12	6
Fcois ROUQUIER	40	2	125	6	20	25
His Wife	27					
Jh Marie	4½					
Aimée	3					
Tonton	1					
Dame Widow PRUDHOMME	50	3	14	24	12	20
Antoine PRUDHOMME	21					
Dominque	18					
Anette	16					
Susette	13					
Widow PAVIE	34	1	1	6	4	2
Helene	5					
Étienne	1					
Jean de LA HAYE, employee	45	0	0	0	0	0

Legajo 201, PPC-AGI, Seville.

1787 Census of Natchitoches

Names	Age	Tracts	Arpents	Slaves	Cows	Horses
Dame Widow BORME	58	2	12	3	2	4
DARTIGUAX	56	3	57	49	150	30
His wife	57	0	0	0	0	0
DARTIGUAX, the son	22	2	60	0	0	0
Jh. CAPURAN	31	4[?]	41	4	0	0
METOYER	40	3	40	19	10	18
A Negress at the home of the same, with her three [free] infants [Marie Thérése COINCOIN Antoine Joseph METOYER Pierre Toussaint METOYER François METOYER]	35	1	6	0	0	0
Dame CAPURAN	36	0	0	0	0	0
Jn Bte LARENAUDIER	28	1	1	0	25	0
His Wife	25	0	0	0	0	0
Gaspard FIOL	52	3	13	3	160	0
His wife	40	0	0	0	0	0
Bte Mathurin [DAVID], orphan	12	0	0	0	0	0
Marie Mathurin [DAVID], orphan	15	0	0	0	0	0
Mr. Jean André VERDALAY	32	0	0	0	0	0
Benoit MONTANARY	28	0	0	0	0	0
[Gaspard FIOL] CADET, his nephew	16	0	0	0	0	0
Maurice DEMOUY	33	0	0	0	0	6
MARCOLAY	38	1	1	0	0	0
*						
Fçois CALLÉ	44	0	0	0	0	0
Fçois NAIGLE	55	0	0	0	0	0
Jn Bte LE DUC	35	0	0	0	0	0

* Past this point, the enumerator rarely showed divisions between households.

1787 Census of Natchitoches

Names	Age	Tracts	Arpents	Slaves	Cows	Horses
Fçois LE MAITRE	53	1	1	0	0	0
His Wife	23	0	0	0	0	0
François	9	0	0	0	0	0
Baptiste	5	0	0	0	0	0
Victoire	3	0	0	0	0	0
Eufrosine	1	0	0	0	0	0
Nicolas LAGNON	—					
Joseph MALIGE	44	1	2	4	0	0
His wife	30	0	0	0	0	0
Angelique	15	0	0	0	0	0
Josette	12	0	0	0	0	0
Manette	5	0	0	0	0	0
Roseline	3	0	0	0	0	0
Eulalie	1	0	0	0	0	0
[Pierre SOREL *dit*] Marly	55	5	14	5	10	10
Luc	17	0	0	0	0	0
Dominique	13	0	0	0	0	0
Marie Geneviève	21	0	0	0	0	0
Marie Jeanne	19	0	0	0	0	0
[Pierre Joseph] MAËS	30	3	25	4	28	3
His wife	—					
Baptiste BARKAR	40	0	0	0	0	0
Joseph SANSON [JANSON]	35	0	0	0	0	0
NICOLAS [PICQUERY?], free mulatto	22	0	0	0	0	0
Widow RAMBIN	55	0	0	0	0	0
Fçois RAMBIN	31	1	⅓	0	0	0
André RAMBIN	36	1	¾	5	7	4
His Wife	32	0	0	0	0	0
Marie Louise Euphrasie	8	0	0	0	0	0
André	7	0	0	0	0	0
Adelaïde	6	0	0	0	0	0
Jean Baptiste	4	0	0	0	0	0
Zité	1	0	0	0	0	0

1787 Census of Natchitoches

Names	Age	Tracts	Arpents	Slaves	Cows	Horses
[Joseph Marie] ARMANT	64	1	1½	4	2	0
His Wife	45	0	0	0	0	0
Athanase	11	0	0	0	0	0
Jn Baptiste	10	0	0	0	0	0
Adelaïde	9	0	0	0	0	0
Valery	7	0	0	0	0	0
Doctrouve	5	0	0	0	0	0
Emilie	2	0	0	0	0	0
Louis FORTIN	36	0	0	0	0	0
Ignace BELLE AVANCE	35	0	0	0	0	0
François CHABUS	28	1	½	0	0	1
[François] LACAZE	55	1	½	0	0	0
DIARD	50	1	½	0	0	0
DUBOIS, the father	—	1	½	1	14	8
His wife	—	0	0	0	0	0
Antoine DUBOIS	18	0	0	0	0	0
Jn Bte. MORIN	50	1	½	0	0	0
Louis DURAND	22	0	0	1	0	0
His wife	24	0	0	0	0	0
Etienne Vincent [DURAND]	1	0	0	0	0	0
Elie BERNARD	42	1	1	0	3	1
His wife	30	0	0	0	0	0
Pierre	13	0	0	0	0	0
Marie Josephe	1	0	0	0	0	0
Joseph MARTIN	25	0	0	0	0	0
François FREDERIC	—	2	1⅓	0	3	3
His wife	42	0	0	0	0	0
Marie [RIS]	14	0	0	0	0	0
Genevieve [RIS]	12	0	0	0	0	0
Marie Jeanne [FREDERIC]	3	0	0	0	0	0
Joseph RIS	22	0	0	0	10	7
Widow CHAGNAUX	—	0	0	0	0	0
Michel CHAGNAU	20	2	1⅓	0	19	20
Widow Bastien PRUDHOMME	50	1	4	1	4	3

1787 Census of Natchitoches

Names	Age	Tracts	Arpents	Slaves	Cows	Horses
Bastien PRUDHOMME, the son	24	0	0	0	5	5
Jn Bte. PRUDHOMME	20	0	0	0	12	2
Jacques	18	0	0	0	22	2
Catherine	22	0	0	0	9	1
Marie Louise	14	0	0	0	2	0
Widow Bte. TRICHE	43	1	11	20	25	6
Gilbert CLOSO	23	0	0	0	0	1
Louis CLOSO	20	0	0	0	0	3
Therese CLOSO [TRICHE]	15	0	0	0	0	0
Marie Josette [TRICHE]	13	0	0	1	0	0
Jn Bte & Françoise, twins [TRICHE]	12	0	0	0	0	0
Fanchonette [TRICHE]	10	0	0	0	0	00
Manuel [TRICHE]	8	0	0	0	0	0
Etienne [TRICHE]	6	0	0	0	0	0
Jean DESSOLES	56	0	0	0	0	0
Guill^me CHEVERT	37	1	3	2	20	12
His wife	28	0	0	0	0	0
Bertr^d PLAISANCE	9	0	0	0	0	0
Louis [PLAISANCE]	8	0	0	0	0	0
Jn Baptiste [PLAISANCE]	7	0	0	0	0	0
Pierre GAGNÉ	51	1	3	5	6	4
His wife	40	0	0	0	0	0
Pierre GAGNÉ, the son	19	0	0	0	0	1
Joseph	13	0	0	0	0	0
Jn Baptiste	1	0	0	0	0	0
Marie	15	0	0	0	0	0
Susanne	10	0	0	0	0	0
Henriette	5	0	0	0	0	0
Pre. BADIN	–	2	8	18	60	2
His wife	34	0	0	0	0	0
Pre. GAIGNON	39	0	0	0	0	0
His wife	20	0	0	0	0	0
Marie Louise	1	0	0	0	0	0
André VALENTIN, orphan	15	0	0	0	0	0

1787 Census of Natchitoches

Names	Age	Tracts	Arpents	Slaves	Cows	Horses
Guillaume WARDER	—	0	0	0	0	0
His wife	34	0	0	0	0	0
Emanuel PRUDHOMME	23	2	10	15	10	2
His wife	22	0	0	0	0	0
Jn Baptiste	2	0	0	0	0	0
Widow ST. DENIS	—	1	3¾	7	0	4
Marie Antoinette, orphan	16	0	0	0	0	0
Louis BUARD	43	3	17½	20	15	10
His wife	29	0	0	0	0	0
Jean Louis	10	0	0	0	0	0
Baptiste	8	0	0	0	0	0
Silvestre	6	0	0	0	0	0
Auguste	1	0	0	0	0	0
Eugenie	3	0	0	0	0	0
Joseph LAMBRE, orphan	6	0	0	0	0	0
Louis LAMBRE	20	1	1¾	5	1	3
Antoine LAMBRE	15	0	0	1	2	2
Marie SALVAN, orphan	17	0	1[?]	0	0	0
Nicolas ROUSSEAU	35	4	80	6	6	4
His wife	16	0	0	0	0	0
Widow LAMBRE	47	2	34	53	30	3
Marie LAMBRE	12	0	0	0	0	0
Pelagie BALLOUX	10	0	0	0	0	0
Remy POISSOT, the father	-	0	0	0	0	0
Remy LAMBRE	26	1	8	6	4	8
Antoine GUICHARD	45	1	2	1	3	1
[Marie] BERNARDE, free negress & her three mulatto children [DeMézières]	40	0	0	0	0	0
André DAVID	40	1	2	0	0	1
Joseph MARTIN	34	0	0	0	0	0
François DENIS	37	0	0	0	0	0
Jacques Daniel BERRIER	35	0	0	0	2	1
His wife	18	0	0	0	0	0
Pre. [LAMALATHIE *dit*] JOBAR, orphan	—	0	0	0	0	0

1787 Census of Natchitoches

Names	Age	Tracts	Arpents	Slaves	Cows	Horses
Widow BUARD	—	3	18	22	20	8
Jn Bte. BUARD	24	0	0	0	5	2
Augustin	20	0	0	0	5	2
Françse BUARD	35	0	0	6	0	0
Marie Jeanne	28	0	0	1	0	0
Denis	17	0	0	0	1	1
Pierre MICHEL [ZARICHI]	40	0	0	0	0	0
Ls COMBAS	34	0	0	0	0	0
Joseph LUÑA	20	0	0	0	0	0
Marin GRILLET	—	2	15	6	12	3
His wife	45	0	0	0	0	0
Antoine	10	0	0	0	0	0
Jn Baptiste	4	0	0	0	0	0
Magdelaine	7	0	0	0	0	0
Marie Barbe	13	0	0	0	0	0
Jean MORIN	54	1	4½	0	0	0
His wife	46	0	0	0	0	0
VAUGINE	32	2	8	10	8	4
Joseph MARIANO	30	0	0	0	0	0
Edouard MURPHY	26	2	11¾	3	0	5
Marianne BUARD	27	0	0	2	0	0
Remy POISSOT, the son	49	2	2	10	10	2
His wife	35	0	0	0	0	0
Marie	13	0	0	0	0	0
Paul & Victorie, twins	7	0	0	0	0	0
Modeste	1	0	0	0	0	0
LAVIGNE	48	0	0	0	0	0
Étienne VERGE	44	2	7	4	7	2
His wife	28	0	0	0	0	0
Étienne	7	0	0	0	0	0
Celeste	9	0	0	0	0	0
Étienne RACHAL, orphan	10	0	0	0	0	0
Pierre CHALAIR	20	0	0	0	2	2
His wife	24	0	0	0	0	0

1787 Census of Natchitoches

Names	Age	Tracts	Arpents	Slaves	Cows	Horses
Pre. DERBANNE, the father	54	3	37	38	2	27
His wife	50	0	0	0	0	0
Joseph	20	0	0	0	13	2
Louis	18	0	0	0	0	1
Emanuel	10	0	0	0	0	0
Fçois LAVESPERE	40	0	0	0	0	0
His wife	26	0	0	0	0	0
Widow Barth^y RACHAL	45	3	20	11	12	8
Barthelemy	18	0	0	0	0	0
Noel	14	0	0	0	0	0
Etienne	8	0	0	0	0	0
Antoine	6	0	0	0	0	0
Marie Louise	17	0	0	0	0	0
Marie Françoise	12	0	0	0	0	0
Pierre LACOUR	52	2	10	0	4	2
His wife	35	0	0	0	0	0
Pierre	18	0	0	0	3	4
Gaspard	14	0	0	0	0	4
Louis ANTY	24	1	2	0	5	3
His wife	20	0	0	0	0	0
Louis Cesaire	1	0	0	0	0	0
Widow LA LIME	54	0	0	0	0	0
Pre DERBANNE, the son	34	2	4	1	0	8
His wife	26	0	0	0	0	0
Pierre	[sic] 18	0	0	0	3	4
Cyprienne	1	0	0	0	0	0
François BOSSIÉ	29	2	30	10	6	5
His wife	25	0	0	0	0	0
Jn François	4	0	0	0	0	0
Ildebert	1	0	0	0	0	0
Eulalie	6	0	0	0	0	0
Marie LAMBRE, orphan	13	0	0	1	4	0
Silvestre BOSSIE	20	0	0	0	0	3
Soulange BOSSIE	—	0	0	0	0	2

1787 Census of Natchitoches

Names	Age	Tracts	Arpents	Slaves	Cows	Horses
Jn POMMIER	44	2	8½	5	7	3
His wife	20	0	0	0	0	0
Cecille DUPRE	12	0	0	0	0	0
Louis RACHAL, the son	29	2	4	0	10	8
His wife	25	0	0	0	0	0
Melanie	1	0	0	0	0	0
Marie RACHAL	15	0	0	0	0	0
Julien RACHAL	27	2	14	0	2	10
His wife	23	0	0	0	0	0
Jn Baptiste	3	0	0	0	0	0
Julien RACHAL	1	0	0	0	0	0
Joseph LINGLEISE	25	0	0	0	0	0
Louis MONET	34	2	20	21	50	20
His wife	30	0	0	0	0	0
Manuel DAVION	23	0	0	1	20	3
"Louis RACHAL, the son – I say the father" [Louis I]*	–	1	5	5	5	2
His wife	50	0	0	0	0	0
Simeon	15	0	0	0	0	6
Jn Baptiste	10	0	0	0	0	2
Felicité	6	0	0	0	0	0
Barthe RACHAL [son of Louis, Sr.]	32	1	3	0	0	3
His wife	18	0	0	0	0	0
Isabelle	1	0	0	0	0	0

*In all probability, each district's *syndic* made an original enumeration of his district, from which the commandant or his clerk compiled a consolidated list—as is known to be the case with the 1795 census of slaveholders. The peculiar identification of Louis Rachal above suggests that the *syndic* of the Grande Côte erroneously identified the head of this household as Louis Rachal *fils* rather than Louis Rachal *père*. Then the commandment, in creating his master list, recorded the entry as written and added his own note indicating that the head of the household should be the father rather than the son.

1787 Census of Natchitoches

Names	Age	Tracts	Arpents	Slaves	Cows	Horses
Pierre LARENAUDIERE	35	2	11	2	8	6
His wife	22	0	0	0	0	0
Severin	1	0	0	0	0	0
Poupone	3	0	0	0	0	0
Jn Bte LABERY	55	2	22	28	40	3
His wife	55	0	0	0	0	0
Magdelaine	16	0	0	0	0	0
Guillaume LESTAGE	52	1	6	3	5	3
His wife	46	0	0	0	0	0
Fç GONIN	15	0	0	0	0	0
Jn Baptiste [LESTAGE]	8	0	0	0	0	0
François [LESTAGE]	6	0	0	0	0	0
Barthelemy [LESTAGE]	4	0	0	0	0	0
Barnabé [LESTAGE]	2	0	0	0	0	0
Geneviève [GONIN]	17	0	0	0	0	0
Agate [LESTAGE]	1	0	0	0	0	0
Françs LE CONTE	55	2	8	0	2	1
His wife	34	0	0	0	0	0
Reine Barbe	9	0	0	0	0	0
Marie Louise	7	0	0	0	0	0
Rosalie	5	0	0	0	0	0
Eleonore	1	0	0	0	0	0
Pierre	3	0	0	0	0	0
Jean MASSIP	47	2	8½	5	6	1
His wife	26	0	0	0	0	0
Dorothée	9	0	0	0	0	0
Pierre	7	0	0	0	0	0
Elisabeth	5	0	0	0	0	0
Étienne	1	0	0	0	0	0
Bernabé CHELATRE	25	2	4	1	7	3
His wife	24	0	0	0	0	0
Josette	1	0	0	0	0	0
Widow CHELATRE	—	2	14	2	8	1
Paul CHELATRE	18	0	0	0	1	5
Fanchon	24	0	0	0	4	1

1787 Census of Natchitoches

Names	Age	Tracts	Arpents	Slaves	Cows	Horses
Rosalie CHELATRE	20	0	0	0	0	2
Jn Bte DUBOIS	30	0	0	0	0	8
Pierre COUVIE	43	0	0	1	0	5
B^d BALLOCHE	30	0	0	0	0	0
Josh. LATIE, the father	58	2	12	1	4	1
Jn Baptiste	16	0	0	0	0	0
Françoise	11	0	0	0	0	0
Giles RIGUER	26	0	0	0	0	0
Widow BAILOUX	28	1	5	6	3	4
Augustin	6	0	0	0	0	0
Jn Louis	4	0	0	0	0	0
Helenne	8	0	0	0	0	0
André FREDERIC	30	2	11	0	3	5
Pre CHELATRE	22	2	2	0	7	4
His wife	20	0	0	0	0	0
Marie Pelage	2	0	0	0	0	0
Jean Pierre	1	0	0	0	0	0
Joseph LATIE, the son	20	0	0	0	2	2
Philip FREDERIC, the father	—	2	15	2	20	4
His wife	36	0	0	0	0	0
Jn François	12	0	0	0	0	0
Jn Baptiste	4	0	0	0	0	0
Pelagie	18	0	0	0	0	0
Rosalie	15	0	0	0	0	0
Marie Catherine	6	0	0	0	0	0
Philippe FREDERIC, the son	33	2	10	2	20	3
His wife	30	0	0	0	0	0
André	7	0	0	0	0	0
Marie Barbe	5	0	0	0	0	0
Marie Pelagie	2	0	0	0	0	0
Gaspard BODIN, orphan	18	0	0	0	0	0
Geneviève BODIN, orphan	8	0	0	0	0	0
Jacques FORT	47	2	14	2	8	4
His wife	35	0	0	0	0	0
Marie Marthe	9	0	0	0	0	0

1787 Census of Natchitoches

Names	Age	Tracts	Arpents	Slaves	Cows	Horses
Marie Louise [FORT]	3	0	0	0	0	0
Fanchonette	1	0	0	0	0	0
Antoine HYMEL	38	2	15	3	8	4
His wife	36	0	0	0	0	0
Elenore	14	0	0	0	0	0
Antoine	9	0	0	0	0	0
François	7	0	0	0	0	0
Bte. DELOUCHE	34	2	12[?]	0	2	0
His wife	30	0	0	0	0	0
Jn Louis	1	0	0	0	0	0
Pre SUPERVILLE	30	0	0	0	0	0
Louis THOMASSINO	39	2	20	3	6	3
His wife	23	0	0	0	0	0
Louis	3	0	0	0	0	0
Catherine	1	0	0	0	0	0
Simon GOUELLE	37	0	0	0	0	0
Jn. CASTLEVIE	45	0	0	0	0	0
Michel HERNANDEZ	24	2	12	0	0	0
His wife	30	0	0	0	0	0
Jean Paul [COUTY]	10	0	0	0	0	0
Paul BAILLY	40	0	0	0	0	0
Fçois POULIDO	44	2	10	0	0	0
Louis VERCHAIR	38	3	18½	2	8	5
His wife	36	0	0	0	0	0
Rosalie	13	0	0	0	0	0
Adelaïde	9	0	0	0	0	0
Jean Louis	11	0	0	0	0	0
Jean Pierre	7	0	0	0	0	0
Jacques	5	0	0	0	0	0
Joseph	3	0	0	0	0	0
Ls. Barthy. RACHAL [son of Bmy.]	28	2	12	1	8	7
His wife	20	0	0	0	0	0
Marie Louise	1	0	0	0	0	0
Elisabeth DAVID	10	0	0	0	0	0
Gaspard PHILBERT	20	0	0	0	0	3

1787 Census of Natchitoches

Names	Age	Tracts	Arpents	Slaves	Cows	Horses
Jacques [LE] VASSEUR	37	3	12	2	2	1
His wife	18	0	0	0	0	0
Victorin	1	0	0	0	0	0
PIERRE, free Negro	25	0	0	0	0	0
Jean VARANGUE	30	3	30	8	6	6
His wife	50	0	0	0	0	0
Pre. DUPRE	19	0	0	0	3	4
Athanase [DUPRE]	11	0	0	0	0	0
Jn Baptiste [DUPRE]	8	0	0	0	0	0
DAVID [DUPRE]	6	0	0	0	0	0
Jn Bte VARANGUE	1	0	0	0	0	0
Marie Louise DUPRE	24	0	0	0	5	0
Marie DUPRE	14	0	0	0	0	0
Marie [JACOB] RACHAL, orphan	16	0	0	0	0	0
Charles [LE] MOINE, the father	50	2	16	0	8	0
Charles LEMOINE, the son	24	0	0	0	5	5
Ante LEMOYNE	22	0	0	0	1	1
Jn. Bte. LEMOYNE	20	0	0	0	1	1
Antoine RACHAL	23	2	6	0	2	2
His wife	18	0	0	0	0	0
Domque RACHAL	22	2	12	0	0	2
Jn Bte RACHAL	20	2	12	0	0	1
Agnes [POISSOT], free mulattress	16	0	0	0	0	0
Jh RABALAIS	23	2	12	0	0	1
His wife	20	0	0	0	0	0
Marie Jeane	1	0	0	0	0	0
Guillaume LEBRUN	50	2	40	3	3	1
Anete	9	0	0	0	0	0
Elisabeth	7	0	0	0	0	0
Jn Bte LOISEL	-	0	0	0	0	0
Fçoise BOUCHÉ	35	0	0	0	0	0
One named LEBRETON at the home of Mr. DARTIGAUX	35	0	0	0	0	0

1787 Census of Natchitoches

Names	Age	Tracts	Arpents	Slaves	Cows	Horses
Riviére aux Cannes:						
Madame Widow LECONTE [LE COMTE]	50	0	0	14	60	4
Ambroise LECONTE	37	0	64	4	15	20
His wife	18	0	0	0	0	0
Jn Bte LECONTE	1	0	0	0	0	0
Widow Joseph DUPRE [*née* LE COMTE]	25	0	0	5	15	15
Joseph DUPRE [III]	4	0	0	0	0	0
Jacques [LECOMTE] orphan [*mestizo*]	8	0	0	0	0	0
Marguerite [LECOMTE] orphan [*mulata*]	7	0	0	0	0	0
By LECOUR	25	0	30	12	15	20
Athanase LECOUR	21	0	0	0	0	0
Fanchonette LECOUR	18	0	0	0	0	0
Cecile [LECOURT]	14	0	0	0	0	0
Pelagie [LECOURT], orphan [*quadroon*]	3	0	0	0	0	0
Franç^s HUGUES	50	0	4	0	6	4
His wife	26	0	0	0	0	0
Conception [Peres]	20	0	0	0	0	0
Jn Bte ANTY	30	0	5	2	8	10
Jn Bte ANTY, the son	8	0	0	0	0	0
Valery	4	0	0	0	0	0
Pre COUTANT	30	0	2	0	2	1
Pre CHARPENTIER	33	0	5	1	15	5
His wife [Widow CLOUTIER-GALLIEN]	50	0	0	0	0	0
Alexie CLOUTIER	—	—	—	—	—	—
Marguerite	14	0	0	0	1	1
Jn Pre CLOUTIER	10	0	0	0	1	1
Michel ROBIN	37	0	10	7	25	5
His wife	23	0	0	0	0	0
Anne	14	0	0	0	0	0
Manuel	[*sic*] 3	0	0	0	0	0

1787 Census of Natchitoches

Names	Age	Tracts	Arpents	Slaves	Cows	Horses
Jn Bte DENIS	50	0	4½	0	1	2
His wife	[sic] 30	0	0	0	0	0
Jn Bte	[sic] 14	0	0	0	0	0
Pre [CASEAU *dit*] FAULEVEN	38	0	30	0	10	5
His wife	30	0	0	0	0	0
Pre BAUDOUIN	17	0	0	0	1	5
Nicolas BAUDOUIN	13	0	0	0	0	0
Thérèse	12	0	0	0	0	0
Marie Jeane	10	0	0	0	0	0
Nicolas Paul	50	0	0	0	0	0
Nicolas GALIEN	26	0	0	2	8	4
His wife	27	0	0	0	0	0
Joseph TORRES	40	0	0	0	1	1
His wife	30	0	0	0	0	0
Jh Marie TORRES`	19	0	0	0	0	0
Two twins	14	0	0	0	0	0
Dolores	12	0	0	0	0	0
Conception	8	0	0	0	0	0
Marcello	5	0	0	0	0	0
Jh MARIANO	40	0	0	0	0	0

Grande Écore:

Names	Age	Tracts	Arpents	Slaves	Cows	Horses
Fs. LEVASSEUR	48	0	10	9	8	1
His wife	30	0	0	0	0	0
Françoise	18	0	0	0	0	0
Jacques	16	0	0	0	0	0
Jn François	14	0	0	0	0	0
Louis	9	0	0	0	0	0
Manuel	7	0	0	0	0	0
Geneviève	12	0	0	0	0	0
MAILLOUX	49	0	13	0	3	3
His wife	37	0	0	0	0	0
Laurent	17	0	0	0	0	0

1787 Census of Natchitoches

Names	Age	Tracts	Arpents	Slaves	Cows	Horses
Pierre [MAILLOUX]	10	0	0	0	0	0
Thérèse	9	0	0	0	0	0
Cecile	5	0	0	0	0	0
Lestasie	2	0	0	0	0	0
Antoine LENOIR	40	0	2	0	0	0
His wife	35	0	0	0	0	0
Ant^e VASCOCU, the father	60	0	10	0	0	0
François	18	0	0	0	0	0
Eulalie	14	0	0	0	0	0
Ant^e PLAUCHÉ	50	0	0	2	0	0
His wife	25	0	0	0	0	0
Étienne	3	0	0	0	0	0
Marie	1	0	0	0	0	0
André VASCOCU	28	0	8	0	2	1
His wife	18	0	0	0	0	0
André, orphan [RAIMOND?]	7	0	0	0	0	0
Michel RAMBIN	22	0	0	0	0	5
Gme. BARBAROUX	40	0	4	0	1	2
His wife	28	0	0	0	0	0
A boy	7	0	0	0	0	0
DORTHOLAND	37	0	4½	6	7	3
His wife	30	0	0	0	0	0
A boy	10	0	0	0	0	0
Chevalier	7	0	0	0	0	0
Athanase	5	0	0	0	0	0
François	1½	0	0	0	0	0
François PRUDHOME	52	0	7	2	12	10
His wife	25	0	0	0	0	0

1787 Census of Natchitoches

Names	Age	Tracts	Arpents	Slaves	Cows	Horses
A boy	6	0	0	0	0	0
Cezaire [PRUDHOMME]	4	0	0	0	0	0
Deneige	2	0	0	0	0	0
Pre ALORGE	33	0	0	3	0	0
Etienne GAIGNÉ	58	0	8	4	15	6
His wife	37	0	0	0	0	0
Ursule	15	0	0	0	0	0
Pelagie	13	0	0	0	0	0
Basile	11	0	0	0	0	0
Louis DAVION	25	0	1	2	15	3
His wife	17	0	0	0	0	0
Louis BERTRAND	33	0	3	1	10	4
His wife	25	0	0	0	0	0
Hyacinthe	4	0	0	0	0	0
Marie Louise	2	0	0	0	0	0
Pre. BERTRAND	35	0	0	0	0	0
DAVION [Jean Baptiste II]	34	0	6	1	15	2
D^{que} DAVION	30	0	0	1	10	1
Louis MERCIER	32	0	6	0	2	1
His wife	26	0	0	0	0	0
Josete	3	0	0	0	0	0
Felicité	1½	0	0	0	0	0
Nic^{ls} MERCIER	26	0	0	0	0	0
Louis CAVALIER	37	0	0	0	0	12
Franç^s GRAPE	38	0	0	9	60	20
Julien BESSON	40	0	18	3	30	15
His wife	28	0	0	0	0	0
Jn Bte	5	0	0	0	0	0
Pre BODIN, orphan	10	0	0	0	0	0

1787 Census of Natchitoches

Names	Age	Tracts	Arpents	Slaves	Cows	Horses
Imanuel TRICH	50	[?]	20	14	30	8
His wife	37	0	0	0	0	0
Thérèse	16	0	0	0	0	0
Henry	14	0	0	0	0	0
Joseph	12	0	0	0	0	0
Manuel	10	0	0	0	0	0
Athanase	7	0	0	0	0	0
Alexis	3	0	0	0	0	0
Ls LAMALATIE	49	0	27	3	2	13
DAVID, orphan	16	0	0	0	0	4
Ls FONTENEAU	36	0	20	13	15	12
His wife	26	0	0	0	0	0
A boy	7	0	0	0	0	0
Modeste	1½	0	0	0	0	0
LAVIGNE, orphan	15	0	0	0	0	0
Jean ADLET	35	0	10	0	0	5
His wife	34	0	0	0	0	0
A boy	10	0	0	0	0	0
Valentine	8	0	0	0	0	0
François	6	0	0	0	0	0
Jn Bte	4	0	0	0	0	0
Thimothée	2	0	0	0	0	0
Pierre	2	0	0	0	0	0
Franç^s DUBOIS	26	0	12	0	24	6
His wife	21	0	0	0	0	0
Jn Bte [LEGER *dit*] Piedferme	46	0	15	1	60	5
His wife	35	0	0	0	0	0

1787 Census of Natchitoches

Names	Age	Tracts	Arpents	Slaves	Cows	Horses
Pre CARLES [in Piedferme household]	17	0	0	0	5	6
Maximillien [DE ARZE], orphan	5	0	0	0	0	0
Jacques, orphan	10	0	0	0	0	0
Widow GRAPPE	87	0	20	18	8	0
Françoise	26	0	0	0	0	0
Jn Bte	24	0	0	0	3	12
Jn Bte DAVION, orphan	18	0	0	0	0	0
Silvie [GUTIERREZ?], orphan	13	0	0	0	8	7
Pascal TURGEON	55	0	0	0	0	1
DURAND [dit] Vigé	46	0	0	0	0	0

Lac Noir:

Names	Age	Tracts	Arpents	Slaves	Cows	Horses
Gaspard DERBANE	36	0	0	0	8	8
His wife	25	0	0	0	0	0
Marie	2	0	0	0	0	0
Fs PERAULT	40	0	0	0	23	9
His wife	30	0	0	0	0	0
A boy	1	0	0	0	0	0
Jn LALANDE	64	0	16	2	100	14
His wife	58	0	0	0	0	0
Remy PERRAULT	20	0	0	0	6	3
Jn LALANDE, the son	15	0	0	0	1	4
Magdne PERRAUT	17	0	0	0	0	0
Marie Jeane LALANDE	13	0	0	0	0	0
Chrisostomé PERRAU	29	0	3	2	50	10
His wife	23	0	0	0	0	0
Felicité	5	0	0	0	0	0
Faustin	2	0	0	0	0	0

1787 Census of Natchitoches

Names	Age	Tracts	Arpents	Slaves	Cows	Horses
Catherine [SALVANT], orphan [in Chrisostomé Perrau household]	12	0	0	0	0	0
Jques. CRISTIL	45	0	0	0	8	5
His wife	35	0	0	0	0	0
François	5	0	0	0	0	0
Magdelaine	3	0	0	0	0	0
Jacques	2	0	0	0	0	0
Bayou aux Pierre:						
Bouët LAFITE	42	0	84	2	350	70
His wife	23	0	0	0	0	0
Pierre	15	0	0	0	0	0
Bapt^e	11	0	0	0	0	0
Marie	4	0	0	0	0	0
Denege	2	0	0	0	0	0
Ath^{ne} POISSOT	42	0	84	2	340	40
His wife	32	0	0	0	0	0
Athanase	11	0	0	0	0	0
Silvestre	6	0	0	0	0	0
Gim OCONOME [O'CONNOR?]	30	0	0	0	0	0
Michel HOPOK	40	0	0	0	0	0
[Jacob ?] HOPOK	35	0	0	0	0	0
Pre DOLET	28	0	40	2	130	20
His wife	20	0	0	0	0	0
Dulino [DOLET]	3	0	0	0	0	0
Pierre	1	0	0	0	0	0
JONCA, employee	40	0	0	0	0	0
WALLIS [WALLACE]	60	0	0	0	0	0
His wife	40	0	0	0	0	0
4 children	0	0	0	0	0	0

1787 Census of Natchitoches

Names	Age	Tracts	Arpents	Slaves	Cows	Horses
Remy TOTIN	33	0	0	0	0	0
His wife	25	0	0	2	20	0
2 children	-	0	0	0	0	0
Fçois MORVANT	55	0	0	0	0	0
Jn CONECHIN [CONELTY/QUINELTY]	40	0	0	0	0	0
His wife	50	0	0	0	0	0
4 children	-	0	0	0	0	0

Town of Natchitoches

Names	Age	Tracts	Arpents	Slaves	Cows	Horses
Athanase DE MÉZIÈRES	31	0	40	15	2	1
Mlle. Mᵉ Felicité	40	0	0	0	0	0
Mlle. Marie Josephe	25	0	0	0	0	0
Ls CHAMART	45	0	½	3	0	0
His wife	38	0	0	0	0	0
Marie	19	0	0	0	0	0
[Michel] CHAMART	9	0	0	0	0	0
André	5	0	0	0	0	0
Melite	3½	0	0	0	0	0
Catherine BARDON	30	0	0	0	0	0
Widow BARDON	55	0	0	0	0	0
Ls LAFORET, employee	25	0	0	0	0	0
BORME, the son	33	0	0	0	0	0
Mlle. Clemence	35	0	0	0	0	0
BAPTISTE, employee	35	0	0	0	0	0
Total Whites: 661			1918	734	2777	1018

[Signed] Josef DE LE PENA

1787 Militia Roll of Natchitoches
9 December 1787

Roll of the Company of Infantry of the Natchitoches Militia, inspected 9 December 1787.

Absent	Troops	Present
	Major Officers	
	Captain V[AUGINE]	P
	Jean B^te AILHAUT S^TE ANNE, Aide-Major	P
	Joseph CAPURAN, Sub-Lieutenant	P
	Baptiste DARTIGAUX, Color-Bearer	P
	Sergeants	
	Paul MARCOLLAY, First	P
	F^çois RAMBINT	P
	F^çois BOSSIER	P
	Corporals	
	Guillaume BARBAROUX, First	P
	Ignaisse MAILLOUX	P
	Louis VERCHAIR	P
	Pierre GAGNON	P
	Riflemen	
	Louis VIGE, First	P
	Ellie BERNARD	P
A	Jean B^te MORIN	
	André FREDERIC	P
Sick at home	Pierre GAGNIE	P
	Jean MASSIP	P
	FORTIN, *le petit*	P
Sick at home	Jacque FORT	P
	Philippe FREDERIC	P
	Bernabé CHELÊTRE	P
A [with permission]	Louis ANTY	
	Louis FONTENEAU	P

Roll 8, Jack D. L. Holmes Collection; citing leg. 193-A, PPC-AGI.

1787 Militia Roll of Natchitoches

Absent	Troops	Present
Sick at home	Jean Baptiste DENIS	
Sick at home	Jean POMMIER	
	Joseph Jean RIS	P
	Pierre CHELETRE	P
	Manuel PRUDHOMME	P
A	Michel CHAIGNOT	
Sick at home	Joseph DERBANNE	
	Charles LEMOINE	P
Sick at home	Augustin BUART	
	Julien RACHAL	P
	Antoine VASTCOCU, the elder	P
	Louis DAVIONT	P
	Jean Baptiste Bastien [PRUDHOMME]	P
Sick at home	Louis DERBANNE	
Sick at home	Michel RAMBIN	
A	COUTANT, of Riviére aux Cannes	
	Jacques Dominique [RACHAL]	P
	MURPHIL, Irish	P
A	Pierre MAËS	
Sick at home	Luc [SOREL *dit*] Marly	
Sick at home	Louis CLAUSEAU	
	Antoine DUBOIS	P
Sick at home	Jean Baptiste LEMOINE	
	Antoine Remi POISOT	P
	Antoine RACHAL	P
	Jacques VASSEUR, the son	P
	Jean Baptiste LATTIER	P
	Joseph LATTIER	P
A	Athanase LE COUR[T]	
	Pierre [CHALER *dit*] Versaille	P
Sick at home	Pierre DUPRE	
	Louis MERCIER	P
Sick at home	François CHELÊTRE	
A	Pierre BAUDOUIN	
Sick at home	Pierre LACOUR, the son	
	Alexis CLOUTIER	P

1787 Militia Roll of Natchitoches

Absent	Troops	Present
Sick at home	Berthelemy RACHAL	
Sick at home	Jacques Bastien [PRUDHOMME]	
A	Jean LA LANDE	
Sick at home	Jean DE LOUCHE	
Sick at home	Antoine PRUDHOMME	P
	Charles DURET	P
	Jean Baptiste [DAVION *dit*] St. Prie	P
Sick at home	Pierre CARLES	
A	Joseph GALLIEN	

Force				80
Officers	P	3		
Sergeants	P	3		
Corporals	P	4		
Riflemen	P	57		67
Absent		13		

At Natchitoches, 9 December 1787 — AILHAUD S^{TE} ANNE

Roll of the Company of Cavalry of the Militia inspected December 9, 1787.

Messieurs the Officers
Dn Louis Charles DEBLANC, Captain — P
Dn Bernard DORTOLANT, Lieutenant — *
Dn Maurice DE MOUY, Cornet — **

---

*"*En ville* with permission." This phrase *en ville* or *à la ville*, which translates as "in the city" or "at the city," was frequently used in this period to designate New Orleans.

** "At Saint Antoine [San Antonio], with permission."

1787 Militia Roll of Natchitoches

Absent	Troops	Present
	Lower Officers	
	François GRAPPE, Sergeant-Marechal de Logis	P
	J Bte de LARENAUDIERE, Corporal-Brigadier	P
	Remy LAMBRE, Sub-Brigadier	*
	Troops	
	J. Bte BUARD	P
	Louis BUARD	P
	Étienne VERGER	P
	J. Bte ANTY	P
	Gaspard DERBANNE	Hunting with permission
Sick	J. Bte DAVION [II]	
	Pierre DOLET	Hunting with permission
	J. Bte DERBANNE	P
	Louis MONET	P
	Remy TOUTIN	P
	J. Bte DUBOIS [II]	P
	Louis Barthelemy [RACHAL]	P
	François DUBOIS	P
	Jean VARANGUE	P
	J. Bte GRAPPE	Hunting with permission
	Chrisausthomme PEREAULT	" "
	Bastien PRUD'HOMME	P
	François TOUTIN	Hunting with permission
	Guillaume CHEVERT	P
	Dominique DAVION	P
	Louis RACHAL	P
Sick	Gilbert CLOSEAU	
	Remy PEREAULT	Hunting with permission
Sick	Nicolas PONT	
	Embroise LE COMTE	Hunting with permission
A	Barthelemy RACHAL	

* "*En ville* [New Orleans] with permission."

1787 Militia Roll of Natchitoches

Absent	Troops	Present
A	Jullien BESSON	
	Louis BERTRAND	P
	Pierre DERBANNE, Jr.	Hunting with permission
Sick	Andres VASCOCU	
	Antoine LE NOIR	P
	Pierre de LA RENAUDIERE	P
Sick	Louis LAMBRE	
	Manuel DAVION	Hunting with permission
	Dominique PRUDHOMME	P
Sick	Louis VASCOCU	
	Antoine LEMOINE	P
Sick	J. B^te [RACHAL], son of Barthelemy	

	Force of the company	46 men
	Present	<u>44</u>
	Absent	2

At Natchitoches, December 1787 — Louis DE BLANC

1788 Infantry Roll of Natchitoches: Regular Troops
6 January 1788

Detachment of the Infantry Regiment of Louisiana, actually in this post.

From the 6th [Co.] of the 1st Battalion:
Corporal Pedro RAMIS   1

From the 5th [Co.] of the 1st Battalion:
Franco FEBLES   1
Man¹ Goñz. [GONZALES], 2d   1
Andres GALLANDO   1

From the 8th [Co.] of the 1st Battalion:
Distinguished Don Diego DEMEZIERES   1
Absent without leave

From the 1st [Co.] of the 2nd Battalion:
Anto Hernz [HERNANDEZ]   1

From the 2nd [Co.] of the 2nd Battalion:
Venta ARIZAVAL   1
                                                                    7

[Signed] Josef DE LA PENA

༒

Roll 9, Holmes Collection; citing leg. 14, PPC-AGI.

1789 Militia Roll of Natchitoches
22 March 1789

Statement of the Cavalry Company of Militia at the post of Natchitoches, in the order according to how they passed in review.

Rank	Names of Officers & Soldiers
Messieurs, the officers	D[on] Louis Charles DEBLANC, Captain Dⁿ Bernard DORTOLAND, Lieutenant Dⁿ Nicolas ROUSSEAU, Sub-lieutenant Dⁿ Maurice DEMOUŸ, Ensign
Messieurs, the lower officers	F^{çois} GRAPPE, Billeting marshal Baptiste LA RENAUDIERE, Brigadier Remy LAMBRE, Sub-brigadier
Cavalrymen	Jean Baptiste BUARD Louis BUARD Etienne VERGER Gaspar DERBANNE Jean Baptiste ANTY DAVION [Jean Baptiste II] Pierre DOLET Jean B^{te} DERBANNE Louis MONET Remy TOUTIN Jean Baptiste DUBOIS François DUBOIS Jean VARANGUE Crisosthome PERAULT Jean Baptiste GRAPPE Bastien PRUDHOMME François TOUTIN Joseph LAVIGNE Barthelemy LECOUR[T]

Legajo 202, folios 400–5, PPC-AGI, Seville.

1789 Militia Roll

Rank	Names of Officers & Soldiers
Cavalrymen (Cont'd)	Guiliaume CHEVERT
	Dominique DAVION
	Louis RACHAL
	Gilbert CLAUSEAU
	Remy PERAULT
	Nicolas PONT
	Embroise LE COMPTE
	Berthelemy RACHAL
	Julien BESSON
	Louis Berthelemy [RACHAL]
	Pierre DERBANNE
	Louis BERTRAN
	André VACOCU
	Antoine LE NOIR
	Pierre LA RENAUDIERE
	Louis LAMBRE
	Manuel DAVION
	Dominique PRUDHOMME
	Louis VACOCU
	Antoine LE MOINE
	Jean Baptiste Berthelemy [RACHAL]
Force:	47
Recapitulation:	
Officers	4
Under-officers	3
Cavalrymen:	40

[Signed] Louis DEBLANC

1789 Militia Roll

Rank	Names of Officers & Soldiers

Statement of the Infantry Company of Militia at Natchitoches, as passed in review, 22 March 1789.

Messieurs, the officers	Jean Baptiste AILHAUD S^TE ANNE Jean Baptiste DARTIGAUX, Lieutenant Paul MARCOLLAY, Sub-lieutenant
Sergeants	François RAMBIN Jean ADLAY François BOSSIÉ François CALLÉ
Corporals	Guillaume BARBAROUX Ignace MAILLIOUX Louis VERCHÊRE Pierre GAGNON
Riflemen	Jean Baptiste MORIN Ellie BERNARD André FREDERIC Pierre GAGNIE Jean MASIP Louis FORTIN Louis FORTIN *dit* Le Petit Philipe FREDERIC Joseph JAMSON Bernabé CHELÊTRE Louis ANTY Louis FONTENEAU Jean POMIER Pascal TURGEON Joseph MARTIN Joseph JEAN RIS Pierre CHELÊTRE Manuel PRUDHOMME Michael CHAIGNEAUT Joseph DERBANNE

1789 Militia Roll

Rank	Names of Officers & Soldiers
Riflemen (cont'd.)	Charle LE MOINE
	Augustin BUART
	Julien RACHAL
	Antoine VACOCU
	Jean Baptiste Bastien [PRUDHOMME]
	Louis DERBANNE
	Michel RAMBIN
	Gime [Young], an Irlander
	Jacques Dominique [RACHAL]
	Morphil [MURPHY], an Irlander
	Gaspar [FIOL], *cadet* [the younger]
	Pierre MAËS
	Luc [SOREL dit] Marly
	Louis CLAUSEAU
	Antoine DUBOIS
	Jean B^{te} LE MOINE
	Antoine RACHAL
	Jean LE VASSEUR, the son
	Jean B^{te} LATTIER
	Joseph LATTIER
	Athanaze LE COUR[T]
	Pierre [CHALER *dit*] Versailles
	Pierre CHARPENTIER
	Pierre DUPRÉ
	Louis MERCIER
	F^{çois} CHELÊTRE
	Pierre BAUDOUIN
	Pierre LA COUR, the son
	Alexis CLOUTIER
	Berthelemy RACHAL
	Jacque Bastien [PRUDHOMME]
	Jean LA LANDE, the son
	Jean DELOUCHE
	Joseph MARTINAU
	François MONBRUN
	Antoine PRUDHOMME

1789 Militia Roll

Rank	Names of Officers & Soldiers
Riflemen (cont'd.)	Joseph MARTIN, *trafiquan* [peddler]
	Charle LURET
	Jean Baptiste [DAVION, *dit*] St Prix
	Pierre CARLES
	Nicolas GALIEN

Force:	80 [*sic*]
Recapitulation:	
Officers	3 :
Sergeants	4 : 73
Corporals	4 :
Cavalrymen:	62 :

[Signed] J. B^{te} AILHAUD S^{TE} ANNE

Supplement
4 September 1788

Louis CHAMART
Joseph MALIGE
André WERDALAY
Maturin [DAVID]
Pierre GAGNIE, the son
Yves LISSIVOUR [LISSILOUR]
Jean Joseph MARTINEAU
Gasparite LACOUR
Silvestre BOSSIÉ
Soulange BOSSIÉ
Jacques LA CASSE
Gaspart BODIN
François LA VESPERE
Jean Jacob OPOCQUE [HOPPOCK]
Edward GREEN
Benoist MONTANARY
Simeon RACHAL
Jean Denis BUARD
François VACOCU

1789 Militia Roll

Rank	Names of Officers & Soldiers
Supplement (cont'd)	Laurent MAILLOUX
	François GONIN
	André LE BRUN
	François CALINAN
	Pierre BAILLIOT
	Joseph TORES
	Gil IZGUIERDO
	André de St ANDRÉ
	Jean B^{te} LAVIGNE
	Antoine COINDÉ
	François MERCIER
	Antoine LAMBRE
	Pierre TERNIER
	Louis DAVID
	Joseph RABALAY
	Pierre LAVIGNE
	Jean Baptiste SAVERULLE
	Michel HERNANDES
	Richard SIMS
	François LANGLOIS
	Jean Laurent BODIN
	Zakarie MARTIN
	Nicolas MERCIER
	Bouet LAFFITTE, the son
	Antoine POISSOT
	Joseph TRICHEL, the son
	WALES [WALLACE], the son

1790 Church Tax Roll of Natchitoches
1 March 1790*

Assessment relating to the community of residents of Natchitoches made by me, METOYER, syndic of the said post, on account of the 75 piasters that the community has consented to pay to Sieur Jean Baptiste MAURIN, for lengthening the storehouse of the presbytery of this parish as it is stated on the agreement that was pledged and signed by the *ancien habitans** of this post, dated 6 January 1790.

After having carefully examined the census that has been given me, I have found that each white male who has attained the age of 14 years or over is due to pay one *real* for himself, as are widows and free people of color, and the same sum for each of their slaves, the small ones as well as the large, as it itemized hereafter, to wit:

Names of Mrs the residents	Whites	Slaves	Reales	Silver Received
The Town:				
P. AILHAUD Ste Anne	1	14	14	14
P. D'ORTHOLANT	1	7	7	7
P. Polle MARCOLLAY	1	0	1	1
P. Athanzae DE MEZIERES & his two brothers	1	14	15	17
P. François CALLAY	1	0	1	1
Fis LACAZE	1	1	2	0
P. Fris ROUQUIER	1	13	14	0
P. Remy LAMBRE	1	38	38	14
P. Ive LISSILOUR	1	0	1	1
P. SOREL [dit] Marly	1	5	0	0
P. Luque [SOREL dit Marly	0	0	0	0
P. Dominique [SOREL dit] Marly	1	0	0	0

Natchitoches Parish Records Collection, Department of Archives, Hill Memorial Library, Louisiana State University (LSU), Baton Rouge.

* This term *ancien habitans* was used to denote the older families of the community, all Catholic, as opposed to the Anglo-Protestant population that had begun to settle at Natchitoches in the previous decade.

1790 Church Tax Roll

Names of M^rs the residents	Whites	Slaves	Reales	Silver Received
The Town, continued:				
P. Widow DARTIGEAUX	1	17	18	18
P. Antoine [VAS]COCU	1	0	1	1
P. B^te BARGARE [BARKER]	1	1	1	1
P. F^is RAMBIN	1	1	2	2
P. André RAMBIN	1	5	5	5
P. Michel RAMBIN	1	0	1	1
P. ARMANT, the father	1	1	2	2
P. Widow [François] FREDERIC	1	0	1	1
P. Michel CHANIAU	1	0	1	1
P. J. B^te MAURIN	1	0	1	1
P. Louis FORTIN	1	0	1	1
P. F^is NEGLE	1	0	1	1
P. F^is LE MAITRE	1	0	1	1
P. Gaspard FIOL	1	5 :	7	7
P. J. B^te DAVID	1	:		
Rivière aux Cannes:				
P. Nicolas PON	1	1	2	2
P. Richard CHIME [SIMS]	1	0	1	1
P. Antoine COINDÉ	1	0	1	1
P. Simon GOIE	1	0	1	1
P. Pierre TOUTANT	1	0	1	1
P. Charle DANIS	1	0	1	1
P. Josephe TORRE	1	0	1	1
P. F^is DAVION	1	1	2	2
P. Alexis CLOUTIE	1	6	7	7
P. Widow LE COMPTE	1	16	17	17
P. Ambroise LE COMPTE	1	5	6	6
P. Bertelemy LE COURT	1	1 :	3	3
P. Athanaze LECOURT	1	:		
P. Nicolas GALLIEN	1	1	2	2
P. François HUGHE	1	0	1	1
P. B^te ANTY	1	2	3	3
P. Pierre BAUDOIN	1	0	1	1
P. J. B^te DENIS	1	0	1	1
P. Pierre CAJAU	1	:	ᵑ	ᵑ
P. Nicolas BAUDOIN	1	:		

1790 Church Tax Roll

Names of M^{rs} the residents	Whites	Slaves	Reales	Silver Received
Rivière aux Cannes, continued				
Jean HORNIE	1	4	5	0
Ille à Brevel:				
P. Pierre BROSSET	1	2	3	3
P. J. B^{te} DELOUCHE	1	0	1	1
P. Louis RACHAL, Jr.	1	1	2	2
P. B^y RACHAL, son of Louis	1	1	2	2
P. André ST. ANDRÉ	1	0	1	1
P. Jean POMMIE	1	5	6	6
P. Louis LAMBRE	1	5	6	6
P. Pierre LA RENODIERE	1	2	3	3
Louis RACHAL, Sr.	1	1 :	3	0
Simeon RACHAL, the son	1	:		
P. Jullien RACHAL	1	3	4	4
P. Jean VARANGUE	1	8	9	9
P. Pierre DUPRE	1	0	1	1
P. Jaque LACASSE	1	1	1	0
P. Antoine RACHAL	1	1	2	2
P. Charle LE MOINE, Sr.	1	0	1	1
P. Charle LEMOINE, son	1	1	2	2
P. Antoine LEMOINE	1	0	1	1
P. J. B^{te} B^y RACHAL	1	0	1	1
P. Dominique RACHAL	1	0	1	1
P. Remy POISOT	1	12	13	13
P. Baptiste LAVIGNE	1	0	1	1
P. Josephe RABALLAY	1	1	2	2
P. Guilhomme LEBRUN	1	3 :	5	5
P. LOISET	1	:		
P. Pierre [CHALER *dit*] Versaille	1	0	1	1
P. Jaque LEVASSEUR	1	3	4	4
Grande Cotte:				
P. Louis Bertelmy RACHAL	1	2	3	3
P. Bertel^y RACHAL, son of the widow	1	0	1	1
P. Louis VERCHERE	1	2 :	4	4
P. J. Louis VERCHERE, the son	1	:		
P. Nicolas [DOCLAS], free Negro	1	0	1	1

1790 Church Tax Roll

Names of Mrs the residents	Whites	Slaves	Reales	Silver Received
Grande Cotte (cont'd.)				
P. Michelle HERNANDES	1	1	2	2
P. Louis THOMASINO	1	3	4	4
P. Pierre MIGUEL [MICHEL dit ZARICHI]	1	0	1	1
P. Pierre SUPERVIL	1	0	1	1
P. Marie Thérèse [COINCOIN], Free Negresse	1	0	1	2
P. Antoine HIMEL	1	3	4	4
P. Jaque FORT	1	4	5	5
P. Phelipe FREDERI, the son	1	2	3	3
P. Phelipe FREDERI, the father	1	2 :	4	4
P. François FREDERI, the son	1	:		
P. Gaspart BODIN	1	0	1	1
P. Pierre CHELET	1	0	1	1
P. Gaspart DERBANNE	1	0	1	1
P. Pierre MAIES	1	13	14	14
P. André FREDERIQUE	1	7	8	8
P. Jhe LATTIÉ, the father	1	1 :		
P. Bte LATTIÉ, the son	1	:	4	4
P. Fis LATTIÉ, the son	1	:		
P. Pierre BOUVIÉ	1	1	2	2
P. Widow CHELET	1	2 :	4	4
P. J. Bte DUBOIS	1	:		
P. Bernabé CHELET	1	0	1	1
P. Polle CHELET	1	3 :	5	5
P J. MASSIP	1	:		
P. J. Bte LE MOINE	1	0	1	1
P. François [SAIDEC dit] LECONTE	1	3 :	5	5
P. Guilhomme LESTAGE	1	:		
P. François GONNIN, his step-son	0	:		
P. J. Bte LABERY	1	28	29	29
Jean Jhe MARTINAU, exempt	1	0	1	1
P. Louis MONET	1	26	27	27
Silveste BOSSIE	1	7	8	6
François BOSSIE	1	12 :		
Plaside BOSSIE	1	0 :	16	0
Antoine LAMBRE	1	1 :		

1790 Church Tax Roll

Names of Mʳˢ the residents	Whites	Slaves	Reales	Silver Received
Grande Cotte (cont'd.)				
P. Soulange BOSSIE	1	0	1	1
P. Pierritte DERBANNE	1	4	5	5
P. Louis ANTY	1	0	1	1
P. Pierre LACOURT, the father	1	:		
P. Gasparitte LACOURT	1	:	3	3
P. Pierre LACOURT, the son	1	:		
P. Widow Bertʸ RACHAL	1	11 :	13	13
P. Manuel RACHAL	1	:		
P. Pierre DERBANNE	1	38 :		
P. Jʰᵉ DERBANNE	1	:	42	42
P. Louis DERBANNE	1	:		
P. Manuel DERBANNE	1	:		
P. François LAVESPERE	1	0	1	1
P. Etiene VERGE	1	3	4	4
P. Etiene RACHAL	1	0	1	1
P. Edouard MORPHY	1	5	6	6
Athanaze POISOT	1	8	9	0
P. Marin GRILLET	1	10 :	12	12
P. Antoine GRILLET	1	:		
P. Gaspart FILIBERT	1	0	1	1
P. François F̶I̶L̶I̶ LEVASSEUR [sic]	1	9 :	11	11
P. J. Fⁱˢ LEVASSEUR	1	:		
P. Widow BUARD	1	26	27	27
P. Mariane BUARD	0	3	3	3
P. Bᵗᵉ BUARD	1	1	2	2
P. Augustin BUARD	1	0	1	1
P. Denis BUARD	1	0	1	1
François MONGINAUT	1	9	10	0
P. Widow [Jacob] LAMBRE & Marie, her daughter	1	17	18	18
Jʰᵉ CAPURANT	1	10	11	0
P. Widow ST. DENIS	1	5	6	6
P. Louis BUARD	1	20 :	22	22
P. Louis Jʰᵉ LAMBRE	0	1 :		
P. Manuel PRUDHOMME	1	36	36	37
P. Dominique PRUDHOMME	1	1	2	2

1790 Church Tax Roll

Names of M^rs the residents	Whites	Slaves	Reales	Silver Received
Grande Cotte (cont'd.)				
P. Pierre BADIN	1	1	9	20
P. Remy TOUTIN	1	2	3	3
Pierre GANNIÉ	1	5 :		
His son Pierre	1	:	8	0
Josephe GANNIÉ	1	:		
P. Guilhomme CHEVERRE[?]	1	5 :	7	7
P. Bertrant PLAISENCE	1	:		
P. Widow TRICHLE	1	21 :		
P. Gilbert CLAUSEAU	1	:		
P. Louis CLAUSEAU	1	:	27	27
P. Marie Josephe TRICHLE	0	2 :		
P. J. B^te TRICHLE	1	:		
P. Antoine PRUDHOMME	1	3	4	4
P. Bastien PRUDHOMME	1	:		
P. Widow Bastien PRUDHOMME	1	1 :	5	5
P. B^te Bastien PRUDHOMME	1	:		
P. Jaque PRUDHOMME	1	:		
Guilhomme VARDET [WARDEN]	1	0	1	0
Charles DURET	1	0	1	0
P. Antoine LUSSIÉ	1	0	1	1
P. Diegue RAMEAU	1	0	1	1
Grande Ecore:				
Antoine PLOCHÉ	1	0	1	0
P. Iniasse MAYOU	1	:	2	2
P. Lorand MAYOU	1	:		
P. André [VAS]COQU	1	0	1	1
P. Antoine VASCOQU, the father	1	0	1	1
P. Jean Louis [VAS]COQU	1	0	1	1
P. François [VAS]COQU	1	0	1	1
P. Josephe Jean RIS	1	0	1	1
P. Guilhomme BARBEROUX	1	0	1	1
P. F^is PRUDHOMME	1	2	3	3
P. Pierre ALORGE	1	3	4	4
P. Louis DAVION	1	2	3	3

1790 Church Tax Roll

Names of M^{rs} the residents	Whites	Slaves	Reales	Silver Received
Grande Ecore, continued:				
P. Etiene GANNIÉ	1	4	5	5
P. Louis BERTRANT	1	1	2	2
P. J. B^{te} DAVION	1	1	2	2
P. Dominique DAVION	1	1	2	2
P. Louis MERCIÉ	1	0	1	1
P. J^{he} MARTIN	1	0	1	1
Cameté [Campti]:				
P. Elie BERNARD	1	0	1	1
P. Pierre BERNARD	1	0	1	1
P. François GRAPE	1	9	10	10
P. Widow GRAPE	1	17 :	19	19
P. J. B^{te} GRAPE	1	:		
P. B^{te} DAVION, for a slave	0	1	1	1
P. Benoit MONTANARY	1	1	2	2
Manuel TRICHLE	1	13 :		
Anris [Henri] TRICHLE	1	3 :	19	19
Joseph TRICHLE	1	:		
P. Louis LAMALATIE	1	4 :	6	6
P. Louis DAVID	1	:		
P. Louis FONTENAU	1	18 :		
P. Pierre TESSIE, hireling	1	:	22	22
P. Jean DE LA EST, hireling	1	:		
Michel VINCANT, hireling	1	:		
P. Jullien BESSON	1	2	3	3
P. J. B^{te} [LEGER *dit*] Piedferme	1	1 :	3	3
P. Pierre CARLES	1	:		
P. Jean ADELET	1	0	1	1
P. François DUBOIS	1	0	1	1
P. Antoine DUBOIS	1	0	1	1
P. J. B^{te} LARENODIERE	1	0	1	1
P. Antoine LENOIRE	1	1	2	2

1790 Church Tax Roll

Names of Mrs the residents	Whites	Slaves	Reales	Silver Received
Lac Noire:				
P. Jean LALANDE	1	2 :		
P. Remy PERAU	1	:	5	4
P. J. Pierre LALANDE	1	:		
P. François PEREAU	1	0	1	1
P. Jaque CRISTY	1	0	1	1
P. Jean Crisostome PEREAU	1	1	2	2
Fause Rivière:				
Baptiste BREVEL	1	11 :	12	12
Baltazar BREVEL	1	:		
Antoine Remy POISOT	1	0	1	5
P. J. Bte Gaspart DERBANNE	1	1	2	2
Jaque JEUIN *dit* Gime Lengles [James YOUNG called Jim, the Englishman]	1	0	1	1
Total	220	606	922	

The present assessment amounts to nine hundred twenty-two reales which makes the sum of one hundred fifteen piasters and two reales. From this sum there has been paid to Mr. J. Bte MAURIN, seventy-five piasters; the rest, which amounts to forty piasters and two reales, will be used toward several persons in need and the preservation of the church and the presbytery of this parish. (It has been supposed that each individual has paid their own share, for which reason a checkmark is carried on the present assessment.) At Natchitoches, 3 March 1790.

METOYER

Publication has been made at the parish mass . . . . The present copy has been remitted to Mr. Antoine HIMELLE, for him to read it and then to pass it to his neighbor, from where it will go from neighbor to neighbor until it reaches the home of Mr. Antoine PRUDHOMME—who will communicate it

1790 Church Tax Roll

to M^{d.} Bastien [PRUDHOMME] and Charles DURET, and then it will be returned to me. Certified by my hand the day that is above, at Natchitoches, 3 March 1790.

A copy has been sent to M^d THOMASINE, in the absence of her husband, for it to circulate to the last habitation of Rivière aux Cannes. Likewise, a copy has been sent to Mr Iniasse MAYOU for advertising at Grand Écore and Campti. Natchitoches, 3 March 1790.

METOYER

1790 Deliquent Tax Roll of Natchitoches
30 November 1790

List of the persons who have not paid their share of assessment of 75 piasters that the community owes to Sr. J. B^te MAURIN for the lengthening that was made on the storehouse of the presbytery.

	Name	Polls	Piasters
	François LACAZE	2	2
	Jean HORNIE	5	5
	Louis RACHAL Sr. & his son Simeon	3	3
P^d	F^is BOSSIE and his brothers	16	16
	J. J^he MARTINAUT, exempt by request	0	1
	Athanaze POISOT, exempt because he paid more than his share for the assessment on the church	0	9
	F^is MONGINAUT, exempt by contrary request	0	10
	J^he CAPURANT	11	11
	Pierre GANNIE and his two sons	8	8
	Guilhomme VARDET [WARDEN]	1	1
	Charle DURET	1	1
	Antoine PLOCHÉ, contrary request	0	1
	Manuel TRICHLE and his children, exempt by *lavante* of [on?] his land	0	19
	Michel VINSANT at the home of Mr. FONTENAUT, an itinerant	1	1
	B^te BREVEL and his son	13	13
	Antoine Remy POISOT	1	1
	Jaque JEUIN *dit* Gime l'Angles [James YOUNG called Jim, the Anglo]	1	1
	Silveste BOSSIE, being taxed at 8 reales, he has paid only 6, and owes	2	2

[Signed] METOYER

Folder 705, Melrose Collection, NSU Archives.

1791 Militia Roll of Natchitoches
4 November 1791

Roll of the Infantry Company of Natchitoches Militia, taken at review, 4 November 1791.

Officers

Captain	D^n Jean Bap^{te} AILHAUD S^{TE} ANNE
Lieutenant:	D^n Jean Bap^{te} DARTIGAUX
Sublieutenant:	D^n Paul MARCOLLAY
Color Bearer:	D^n Pierre METOYER

Sergeants

François RAMBIN
Jean ADLET
François BOSSIÉ
François CALLÉ

Corporals

Guillaume BARBAROUX
Louis VERCHAIR
Jean Joseph MARTINEAU
Le Petit FORTIN

Riflemen

Ellie BERNARD
Jean MASSIP
Philippe FREDERIC
Bernabé CHELETRE
Louis FONTENEAU
Pascal TURJON
Joseph Jean RIS

André FREDERIC
Louis FORTIN
Joseph JANSON
Louis ANTY
Jean POMMIER
Joseph MARTIN
Pierre CHELETRE

Roll 8, Jack D. L. Holmes Collection; citing leg. 193-A, PPC-AGI.

1791 Militia Roll of Natchitoches

Riflemen (cont'd.)

Manuel PRUD'HOMME
Charles LE MOINE
Julien RACHAL
Jean Bap^te Bastien [PRUDHOMME]
Michel RAMBIN
Jaques [LE] VASSEUR
Gaspard *Cadet* [FIOL]
Luc [SOREL *dit*] Marly
Antoine DUBOIS
Antoine RACHAL
Athanase LE COURT
Pierre DUPRE
François CHELETRE
Pierre LA COUR Jr.
Berthelmy RACHAL
Joseph MARIANO
Antoine PRUD'HOMME
Jean Bap^te DAVION
Louis CHAMARD
André VERDELAY
Pierre GAGNIÉ Jr.
Jean [LE] VASSEUR, the son
Silvestre BOSSIÉ
Jacques LA CASSE
François LAVESPÈRE
Benoit MONTHANARY
Jean Denis BOUARD
Laurant MAILLOUX
André VALENTIN
Gil IZQUIERDO
Jean B^te LAVIGNE
François MERCIER
Richard SIMS
Louis DAVID
Pierre LAVIGNE
Jean FABRE
François MORVANT Jr.

Joseph DERBANNE
Augustin BUARD
Antoine VASCOCU
Louis DERBANNE
Gimes JOUNG [James YOUNG]
Eduard MURPHY
Pierre MAES
Louis CLAUSEAU
Jean B^te LE MOINE
Jean B^te LATTIÉ
Pierre [CHALER *dit*] VERSAILLES
Louis MERCIER
Pierre BAUDOUIN
Alexi CLOUTIER
Jean DE LOUCHE
François MONBRUN
Charles DURET
Nicolas GALIEN
Joseph MALIGE
Maturin BOISSOT
Ives LISSILOUR
Gasparit LA COURT
Soulange BOSSIÉ
Gaspard BODIN
Jacob OBHOR [HOPPOK]
Simeon RACHAL
François VASCOCU
François GONIN
Joseph Marie TORRES
André de ST. ANDRÉ
Antoine COINDÉ
Antoine LAMBRE
Pierre TERNIER
Joseph RABALAY
Jean Bap^te DAVID
Michel HERNANDEZ
Jean B^te SAVOYE

MILLS • NATCHITOCHES COLONIALS | 143

1791 Militia Roll of Natchitoches

Recapitulation:

Officers	4
Sergeants	4
Corporals	4
Riflemen	88
Force	100

[Signed] J. B^te AILHAUD Ste ANNE
Louis DE BLANC

Roll of the Cavalry Company of Natchitoches Militia taken in review, 4 November 1791.

Captain:	D^n Louis Charles DE BLANC
Lieutenant:	D^n Bernard D'ORTOLANT
2s Lieutenant:	D^n Maurice DE MOUY

Under-Officers

Marechal de Logis:	François GRAPPE
Brigadier:	Jean B^te LA RENAUDIERE
Under-Brigadier:	Remy LAMBRE

Cavalrymen

Louis BOUARD	Bap^te BOUARD
Etienne VERGER	Louis LAMBRE
Jean Bap^te DERBANNE	Jean Bap^te GRAPPE
Crisostome PEROT	Remy PEROT
Jean LALANDE Jr.	Louis MONET
Bap^te ANTY	Gilbert CLAUSSEAU
Dominique PRUD'HOMME	Bastien PRUD'HOMME
Gasparite DERBANNE	Jacques Bastien [PRUDHOMME]
François DUBOIS	Louis SEMPRY [DAVION *dit* St. Prix]
Louis BERTRAND	Jullien BESON
Remy TAUTIN	François TAUTIN

1791 Militia Roll of Natchitoches

Cavalrymen (cont'd.)

Jean Bap^{te} DUBOIS
Dominique Sempry
  [DAVION *dit* St. Prix]
Louis RACHAL *dit* Barthelemy
Louis RACHAL [son of Louis]
Ambroise LE COMPTE
Barthelemy LE COUR[T]
Louis VASCOCU
Michel CHEGNAU
Pierrite CARLES

Pierrite DERBANNE
Jean VARANGUE
Bap^{te} RACHAL [son of Barthelemy]
Barthelemy RACHAL
Antoine LEMOINE
Enrry TRICHEL
Manuel SEMPRY [DAVION *dit* St. Prix]
Pierre LARRENAUDIERE
Jean Bap^{te} DAVION

Recapitulation:
Officers:	3
Lower Officers:	3
Cavalrymen:	<u>40</u>
Force:	43

[Signed] Louis DE BLANC

1793 Delinquent Tax Roll of Natchitoches
[*ca.* December 1793]

Statement of the various debtors to the old tax, who have not given their notes and who nevertheless have been regarded as enumerated during this time, as certified by the attached account of Mr. Maës.

Names of the Messieurs	Piasters	Escalins
Simeon RACHAL		5
Athanase DUPRE		4
Piere BEAULIEU		4
Nicholas Martin BODIN		4
Margueritte [LE COMTE], free Negress		4
Nicolas BEAUDOUIN		4
MARIOTE, free Negress		4
Antoine BERJON		4
François HUGHES *dit* Tonnan		4
Barthelemy LE COUR		6
Joseph TORES		4
Pierre COUTANT		4
Louis LAMBRE	1	2½
André ST. ANDRÉ		4
Louis Berthelemy RACHALE		1½
François TOTIN		4
Pierite DERBANNE	1	

Folder 735, Melrose Collection, NSU Archives. The document is undated; however an analysis of the enumerated individuals indicates that the original tax list was drawn in late 1793. According the Register 15, page 8, Archives of Immaculate Conception Church, Natchitoches, "Louis PLAISANCE, deceased," passed away on 29 November 1793 while Register 15, page 9 indicates that "Gaspard FIOL," who was still alive at the time of enumeration, died 22 December 1793. Thus, it would appear that the original enumeration occurred in December 1793, but no determination can be made of the date upon which Pierre Joseph Maës enumerated the delinquents. The roll itself is unsigned. The handwriting and various peculiar misspellings of names are those of BOSSIÉ, syndic, who drafted and signed several other rolls of this period.

1793 Delinquent Tax Roll of Natchitoches

Names of the Messieurs	Piasters	Escalins
Joseph DERBANNE	0	4
François LAVESPÈRE	0	6
Antoine BORDELON	0	4
Louis [DURAND, *dit*] Vigé		04
Louis PLAISANCE, deceased	0	4
Bertran PLAISANCE	0	4
Piere GAGNÉ and his two sons	1	0
Btiste. BREVELLE, the father	1	4
Baltazard BREVELLE	0	1
James [Jacques] VACHERE, at Mr. ROUQUIER's	0	1
Gaspart FIOLE	1	6
Widow LANGLOIS *dit* Sans Regret	0	? ½
Pedro ALEMAND	0	4
Pedro RAMISE, corporal	0	4
Joseph Marie ARMANT	0	6
Antoine DUBOIS	0	4
Succession of Widow François FREDERIC	0	4
Pascale TURGEON	7	1
Ignace MAILLOUX and his two sons	1	4
François PRUDHOMME	0	6
François MERCIER	0	4
Louis MERCIER	0	4
Widow ROBLO	0	4
Btiste. DAVION, the younger	1	0
Pierre ALORGE	1	0
François DUBOIS	0	4
Widow GRAPE	4	2
François GRAPE	2	6
Btiste. GRAPE	0	4
Benoit MONTANARY	0	6
Widow or the succession of Manuelle TRICHLL	4	0
Henry TRICHLL	1	4
Joseph TRICHLL	0	4
Louis LAMALATY	1	6
Louis DAVID	0	4

1793 Delinquent Tax Roll of Natchitoches

Names of the Messieurs	Piasters	Escalins
Btiste. DAVID	0	4
Jean PALVADO	0	4
Louis FONTENAU	6	0
Julien BESSON	1	4
Piere BODIN	0	4
Btiste. LAGÉ [dit] Piedferme	0	6
Piere CARLE	0	4
Jaque, orphan	0	4
Jean LALANDE	1	0
Remy PERO	0	4
François PERO	0	4
Jaque CRISTY	0	4
Gaspart DERBANNE	0	4
Bastienitte PRUDHOMME	0	4
Etiene DUGUETE	0	4
Gme. SCNODAY [William SNODDY]	0	4
Antoine POISOT	0	4
Michele VINCENT	0	4
	66	3½

Notes remitted to me by Mr. Maës for the community

By:		Piasters	Escalins
	Mr. DEBLANC	1	4
	Antoine RACHAL	0	3
	DARTIGAUX	7	2
	Widow DARTIGAUX	8	0
	DARTIGAUX	1	4
	TAUZIN	1	6½
	MÉTOYÉ	13	0
	Remy TOTIN, 2 notes	10	0
	DARTIGAUX	42	2
	TAUZIN	6	5½
	BOSSIÉ	17	2
		109	5

1793 Militia Roll of Natchitoches
1 December 1793

First Company of Cavalry of the Militia at the Post of Natchitoches taken in review, 1 December 1793.

Captain	D^n Louis Charles DE BLANC
Lieutenant	D^n Louis Mª Cezerio DE BLANC
Sublieutenant	D^n Maurice DE MOUY
Marechal de Logis	Athanaze POISSOT
Brigadier	Barthelmy LECOURT
Under-Brigadier	Baptiste GRAPPE

Baptiste BUARD
J^n B^{te} DERBANNE
Remy PERREAULT
Louis MONET
Gilbert CLOZEAU
Basthien PRUD'HOMME
Jacques Basthien [PRUDHOMME]
Louis SEMPRY [DAVION dit
   St. Prix]
Remy TOUTIN
Jean B^{te} DUBOIS
Dominique DAVION
B^{te} RACHAL [son of Barthelemy]
Antoine LE MOINNE
Enrry TRICHEL
Louis VACOCU
Michel CHEIGNAU
Pierre CARLES
Athanaze LE COURT
Augustine BUARD

Athanaze DUPRÉ
Crisosthomme PERREAULT
Jean LALANDE, Jr.
Bap^{te} ANTY
Dominique PRUD'HOMME
Louis CLOZEAU
François DUBOIS
Louis BERTRAND
Balthazar BREVEL
François TOUTIN
Pierrit DERBANNE
Jean VARRANGUE
Louis RACHAL [son of Barthelemy]
Ambroise LE COMTE
Emmanuel SEMPRY [DAVION dit
   St. Prix]
J^n B^{te} DAVION
André VACOCU
Louis DERBANNE

Legajo 159-A, PPC-AGI.

1793 Militia Roll of Natchitoches

Recapitulation:

Marechal de Logis	1
Brigadier	1
Under-Brigadier	1
Cavalrymen	40
Force	43

Natchitoches, 1 December 1793
[Signed] Louis DEBLANC

Roll of the Infantry Company of Militia at the Post of Natchitoches, 1 December 1793

Messieurs, The Officers

Jⁿ B^{te} AILHAUD ST. ANNE, Captain
Jⁿ B^{te} DARTIGAUX, Lieutenant
Paul MARCOLLAY, Sub-Lieutenant

Sergeants

Emmanuel PRUDHOMME
Silv^{tre} BOSSIER
Jⁿ HORNNE

First Class Corporals

Louis VERCHAIRE
Jⁿ Joseph MARTINEAU
Soulange BOSSIER
Louis RENOUL

Second Class Corporals

Jacques LEVASSEUR
François LAVESPÈRE
Jean POMIER
Bernabé CHELETTRE

1793 Militia Roll of Natchitoches

Riflemen

Jean MASSIP
Phelippe FREDERIC
Augustain FREDIEU
Julien RACHAL
Antoine RACHAL
Pierre CHALERE
François CHELLETTRE
Pierre LA COUR Jr.
Berthelemy RACHAL
Jean DELOUCHE
Antoine PRUDHOMME
Ives LISSILLOURD
Jacques LACASSE
Gabriel TORRES
Gil IZCUERDO
Jn Bte LAVIGNE
Antoine LAMBRE
Pierre LAVIGNE
Richard SIMES
Jouachin DENOIR
François LATTIER
Jean Louis VERCHAIRE
Louis TAUTAIN
Pierre SUPERVILLE
Simon GOUILLE
Pierre BEAULIEU
Pierre COUTAN
Jacques LEPINE
Antoine L'HUISSIER
François ST. GERMAIN
Joseph DERBANNE
François HUGHES
Louis LAMBRE

Andre FREDERIC
Pierre CHELLETTRE
Charle LEMOINE
Jean Bte LEMOINNE
Jn Bte LATTIER
Piere DUPRÉ
Pierre BEAUDOUIN
Alexis CLOUTIER
Fifi [Jean Pierre] CLOUTIER
Pierre BROSSET
Nicolas GALIEN
Gasparitte LACOUR
François GONAIN
Joseph Marie TORRES
André de ST. ANDRÉ
Antoine COINDÉ
Joseph RABALAY
Miguel ERNANDES
Placide BOSSIER
Ma[nue]l RACHAL, son of Bmy.
Antoine RACHAL [son of Bmy.]
Joseph LATTIER, the son
Paul COUTY
Jacques ST. ANDRÉ
Antoine BERGERON
Nicolas BEAUDOIN [BAUDIN/BODIN]
Jean Bte RACHAL [son of Bmy.]
Nicolas MORRON [MORIN? MORROW?]
Nicolas BEAUDOUIN
Jean BONNET
François MONBRUN
Louis ANTY

1793 Militia Roll of Natchitoches

Recapitulation:

Sergeants	3
Corporals, 2d class	4
Corporals, 1st class	4
Riflemen	65
Force	76

Natchitoches, 1 December 1793
[Signed] Jn Bte AILHAUD STE ANNE

Roll of the review of the Second Company of the Cavalry of the Militia, taken 1 December 1793.

Messieurs, The Officers

Bernard D'ORTOLANT, Captain
Marcel DE SOTO, Lieutenant
Remy LAMBRE, Under-lieutenant

First Sergeant

Louis FONTENAUT

Second Sergeants

Jean ADELAY
Guilhaume BARBEROUSE

First Corporals

Antoine LE NOIR
Ellie BERNARD
Louis DAVID
Louis FORTIN *dit* Le Petit

Second Corporals

Guilhaume CHEVERT
Antoine DUBOIS
Pierre TERNIER
Antoine BORDELON

1793 Militia Roll of Natchitoches

Cavalrymen

Louis FORTIN *dit* Le Gros
Joseph Jean RIS
Jean B^{te} Bastien [PRUDHOMME]
Eduard MURFPHY
Luc [SOREL *dit*] Marly
Louis MERCIER
Jean B^{te} DAVION
Joseph MALIGE
Pierre GAGNÉ Jr.
Gaspard BODIN
Jean Denis BUARD
Laurent MALLOUX
Jean Baptiste DAVID
Jean B^{te} SAVOUELLE
Denis CARNES
Jacques ERRIE
NORMANDIN
François ROBZEAN [ROBINSON?]
Antoine BORDON [BARDON?]
Bazile GAGNÉ
Jean B^{te} ARMANT
Joseph TRICHEL
Jean Pierre BODIN
Pierre ROUSILLON
Joseph CALLERE
François Clavier [SAIDEC *dit* LECONTE]
Louis LEVASEUR
Pierre Ellie [BERNARD]
B^{te} TONIN
Jean PALVADEAU
Nicollas COLMA
Michel VINCENT

Joseph MARTIN
Antoine VACOCU
Michel RAMBIN
Gaspard [FIOL *dit*] Cadet
Gasparitte DERBANNE
Charles DURET
Louis CHAMARD
André VERDELAY
Jean LEVASSEUR, the son
Benoit MONTANARY
François VACOCU
François MERCIER
Jean FABRE
François NECESITE
Wuillam BARRE
Jean Marc MARCHAND
Guillaume ETREISEN [ETTREDGE]
Guillaume SNODDY
Jean MAGDANEL [McDANIEL]
Pierre MALLOUX
Jean B^{te} ADLET
Jean B^{te} DUHAMEL
Dominique [SOREL *dit*] Marly
François ETTIE
Pierre ROBLEAU
Antoine GRILLET
Nicolas SORAGE
Cristophe TEAL
Nicolas MERCIER
Joseph ROY
Jean BODIN
Thomas STIL

1793 Militia Roll of Natchitoches

Recapitulation:

Officers	3
1st Sergeant	1
2nd Sergeants	2
1st Corporals	4
2nd Corporals	4
Cavalrymen	65
Force	72

Natchitoches, 1 December 1793
[Signed] Bernard DORTOLANT

1793 Tax Roll of Natchitoches Post
3 February 1794

Assessment consented to by the Community in assembly on 30 November 1793 at the rate of one piaster for each head of family or man over the age of 14 and one *escalin* [also written as *real*] for each arpent of land, to finance the public work for the year 1793. For some persons listed here, the margin carries a note "M^re^" indicating they are on the *memoire* [memorandum] of those who have already contributed. An * in the column for land indicates that there is some objection [from the owner] that the land is not fit for habitation.

Paid	Messieurs	Arpents	Paid by Note Piasters/Escalins
Paid	DE MÉZIÈRES & his brother Jacq.	80	
	F^çois^ ROUQUIER, the elder	121	
	F^çois^ ROUQUIER, the younger	0	
	Dominique PRUDHOMME	0	
	F^çois^ LA CAZE	1	
Paid	Louis CHAMART	1[1]	
~~Paid~~	~~Paul MARCOLLAY~~	~~1~~	
	Gaspard FIOL, or his succession	86	
	J. B^te^ DAVID, nephew of Gaspard FIOL	0	
	Widow LANGLOIS *dit* Sans Regret	1	
	Pedro ALOMAND	0	
M^re^	Pedro RAMIS	1	
Paid	Paul MARCOLAY, officer	1	
	F^çois^ LEMAITRE, the beadle	0	
Paid	Luc [SOREL dit] Marly	0	
Paid	Genevieve [SOREL *dite*] Marly	1[2]	
Paid	Dominique [SOREL dit] Marly	0	
	J. B^te^ BARKAR	0	

Folder 703, Melrose Collection, NSU Archives.

1. "Except the land."
2. "There remains due 1 *escalin* for the land."

1793 Tax Roll of Natchitoches

Paid	Messieurs	Arpents	Paid by Note Piasters/Escalins
	Louis FORTIN [*dit*] Le Petit	0	
Paid	Widow RAMBIN, the mother	0	
	Widow RAMBIN, the younger	1	
	~~André FREDERIC, for himself only~~		
	André RAMBINT	15	
	J^h Marie ARMANT	1½	
	Antoine DU BOIS	½	
Paid	Joseph TAUZIN	1	
M^re	Widow or Succession of		
	Widow [François] FREDERIC	1½³	
	Michel CHANIOT	1½	
	J^h CAPURAN	*	
Paid	F^çois LEVASSEUR	11	
Paid	J^n François LEVASSEUR, the son	0	
	Charles DURET	4	
Paid	Ignace MAILLOUX, the father	7¾	2p
Paid	Laurent MAILLOUX	0	1p
Paid	Pierre MAILLOUX		1p
Paid	Michel RAMBINT	12⁴	
Paid	Antoine LENOIR *dit* Liston	2⁵	
Paid	Marcel DE SOTO	8	
Paid	Joseph JANRIS	7	
Paid	Antoine VAST-COCU, the father	0	
Paid	Louis VASTCOCU, the son	5	
Paid	André VAST-COCU	3¾	
Paid	G^me BARBEROUSSE	4	1p 4e
Paid	Bernard DORTHOLANT, officer	4	1p 4e
	François PRUDHOMME	12	
	François MERCIER	6	
Paid	N^as MERCIER	0	
Paid	Louis MERCIER	3	
	Widow ROBLOT	3	
	Pierre ROBLOT	0	

---

3. Comment: "For the land only."
4. Comment: "Paid for himself only."
5. Comment: "Due for the land that he has not declared."

1793 Tax Roll of Natchitoches

Paid	Messieurs	Arpents	Paid by Note Piasters/Escalins
Paid	Joseph ROY	0	
Paid	Widow [TERNIER dit] Grenoble	0	
Paid	Pierre TEURNIER	5	
Paid	Louis DAVION	2½	
Paid	Étienne GAGNEZ	12	
Paid	Bazile GAGNEZ	0	
Paid	J. B^{te} DAVION, the elder	18	
Paid	Dominique DAVION	7	
Paid	Louis BERTRAND	3	
	J. B^{te} DAVION, the younger	5	
	François VAST-COCU	3	
	Pierre ALORGE	6	
	Elie BERNARD	6½	|
	Pierre BERNARD	0	|6
Paid	J^h MARTIN	0	
	François DU BOIS	7[7]	
	Ant^e VAST-COCU, elder son	3	
Paid	Antoine PLAUCHET	22	
Paid	Widow J. B^{te} TRICHEL	11	
Paid	Gilbert CLAUSO	30	
Paid	Louis CLAUSO	16	
Paid	D^{lle} Marie J^{he} TRICHEL	0	
Paid	J. B^{te} TRICHEL	0	
Paid	G^{me} CHEVERT	4	
Paid	Bertrand PLAISANCE	0	
Died	Louis PLAISANCE	0	
	Pierre GAGNEZ, the father	3	
	Pierre GAGNEZ, the son	0	
	Joseph GAGNEZ	0	
Paid	Estate of Remy TOUTIN	2	
	Pierre BADIN	22	
Paid	Louis BUARD	26	

---

6. Comment: "Paid in part by him [Elie] and his son [Pierre] but 1½ escalins remain."

7. Comment: "Has paid 6½ escalins."

1793 Tax Roll of Natchitoches

Paid	Messieurs	Arpents	Paid by Note Piasters/Escalins	
M^re	J^h LAMBRE	0[8]		
	Widow [JUCHEREAU de] St. Denis	1⅓		
	Jacq. PRUDHOMME	4		
	Joseph MALIGE	2		
M^re	Widow of G^me WARDET	0	1	
	Louis VIGÉ	0		
	Marie Anne BUARD	*19[9]		
Paid	Denis BUARD	0		
Paid	J. B^te BUARD	12	2p	4e
Paid	Augustin BUARD	0	1	
Paid	J. Baptiste ANTY	2½		
Paid	Marin GRILLET	13		
Paid	Antoine GRILLET	0		
Paid	Athanas POISOT, the father	36		
Paid	Athanas POISOT, the son	0		
Paid	Edouard MURPHY	11¾		
M^re	Antoine BOURDELON	0		
	François LAVESPÈRE	0		
	Joseph DERBANNE	0		
Paid	Louis DERBANNE	0		
	Manuel DERBANNE	0		
	Widow Barth^my RACHAL	21½		
	Noël RACHAL	0		
	Pierre DERBANNE, the father	37[10]		
Paid	Pierritte DERBANNE	6		
Paid	François BOSSIÉ	51	7p	3e
Paid	Placide BOSSIÉ	0	1	
M^re	Antoine LAMBRE	0[11]		
Paid	Soulange BOSSIÉ	0		
Paid	Silvestre BOSSIÉ	8		

---

8. Comment: "On account of his Negro, thus void here [?]."
9. Comment: "Credited or secured. (She has paid for her land, 7 March 1795)."
10. Comment: "He has already paid."
11. Comment: "Died. Therefore null."

1793 Tax Roll of Natchitoches

Paid	Messieurs	Arpents	Paid by Note Piasters/Escalins
Paid	Louis RACHAL, son of Louis	?4	
	Louis MONET	173½	
	Louis RACHAL, the father	10	
	Barth^{my} RACHAL, son of Louis	0[12]	
	François TOUTIN *dit* Guinoche	0	
Paid	J. B^{te} RACHAL, son of Louis	0	
Paid	J. Baptiste LA BERRY	40	6p
Paid	Louis TOUTIN	0	
Paid	G^{me} LESTAGE	6	2p ?e
	François GONIN	0	
Paid	François LECONTE	8	
Paid	Barnabé CHELETTRE	4	
	Estate of Widow CHELETTRE	14	
Paid	Paul F^{cois} CHELETTRE	10	
Paid	Widow DARTIGAUX	56	8p
Paid	J. B^{te} DARTIGAUX, officer	50	7p 2e
	Joseph CONNAND	0	
Paid	André FREDERIC	0	
M^{re}	Succession of Widow BAILLOU, Wife of [André] FREDERIC	15[13]	
Paid	Pierre CHELETTRE	8	2p
	Succession of Ph^{pe} FREDERIC, Sr.	24	
Paid	François FREDERIC	0	Pd 1p
Paid	Ph^{pe} FREDERIC, the son	14	Pd 2p6e
Paid	Jacq. FAURE	16	
Paid	Widow HIMEL	11	
Paid	P^{re} METOYER	46	
Paid	N^{as} Augustin [METOYER], free mulatto	0	
Paid	Marie Thérèse [COINCOIN], free Negro ~~Pierre, her free mulatto son~~[14]	12	
	J^{n} Baptiste AILHAUD S^{TE} ANNE, officer ~~Jean BONNET, his employee~~	51 0	

12. Comment: "His land is included with that of Bayonne."
13. Comment: "For the land only."
14. This young man, Pierre Metoyer [*fils*], was not yet free, but lived as free.

1793 Tax Roll of Natchitoches

Paid	Messieurs	Arpents	Paid by Note Piasters/Escalins
	Louis THOMASSINO	20	
Paid	Michel HERNANDE	12	
Paid	Jean Paul COUTIE	0	
	Nicolas, or DOCLAS, free Negro	0	
Paid	Louis VERCHERE, the father	22½	
	J^n Louis VERCHERE, his son[15]	0	
Paid	Louis Barthelemy RACHAL, son of B^{my}	12	
Paid	Barth^{my} RACHAL, son of B^{my}	0	
M^{re}	Pierre SUPERVILLE	10	
Paid	Jacq. LEVASSEUR	12	
Paid	Pierre CHALAIRE *dit* Versaille	8	
	Pierre LACOUR, the father	20	
Paid	Pierre LACOUR, the son	0	
Paid	Gaspard LACOUR	0	
Paid	Louis ANTY	0	
Due	Antoine PRUDHOMME	*	
Paid	J^n B^{te} PRUDHOMME	0	
Due	Manuel PRUDHOMME	*	
	Widow Jacquot LAMBRE	0	
	Remy LAMBRE	70	
	Auguste LANGLOIS	0	
	Yves LISSILOUR	20	
Paid	Remy POISOT	54	
Paid	Joseph RABALET	8	
Paid	J. B^{te} RACHAL, son of B^{my}	12	
Paid	Dominique RACHAL	4	
Paid	Charles LEMOINE, the father	0	
Paid	Charles LEMOINE, the son	9	
Paid	Antoine RACHAL	11	2p 3e
Paid	Antoine LEMOINE	0	
	J^n VARANGUE	28	
	Athanas DUPRÉ	0	
Paid	Pierre DUPRÉ	4	

---

15. Comment: "Died in November."

1793 Tax Roll of Natchitoches

Paid	Messieurs	Arpents	Paid by Note Piasters/Escalins
Paid	Étienne VERGÉ	20	
	Étienne RACHAL	0	
Paid	Pierre LARENODIÈRE	16	
Paid	Julien RACHAL	16	
	Simeon RACHAL	0	
Paid	Jean MASSIP	9	
Paid	J. B^te LEMOINE	0	
Paid	Augustin FREDIEU & Ant^e BOURDON	30	
Paid	Jean POMMIER	20	
	Jacq. LACASSE	10	
Paid	Widow MALBERT	10	
Paid	J. B^te LAVIGNE	10	
Paid	Widow Philippe PHREDERIQUE	0	
	Pierre BAULIEU	0	
Paid	J^n Baptiste LATTIER	20	
Paid	Joseph LATTIER, the father	12	
Paid	François LATTIER	0	
Paid	J^n B^te DESLOUCHES	16	
	Gil YSQUIERDO	12	
Paid	Pierre BROSSET	20	
Paid	G^me LEBRUN	31	
	Jean HORN	16	
	N^as Martin BAUDIN	0	
	Margueritte [LE COMTE], free Negro	10	
	Pierre CAZEAU *dit* Faulevant	30	
	J. B^te DENIS	8	
	N^as BAUDOUIN	6	
	Pierre BAUDOUIN	11	
	Antoine BERJON	12	
	[Marie Louise] MARIOTTE, free Negress	0	
	François HUGHES *dit* Tonant	8	
Paid	N^as GALIEN	6	
Paid	Athanas LECOUR	6	
	Barth^my LECOUR	24	
Paid	Widow LECONTE	0	

1793 Tax Roll of Natchitoches

Paid	Messieurs	Arpents	Paid by Note Piasters/Escalins
Paid	Ambroise LECONTE	65[16]	
Paid	Pierre CHARPENTIER	0	Pd 1p cash
Paid	Jⁿ Pierre CLOUTIER	0	Pd 1p cash
Due	Alexis CLOUTIER	*	
Paid	François DAVION	20	Pd 3p4e cash
	Joseph TORRES	20	
	Joacinthe DAVION	20	
	Pierre COUTANT	5	
Paid	Antoine COINDÉ	8	
Paid	Simon GOUEL	11	
	Louis LAMBRE	15	
	André [BOTIEN de] St. André	*	
Paid	Widow Alexis GRAPE	37	
**	François GRAPE	*[17]	
**	J. Bᵗᵉ GRAPE	*[18]	
Paid	Benoist MONTANARY	3	
Paid	Widow or succ. of Manuel TRICHEL	25	
Paid	Henry TRICHEL	0	
Paid	Jʰ TRICHEL	0	
Due	LAMALATI	* 35	
	Louis DAVID, his nephew	0	
**	Jⁿ PALVADOT	*	
	Louis FONTENAU	44	
	Julien BESSON	15	
	Pierre BAUDIN	0	
	J. Bᵗᵉ [LEGER *dit*] Piedferme	59	
	Pierre CARLES	0	
	Jacques, orphan	0	
Paid	Jean ADLET	18	
	Jean LALANDE	6	

---

16. Comment: "Pd 8p 4e for 60 arpents."
17. Comment: "Not excused — paid."
18. Comment: "Not excused."

1793 Tax Roll of Natchitoches

Paid	Messieurs	Arpents	Paid by Note Piasters/Escalins
	Remy PERRAU	0	
	Jⁿ Pierre LALANDE	0	
Paid	François PERRAU	0	
Paid	Jacq. CHRISTIL	1	
	Chrisostomé PERAU	20	
	Gasparitte DERBANNE	0	
	Étienne DUGUETTE	12	
	G^{me} [William] SNODEY	20	
	Michel VINCENT	0	
**	J. B^{te} BREVEL		*19
	Balthazard BREVEL	0	
	Jⁿ Bap^{te} BREVEL, the son	0	
**	Jⁿ Baptiste DERBANNE		*20
**	Sebastien PRUDHOMME		*21
**	TILL, at Quizatché		*22
	Antoine LUISSIER[23]		

Natchitoches, 3 February 1794
[Signed:] MAËS, Syndic

---

19. Comment: "Not excused."
20. Comment: "Not excused."
21. Comment: "Not excused."
22. Comment: "Not excused."
23. Comment: "Not enumerated."

Old Debts: Quarter of Isle Brevelle & Rivière aux Cannes
17 January 1794*

Various debtors to the old public tax ... payable at the time tobacco was marketed in 1792, according to the General Account and additional detail remitted to Monsieur the Commandant.

No.	Paid	Messieurs	DUE Piasters	Reales
95		Simeon RACHAL		5
115	P	Augustin FREDIEU	2	4
94		Athanas DUPRÉ		4
96	P	Jean MASSIP	1	2
97		Pierre BAULIEU		4
98	P	Jean DESLOUCHE		6
99	P	G^me LEBRUN	1	2
63	P	Soulange BOSSIÉ		4
9		Jean HORN	3	2
100		Nicolas Martin BAUDIN		4
101		Marguerite [LECOMTE], free Negress		4
102		Nicolas BAUDOUIN		4
103		Antoine BERJON		4
104		MARIOTTE, free Negress		4
105		François HUGUES *dit* Tonant		4
106	P	Nicolas GALIEN		4
107	P	Athanas LACOUR [LE COURT]		4
108		Barthelemy LE COUR[T]		6
109	P	Pierre CHARPENTIER		4
110	P	J^n Pierre CLOUTIER		4
111		Joseph TORRES		4
112		Pierre COUTANT		4
10		Louis RACHAL, Sr.	5	2
113		Louis LAMBRE	1	2
114		André [BOTIEN] St. André		4
			24	7

[Signed] MAËS, Syndic

*Folder 705, Melrose Collection, NSU Archives.

1794 Public Works Roster
[No day or month] 1794

Roster of Public Labors and Contributions, in alphabetical order.

Types of labor:
1. Work on the road before and around the church, 28 August 1794
2. Work on the ditch around the cemetery and the road-bridge
3. Enclosing the cemetery with a levee, 26 November 1792
4. Work on the crevasse in front of the church, 4 February 1793
5. Repair work on the ditch around the cemetery, 6 May 1793

Type of Labor	Names	Comments	No. of Days
2	AILHAUD STE. ANNE		1
2	ALORGE, Pierre		1
1,2	ANTY, Jean Baptiste		1,1
2	ARMANT, Joseph Marie		1
2	ADLET, Jean		1
	Augustin [METOYER]	free mulatto	
	ANTY, Louis		
	AIMOND	An itinerant	
	ALOMAND, Pierre		
	ARMANT, J. B^{te}, the son		
	ARDOUIN, F^{çois}	An itinerant	
	ARNOULD, Louis		
	ST. ANDRÉ, André		
3	BROSSET, Pierre		1
3	BERTRAND, Louis		1
3	BARBEROUSSE, G^{me}		1
1,3	BADIN, Pierre		2,1
1,3	BUARD, Louis		2,1
3	BUARD, Marianne		1
1,3	BUARD, J. Baptiste		1,1
3	BOSSIÉ, François		1
3	BOSSIÉ, Silvestre		1

---

*Natchitoches Parish Records Collection, Department of Archives, LSU.

1794 Public Works Roster of Natchitoches

Type of Labor	Names	Comments	No. of Days
3	BOSSIÉ, Soulange		1
3	BOSSIÉ, Placide		1
3	BESSON, Julien		1
	BREVEL, the father		
	BREVEL, the son		
2	BERNARD, Elie, the father		1
2	BERNARD, Pierre, the son		1
2	BUARD, Denis		1
2	BUARD, Augustin		1
2	BOURDELON, Antoine		1
	BONNET, Jean	An itinerant	
	BORME, Louis		
	BARKAR, J. B^{te}		
	BORME, Clemence	Through her 2 slaves	
	BAULIEU, Pierre		
	BODIN, N^{as} Martin		
	BAUDOUIN, N^{as}		
	BAUDOUIN, Pierre		
	BERJON, Ant^{e}		
	BAUDIN, J^{n} Pierre		
	BOURDON, Ant.		
1,3	CHEVERT, G^{me}		1,1
3	CAPURAN, Joseph		1
3	CLOUTIER, Alexis		1
3	CHELETTRE, Widow		1
3	CHAMARD, Louis		1
2	CARLE, Pierre		1
	CRISTIL, Jacques		
2	CLAUSO, Gilbert		1
2	CLAUSO, Louis		1
2	CHANIOT, Michel		1
	COLMANNE, Nicholas	Englishman	
	CHELETTRE, Paul		
	CONNAND, Joseph		
	CHELETTRE, Pierre		
	COUTIE, Paul		
	CHALAIRE *dit* Versailles, P^{re}		

1794 Public Works Roster of Natchitoches

Type of Labor	Names	Comments	No. of Days
	~~COLMANN, Nicolas~~	~~Blacksmith~~	
	CASEAU *dit* Faulevant, P^re		
3	CHELETTRE, Barnabé		1
	CHARPENTIE, Pierre		
	CLOUTIER, J^n Pierre		
	COUTANT, Pierre		
	COINDÉ, Ant^e		
3	DENIS, Widow St.		1
4,3	DERBANNE, Pierre, the father		1,1
3	DERBANNE, Pierritte, the son		1
	DAVION, François		1
3	DARTIGAUX, Widow		1
3	DAVION, Louis		1
3	DAVION, Dominique		1
3	DAVION, J. B^te, the elder		1
4	DUGUETTE, Étienne		1
4	DAVID, Louis		1
	DERBANNE, Gaspard		
4	DURET, Charles		1
	DUBOIS, F^çois		
4	DUBOIS, Antoine		
	DERBANNE, Joseph, son of P^re		
	DERBANNE, Louis, son of P^re		
4	DERBANNE, Manuel, son of P^re		
	DUHAMEL, J. Baptiste		
4	DARTIGAUX, J. Baptiste, son		1
	DUPRÉ, Pierre		
	DUPRÉ, Athanase		
	DERBANNE, J. B^te, son of P^re		
	DAVID, nephew of Gaspard FIOL		
	DESLOUCHE, Jean		
	DAVION, Joacinthe		
	DUJARDIN, Manuel		
3	FREDERIC, André		1
3	FREDERIC, Philippe, father		1
3	FREDERIC, Philippe, son		1
3	FAURE, Jacques		1
	DIEGO	Itinerant Spaniard	

1794 Public Works Roster of Natchitoches

Type of Labor	Names	Comments	No. of Days
3	FREDIEU, Augustin		1
3	FIOL, Gaspard		1
3	FONTENAU, Louis		1
4	FORTIN, Louis, *le petit*		1
	FLORIO, F^çois	Mulatto	
	FREDERIC, François, son		
1,3	GAGNEZ, Pierre		1,1
1,3	GRILLET, Marin		1,1
3	GALIEN, Nicholas		1
3	GAGNEZ, Étienne		1
3	GUERBOIS, Louis		1
3	GRAP, Widow Alexis		1
4	GRAP, François		1
4	GRAP, J. Baptiste		1
	GAGNEZ, Bazille	Son of Étienne	
4	GAGNEZ, Pierre	Son of Pierre	1
4	GAGNEZ, Joseph	Son of Pierre	1
	GONIN, F^çois		
4	GRILLET, Antoine, the son		1
	GOUEL, Simon		
3	HIMEL, Widow		1
	HORNE, Jean		
5	JANRIS, Joseph		1
	INGRAND, Joseph	Itinerant	
	ISQUIERDO, Gil		
	Jacques, orphan	At home of Piedferme	
3	LACAZE, F^çois	Surgeon	1
3	LEVASSEUR, François		1
3	LAMBRE, Antoine		1
3	LESTAGE, Guillaume		1
3	LECOUR, Barth^my		1
3	LECONTE, Widow [J. B.]		1
3	LECONTE, Ambroise		1
3	LEVASSEUR, Jacques		1
3	LAMBRE, Remy		1
3	LENOIR, Antoine *dit* Liston		1
3	LEMOINE, Charles, the son		1
3	LARENODIÈRE, Pierre		1

1794 Public Works Roster of Natchitoches

Type of Labor	Names	Comments	No. of Days
4,5	LEBRUN, Guillaume		1
3	LAMALATI, Louis		1
3	LALANDE, Jean		1
4,5	LA BERRY, J. Baptiste		1
	LALANDE, Pierre		
	LISSILLOUR, Yves		
	LAVIGNE-TESSIER		
4,5	LEVASSEUR, J^n François	Son of François	1
4,5	LAMBRE, Joseph		1
3	LAMBRE, Widow		1
	LAVESPÈRE, F^{çois}		
	LACOUR, Pierre, the father		
	LACOUR, Pierre, the son		
	LACOUR, Gaspard, the son		
	LANGLOIS, Auguste		
	LEMOINE, Charles, father		
3	LEMOINE, Antoine, the son		1
	LEMOINE, J. B^{te}		
	LEMAITRE, F^{çois} *dit* La Lime	The beadle	
	L'HUISSIER, Ant^e	An itinerant	
	LA CASSE, Jacq.		
	LAVIGNE, J. B^{te}		
	LATTIER, J. B^{te}, the son		
	LATTIER, François, "ditto"		
	LE COUR, Athanas		
	LAMBRE, Louis		
	L'EPINE	At home of Brevel	
2	MASSIP, Jean		1
2	Miguel HERNANDE		1
2	METOYER, Pierre		1
2	MÉZIÈRE, DE, the elder		1
2	MARLY-SOREL, Luc		1
2	MARLY-SOREL, Génevière		1
4,2	MONGINOT, F^{çois}		1
4,2	MURPHY, Edouard		2
2	MONET, Louis		1
4,2	MONTANARY, Benoit		1
4,2	MAILLOUX, Laurent, the son		1

1794 Public Works Roster of Natchitoches

Type of Labor	Names	Comments	No. of Days
4,2	MAILLOUX, Pierre, the son		1
	MERCIER, Fçois	An itinerant	
4,2	MERCIER, Louis		1
	MERCIER, Nicolas		
	MARTIN, Joseph		
4,2	MARLY-SOREL, Dominique		1
4,2	MALIGE, Joseph		1
	MAURIN, J. Baptiste		
	MACARTY, G^me	An itinerant	
	MATCHASS, Antoine	Free Negro	
	MARCOLAY, Paul	Officer	
2	NORMAND, Louis		1
	NAIGLE, Fçois	Sick	
	Nicolas DAUCLAS	Free Negro	
3	ORTHOLANT, Bernard	Office of the militia	1
4,3	POISOT, Athanas, the father		1,1
	PONT, Nicolas		
3	POMMIER, Jean		1
3	PRUDHOMME, François		1
3	PRUDHOMME, Antoine	Son of J. B^te	1
3	PRUDHOMME, Manuel	Son of J. B^te	1
3	POISOT, Remy, the father		1
3	PIEDFERME		1
3	PERAUT, Chrisostomé	1	
4	PERRAUT, François	1	
4	PERRAUT, Remy	1	
4	PALVADOT, Jean	1	
	POISOT, Antoine	Son of Remy	
4	PRUDHOMME, Jacques	Son of Bastien	
4	PLAISANCE, Bertrand		1
4	PLAISANCE, Louis		1
4	PRUDHOMME, Dominique		1
4	PIQUERY, Nicolas	Mulatto	1
4	PLAUCHET, Antoine		1
	Pierre [METOYER], free mul.	[living as free]	
	PRUDHOMME, J. B^te	Son of Sebastien	
4	POISOT, Ath^as	Son of Athanas	1
	PRUDHOMME, Sebastien	Elder son of Sebastien	

1794 Public Works Roster of Natchitoches

Type of Labor	Names	Comments	No. of Days
3	RACHAL, Louis Barth^my	Son of Barth^my	1
3	RACHAL, Antoine	Son of Louis	1
4,3	RACHAL, Julien	Son of Louis	1
3	ROUQUIER, François	The elder	1
3	RAMBINT, André		
4,3	RACHAL, Widow Barth^my		1,1
4	RACHAL, Louis	Son of Louis	1
4	RACHAL, Barth^my	Son of Louis	1
4	RAMBIN, Michel		1
4	ROY, Joseph		1
4	ROBLOT, Pierre		1
4	ROUQUIER, F^çois	The younger	1
4	RACHAL, Noël	Son of Barth^my	1
	RACHAL, J. B^te	Son of Louis	
	RACHAL, Barth^my	Son of Barth^my	
	RABALET, Joseph		
	RACHAL, Étienne	Son of Jacq.	
	RACHAL, Simeon	Son of Louis	
4	RAMIZ, Pedro, Corporal	By his slaves only	1
	RACHAL, J. B^te	Son of Barth^my	
	RACHAL, Dominique *dit* Coco	Son of Barth^my	
3	SOTO, Marcel de		1
5	SNODEY, G^me, the father		1
5	SAVIO, J. B^te	An itinerant	1
	SUPERVILLE, Pierre		
3	TAUTIN, Remy		1
3	TRICHEL, Widow J. B^te		1
3	Thérèse, COINCOIN	Free Negro	1
3	TAUZIN, Joseph		1
3	TRICHEL, Widow Manuel		1
5	TERNIER, Pierre		1
5	TRICHEL, J. Baptiste		1
	TAUTIN, F^cois		
	TAUTIN, Louis		
	THONIN, J. B^te		
3	TRICHEL, Marie Joseph[e]	By her 2 slaves only	
	TORRES, J^h		
	TRICHEL, Henry	Son of Manuel	

1794 Public Works Roster of Natchitoches

Type of Labor	Names	Comments	No. of Days
	TRICHEL, Joseph	Son of Manuel	
	TESSIE, P^{re}		
3	THOMASSINE, Louis		1
3	VERCHAIRE, Louis	The father	1
3	VERCHAIRE, Jⁿ Louis, son		1
3	VARANGUE, Jean		1
3	VERGÉ, Étienne		1
5	VAST-COCU, Louis		1
	VAST-COCU, André		1
5	VAST-COCU, Antoine		1
	VERDALEY, André		
	VAST-COCU, François		
	VINCENT, Michel		

1795 Delinquent Tax Roll: Bayou Plat through Lac Noir
August 1795*

Statement of various debtors to the public tax (more old accounts than recent ones) whose notes are recorded on the pertinent account rolls, itemized according to the district ascending the river from Bayou Plat to the last residents, including Lac Noir. Remitted by Monsieur Julien Besson, the actual syndic of that district.*

Names of the Messieurs	Piasters	Escalins
François GRAPE	2	6
Benoist MONTANARY		6
Widow or Succession GRAPE	4	2
Widow or Succession of Mlle [Manuel] TRICHLL	4	
J. Btiste. GRAPE	4	4
Henry TRICHLL	1	4
Joseph TRICHLL		4
Louis LAMALTY	6	4
Louis DAVID	1	4
Btiste. DAVID	1	4
Louis FONTENAU	12	4
Julien BESSON	4	3
Piere BODIN	1	4
Btiste. PIEDFERME	8	1
Pierre CARLES	1	4
Jaque, orphan	1	4
Guillaume SCHNAUDAY	4	
Jean PALVADO	1	4
Étiene DUGUETTE	3	
Michelle CHAIGNEAU, by one note or another	6	2½
Widow François RAMBIN	1	
Widow or Succession of LALANDE	2	6
Remy PERO	1	4
Jean Piere LALANDE	1	4

*Folder 715, Melrose Collection, NSU Archives.

1795 Delinquent Tax Roll: Bayou Plat through Lac Noir

Names of the Messieurs	Piasters	Escalins
Gaspart DERBANNE	1	4
Jaque CLISTY [CHRISTY]	1	5
Antoine POISO	1	4
Jean DESSAULE	3	1
Joseph INGRUM	1	
	83	4½

I certify the present account to be true without error or omission, extracted from the general accounts of Natchitoches. August 1795.

BOSSIÉ, Syndic

1795 Delinquent Tax Roll: Isle Brevelle & Rivière aux Cannes
August 1795

Statement of various debtors to the public tax (more old accounts than recent ones) whose notes are recorded on the pertinent account rolls, itemized according to the district descending from Bayou Brevelle to the last resident in the jurisdiction of the post (thereby including Isle Brevelle and Rivière aux Cannes). Monsieur Remy Lambre, the actual syndic, has remitted the present list to me.

Names of the Messieurs	Piasters	Escalins
Sivestre BOSSIE, by notes	2	1
Jaque LE VASSEUR, by the same	2	4
Antoine PRUDHOMME	11	1
Auguste LANGLOIS	1	
Emanuelle PRUDHOMME	6	6
Widow Jaque LAMBRE	1	
Remy LAMBRE	9	6
Remy POISSO, by note	7	2
J. Btiste. Berthelmy RACHALE, by one note or another	14	2
Jean VARANGUE	4	4
Athanase DUPRÉ	1	
Piere LARNAUDIÈRE, by note	3	
Julien RACHALE, by note	3	
Jean MASSIPE, by note	3	3
Jaque LACASE	2	2
Ives LISILLOUR	3	4
Antoine [MATCHASS], free Negro	1	
Piere BEAULIEU	1	
Soulange BOSSIÉ, by note	6	
Gil ISQUIERDO	2	4
Jean DELOUCHE		6

*Folder 716, Melrose Collection, NSU Archives.

1795 Delinquent Tax Roll: Isle Brevelle & Rivière aux Cannes

Names of the Messieurs	Piasters	Escalins
Guillaume LE BRUN, by note		7
Charles LE MOINE, Jr., by note	2	1
Marguerite [LE COMTE], free Negress	2	6
Jean HORN, by one note or another	6	5
Antoine BERGEON	3	
[Marie Louise] MARIOTE, free Negress	1	4
Pierre CASEAU	4	6
Nicolas BEAUDOUIN	2	2
Btiste. DENIS	2	
Pierre BEAUDOUIN	2	3
Pierre LACOUR, Sr.	3	4
Capitaine, civilized Indian resident	1	4
Jean Laurend BODIN	1	
Nicolas BODIN	1	4
François HUGUES	2	4
Berthelmy LE COUR[T]	4	6
Joseph TAURES	4	
Joachim DAVION	3	4
Pierre COUTANT	2	1
Gabrielle TAURES	1	
Simeon RACHAL	1	5
Berthelmy RACHALE, son of Louis	1	
Louis RACHALE, Sr., by one note or another	7	2
Louis MONETTE	22	5½
Louis LAMBRE	4	1
André St. ANDRÉ	1	1
He has several arpents of land on which will be due several *escalins* in addition to what is owed here.		
	179	7½

I certify the present account to be true without error or omission, extracted from the general accounts. Natchitoches, August 1795.

BOSSIÉ, Syndic

1795 Delinquent Tax Roll: Bayou Portage to Bayou Brevelle
August 1795*

Statement of various debtors to the public tax (more old accounts than recent ones) whose notes are recorded on the pertinent account rolls, itemized according to the district from Bayou Portage to Bayou Brevelle. Remitted by Mr. Dartigaux, present syndic of the said district.

Names of the Messieurs	Piasters	Escalins
François LAVESPÊRE	1	6
Piere DERBANNE, Sr., by one note or another	10	6
Joseph DERBANNE	1	4
Louis DERBANNE, by his note	1	4
Emanuelle DERBANNE	1	
Widow Berthelmy RACHALE	3	5½
Emanuelle RACHALE	1	
Piere DERBANNE, Jr., by one note or another	2	6
François TOTIN	1	4
Succession of CHELAYTE	2	6
Succession of Widow BAILLOU	2	
Joseph CONAND	1	
Succession of Philipe FREDERIC	3	
Jaque FORT		2
Widow HIMEL	2	3
J. Btiste. AILHAUD ST. ANNE	7	3
Louis TOMASSINO	4	5
Nicolas DOCLA, free Negro	1	
Louis Berthelmy RACHALE		1½
Antoine BORDELON	1	4
	50	3

I certify the present account to be true without error or omission, extracted from the general accounts. Natchitoches, August 1795.

BOSSIÉ, Syndic

---

*Folder 717, Melrose Collection, NSU Archives. This district is the region variously called the Grand Côte and Joyous Coast—the stretch of river between Natchitoches and Isle Brevelle.

1795 Census of Slaveholders
15 October 1795*

General Census of the Slaves of all ages and of all sexes at the Post of Natchitoches, in accordance with the lists that have been provided by Messieurs the syndics ... .

District	Name of Owner	No. of Slaves
Côte Tulin & including the town; District of Mr. Edouard Murphy, Syndic	The Commandant [DE BLANC]	23
	Mme. Widow TRICHEL	30
	Joseph CAPURAN	8
	François LE VASSEUR	7
	Guillaume CHEVERT	5
	Pierre GAGNER	6
	Mme. Widow Remy TOTIN	4
	Joseph MALIGE	1
	Jean B^{te} ANTY	4
	Marin GRILLET	11
	François MONGINOT	16
	Athanaze POISSEAU	15
	François ROUQUIER, the younger	9
	Denis BUARD	4
	Dominique PRUDHOMME	1
	Joseph TAUZIN	4
	Joseph Marie ARMANT	1
	André RAMBIN	10
	François ROUQUIER, the elder	22
	François LACAZE	1
	Pierre BADIN	21
	Mme. Widow SAINT DENIS	5
	Luc [SOREL dit] Marly & his sister [Geneviève]	2

Legajo 201, PPC-AGI. Côte Tulin, above Natchitoches, was the site of the Grappe family dit Tuline.

1795 Census of Slaveholders

District	Name of Owner	No. of Slaves
	Mme. Widow Gaspard FIOL	4
	Athanaze de MÉZIÈRES	20
	Edouard MURPHY	15
	Pierre RAMIZ	2
		251
Grand Écore and the vacherie of CONAND – District of M. Marcel DE SOTO, Lieutenant of cavalry of the militia and a syndic	François PERRAUT	7
	Jean B^te DAVION	1
	Dominique DAVION	3
	Louis DAVION	4
	Jean B^te DAVION *dit* Fify	2
	Pierre THERNIER	1
	Pierre GAGNE	4
	Antoine LE NOIR	1
	Jean B^te BREVEL	14
	Jean B^te D'ERBANNE	1
	Marcel DE SOTO	7
		45
Camté & Fayard, including the vacheries of Lac Noir [Black Lake] – District of Mr. Julien BESSON, Syndic	François GRAPPE	17
	Benoit MONTANARY	3
	Louis LAMALATHIE	4
	Heirs of deceased Emanuel TRICHEL	17
	Henry TRICHEL	5
	Hypolite BORDELON	1
	Louis FONTENEAU	26
	Jean B^te GRAPPE	4
	Julien BESSON	6
	Chrisosthomé PERRAUT	1
	Mme. Widow LA LANDE	1
	Pierre LA LANDE	1
		86

1795 Census of Slaveholders

District	Name of Owner	No. of Slaves
Côte Joyeuse, including the vacheries of Petite Écore —District of Mr. Jean B^te DAR- TIGAUX, Lieutenant of the infantry of the militia & a syndic	Pierre DERBANNE	33
	Dame Widow Barthelemy RACHAL	10
	Jean B^te BUARD	7
	Augustin BUARD	3
	Pierre DERBANNE, the son	3
	François BOSSIE	16
	Louis RACHAL Jr.	1
	Louis BUARD	24
	Joseph L'AMBRE	1
	Guillaume L'ESTAGE	8
	Joseph CONAND	2
	Barnabé CHELETRE	1
	Jean B^te DARTIGAUX	18
	Pierre MAËS	15
	Pierre CHELETRE	1
	Philipe FREDERIC	3
	Jacques FORT	3
	Dame Widow HYMEL	3
	Pierre METOYER	50
	Marie Thérèse [COINCOIN], free Negro	5
	AILHAUD Ste. Anne	22
	Louis THOMASINO	3
	Michel ERNANDEZ	4
	DOCRAS, free Negro	2
	Louis VERCHER	3
	Louis Barthelmy RACHAL [fils Bmy.]	4
		245
Isle Brevelle, including the bluffs [MONET's Bluff] to Bayou Jean de Jean— District of Mr. Remy LAMBRE, Lieutenant of the cavalry of the militia & a syndic	Dame Widow OPOK	3
	Louis LAMBRE	4
	Antoine RACHAL	1
	Louis MONET	25
	Alexis CLOUTIER	8
	Emanuel DAVION	1
	Dame Widow LE COMTE	18
	Ambroise LE COMTE	14

1795 Census of Slaveholders

District	Name of Owner	No. of Slaves
	GALIEN	1
	Athanaze LE COUR[T]	1
	Pierre BAUDOUIN	2
	Jean HORNE	3
	Pierre BROSSET	2
	Guillaume LE BRUN	3
	Jean DELOUCHE	1
	Jean B^{te} LATTIER	1
	Jacques LA CASSE	2
	Jean POMMIER	4
	Jean MASSIPE	3
	Augustin FREDIEU	9
	Pierre LA RENAUDIÈRE	4
	Julien RACHAL	4
	Étienne VERGER	4
	Dame Widow VARANGUE*	8
	Louis TOTIN	4
	Pierre DUPRÉ	1
	Yves LISSILOURD	1
	Remy POISSEAU	21
	Emanuel PRUD'HOMME	38
	Antoine PRUD'HOMME	26
	Pierre CHALERE	1
	Jacques LE VASSEUR	2
	Silvestre BOSSIÉ	6
	LAUVE, the younger	1
	Remy LAMBRE	39
		266

---

*This taxpayer is Marie de l'Incarnacion Derbanne, the *widow of Joseph Dupré I* who was in 1795 the *wife* (not widow) *of Jean Varangue*. As in other community and tax rolls, she is grouped with her son Pierre Dupré and her son-in-law Jacques Étienne Verger.

1795 Census of Slaveholders

Recapitulation	District of Mr. Edouard MURPHY	251
	District of Mr. Marcel de SOTO	45
	District of Mr. Julien BESSON	86
	District of Mr. J. B. DARTIGAUX	245
	District of Mr. Remy LAMBRE	266
		893

General Census of the Slaves of the Post of Natchitoches taken in the form prescribed by the law of 15 June of the present year, signed by me the commandant and by Messieurs, the syndics, and their witnesses, at the said Post of Natchitoches, 15 October 1795.

Louis DE BLANC

[Signed]

Remy LAMBRE, Syndic	METOYER, witness
Julien BESSON. Syndic	Louis LAMATY, witness
E. MURPHY, Syndic	J^h TAUZIN, witness
DARTIGAUX, Syndic	Slve. BOSSIÉ (X), witness
Marcel DE SOTO, Syndic	PRUDHOMME, witness
	GRILLTE, witness
	Ignase MAILLIOUX, witness
	BARBERRAUX, witness

1795 Church Census
[No date]*

Statistical count of the inhabitants of the parish of St. François des Natchitoches.*

Category	Age Group	Total No.
White males	Aged 1 to 15	253
	Aged 15 and above	167
Free Negro males	Aged 1 to 15	7
	Aged 15 and above	9
Total free males		(436)
White females	Aged 1 to 15	165
	Aged 15 and above	143
Free Negro females	Aged 1 to 15	9
	Aged 15 and above	8
Total free females		(325)
Slaves		904
Total general population		1,665

Clerical notes:

The population in the preceding year has increased by forty. Very few of the parishioners have satisfied their Easter Duty.

The church does not have a fixed fee schedule. The church warden has received 57 *piasters* for the announcement of marriage bans and 32 *piasters* for the care of the church, making a total of 89 *piasters*.

Records of the Diocese of Louisiana and the Floridas, microfilm, 12 rolls (Notre Dame, Ind.: University of Notre Dame Archives, 1967), roll 5.

1795 Church Census

With regard to the catechism that it is necessary to have for children, the major part of the parishioners live a great distance from the post and are not able to come to the instructions that are held for them.

All the inhabitants are Catholic except twelve Anglos.

[Signed] PAVIE, curate of Natchitoches

1796 Tax Roll: Grand Coast & the Town
2 January 1796

Statement of those owing to the public outlays for the District of the Grand Coast and the Town.

Messieurs	Piasters
D^e Vve [Dame Widow] Gaspard FIOL	3. 3. 0
Thil [TEAL], father and son	
"need to adjust the quantity of land"	3. 0. 0
Antoine DUBOIS and his mother	2. 4. ½
Succession of deceased D^e Vve [Dame Widow] FREDERIC	. 5. ½
Joseph Marie ARMAND	1. 7. ½
Dominique PRUDHOMME	1. 0. 0
B^{te} BARKAR	1. 0. 0
Louis FORTIER [FORTIN] *dit* Lepetit	1. 0. 0
Gim LE JEUNE [James YOUNG]	1. 1. 0
André RAMBIN	5. 3. 0
F^{çois} LE MAITRE, the son	1. 0. 0
Pedro RAMIS	. 5. 0
Pedro LALEMAND	1. 4. 0
D^e Vve [Dame Widow] LANGLOIS *dte.* Sanregret	1. 5. 0
Antoine VACOCU, the son	1. 3. 0
Pierre "Grand" GAGNIE	11. 5. 0
F^{çois} LA CAZE	16. 5. 0
F^{çois} ROUQUIER, the elder brother	21. 1. 0
Succession of deceased B^{te} [LE DUC, *dit*] Vilfranche	12. 7. 0
Charle DURET	4. 1. 0
Maurice DEMOUY	9. 0. 0
J^h CAPURAND	8. 6. 0
F^{çois} MERCIER	2. 2. 0
Bertran PLAISANCE	. 4. 0
Athanaze POISOT, the father	6. 4. 0
Pierre BADIN	3. 6. 0
D^e Vve [Dame Widow] [JUCHEREAU de] St. Denis	1. 1. ½
F^{çois} ROUQUIER, the younger brother	2. 0. 0

Doc. 2628, Colonial Notarial Records, Natchitoches.

1796 Tax Roll: Grand Coast & Town

Messieurs	Piasters
Louis VIGÉ	1. 4. 0
J^h MALIGE	1. 2. 0
F^{çois} MONGINOT	2. 3. 0
Jacques PRUD'HOMME	1. 4. 0
Succession of deceased Remi TOTIN	12. 2. 0
Succession of deceased F^{çois} RAMBIN	. 5. 0
J^n TAUZIN, as appears on his promissory note	1. 6. 0

I have received the notes and accounts amounting to
one hundred forty eight *piasters* and six *escalins*.   **148. 6. 0**

Natchitoches, 2 January 1796
MURPHY, Syndic

1796 Church Census
[No date]*

Statistical count of inhabitants, parish of St. François des Natchitoches.

Category	Age Group	Total No.
White males	Aged 1 to 15	175
	Aged 15 and above	274
Free Negro males	Aged 1 to 15	8
	Aged 15 and above	8
Total free males		(445)
White females	Aged 1 to 15	148
	Aged 15 and above	172
Free Negro females	Aged 1 to 15	7
	Aged 15 and above	10
Total free females		(337)
Slaves		912
Total general population		1,694

Clerical notes:

Very few of the inhabitants have satisfied their Easter Duty.

The church does not have a fixed fee schedule. There has been paid 50 *piasters* for the announcement of marriage bans, and 11 *piasters* and 7 *escalins* for the care of the church.

The great distance of inhabitants from the church makes it impossible for fathers and mothers to send their infants to instruction classes. It would be desirable that little catechisms be held for them in their areas by those who know how to read.

PAVIE, curate of Natchitoches

Records of the Diocese of Louisiana and the Floridas, roll 5.

1798 Church Census
[No date]*

Statistical count of inhabitants, parish of St. François des Natchitoches.

Category	Age Group	Total No.
White males	Aged 1 to 15	263
	Aged 15 and above	180
Free Negro males	Aged 1 to 15	8
	Aged 15 and above	12
Negro male slaves		496
Total males		(959)
White females	Aged 1 to 15	180
	Aged 15 and above	154
Free Negresses	Aged 1 to 15	9
	Aged 15 and above	8
Slave Negresses		425
Total free females		(776)
Total general population		1,735

Clerical notes:

The popuation has increased by 34 during this year.

The church does not have a fixed fee schedule. The new vestry board has received nothing, but efforts will be made to collect the little that is due.

I have the sadness of seeing that the major part of my parishioners are not making their Easter duty.

PAVIE, curate of Natchitoches

Records of the Diocese of Louisiana and the Floridas, roll 7.

1799 Church Census
[No date]

Statistical count of inhabitants, parish of St. François des Natchitoches.

Category	Age Group	Total No.
White males	Aged 1 to 15	260
	Aged 15 and above	184
Free Negro & Mulatto males	Aged 1 to 15	9
	Aged 15 and above	10
Negro male slaves		480
Total males		(943)
White females	Aged 1 to 15	182
	Aged 15 and above	160
Free Negresses	Aged 1 to 15	9
	Aged 15 and above	7
Slave Negresses		420
Total females		(778)
Total general population		1,721

Clerical notes:

The vestry-board has not set a fixed fee schedule. They have received 235 *reales* and 30 *escalins* for the announcement of bans.

I have the sadness of seeing that very few persons have satisfied their Easter Duty. It appears to me that the great distance of the inhabitants from the church contribute to this. It is for this reason that I have proposed to the residents of Isle Brevelle to build a small chapel where I can come and say mass several times a year, and where it can be celebrated with more appropriateness than on their plantations, and those settlers from

---

*Records of the Diocese of Louisiana and the Floridas, roll 8.

1799 Church Census

Rivière aux Cannes would be able to come. If this pleases your Reverence [the bishop] I will make all efforts to succeed in this.

[Signed]

PAVIE, curate of Natchitoches

1800 Church Census
4 February 1801

Statistical count of inhabitants, parish of St. François des Natchitoches.

Category	Age Group	Total No.
White males	Aged 1 to 15	178
	Aged 15 and above	258
Free male Mulattoes	Aged 1 to 15	10
	Aged 15 and above	13
Negro male slaves		483
Total males		(942)
White females	Aged 1 to 15	157
	Aged 15 and above	182
Free female Mulattoes	Aged 1 to 15	6
	Aged 15 and above	12
Slave Negresses		425
Total females		(782)
Total general population		1,724

Clerical notes:

The vestry-board does not have a fixed rent. The church administration has received the following:

For its work	122 *piasters* 5 *escalins*
For bans	10 *piasters*
From wills	25 *piasters*
Total	158 *piasters* 5 *escalins*

The residents have not given me the satisfaction I hoped for in the fulfillment of their Easter duties. I see with sadness that my teachings and my exhortations are for the most part useless with them. In faith of which I have signed at Natchitoches 4 February 1801. [Signed] PAVIE.

Records of the Diocese of Louisiana and the Floridas, roll 9.

1801 Church Census
15 March 1802

Statistical count of inhabitants, parish of St. François des Natchitoches. .

Category	Age Group	Total No.
White males	Aged 1 to 15	191
	Aged 15 and above	267
Free Negro & Mulatto males	Aged 1 to 15	12
	Aged 15 and above	18
Negro & Mulatto male slaves		506
Total males		(994)
White females	Aged 1 to 15	159
	Aged 15 and above	187
Free Negro & Mulatto females	Aged 1 to 15	8
	Aged 15 and above	10
Female Negro & Mulatto slaves		430
Total females		(794)
Total general population		1,738

Clerical notes:

The population has increased by sixty-four. I am not able to give you the satisfaction that I wish for the completion of the Easter Duty. The church does not have a fixed fee schedule. The vestry-board has received 3 *piasters* for the announcement of bans and 87 *piasters* and 7 *escalins* for the care of the church. In faith of which I have signed, this fifteenth of March 1802.

P. PAVIE

Records of the Diocese of Louisiana and the Floridas, microfilm, roll 10.

1801 Church Census

Attachment:
Burials which have been made in the Church of St. François of the Post of Natchitoches in the year 1801.

		Piasters	Escalins
2 April	Jacques Cadet FORT		
	Removal of the body from the residence	3	2
	The cope	2	4
	The cross	1	4
	The incense		4
	The vigils	4	
	The last response	2	
	For the grave	1	4
	For the mortuary cloth	1	
	The bells	3	
	The lights	1	
		20	2
11 June	Étienne VERGÉ		
	Removal of the body from the residence	3	2
	The cope	2	4
	The cross	1	4
	The incense		4
	The vigils	4	
	The last response	2	
	For the grave	1	4
	For the mortuary cloth	1	
	The bells	3	
	The lights	1	
		20	2

Burials of Negroes:

24 February	Pierre, slave of Mr. ROUQUIÉ, aged 30		
	Removal of the corpse	2	
	The grave	1	4
		3	4

1801 Church Census

18 March	Augustin, slave of Mr. ROUQUIÉ, aged 28		
	Removal of the corpse	2	
	The grave	1	4
		3	4

10 April	A negro boy who died after having been privately baptized, slave of Mr. ROUQUIÉ		
	Removal of the corpse	1	4
	The grave		6
		2	2

26 August	Michel, slave of Mr. TRICHE, aged 40		
	Removal of the corpse	2	
	The grave	1	4
		3	4

25 December	A negro boy, aged 2 months, slave of Mr. DAVION		
	Removal of the corpse	1	4
	The grave		6
		2	2

Marriages

1 January	ERRIÉ with MAILLOU
8 January	VERCHER with GALLIEN
12 January	VALERI with TORRES
9 February	Louis [METOYER], free mulatto, with Thérèse [LECOMTE], daughter of an Indian*
5 May	GAGNÉ with LALANDE
6 May	LEVASSEUR with MERCIÉ
1 June	Antoine [METOYER], with Pelagie [LE COURT], free mulattoes*

---

*For more on the identity of these two couples, see Gary B. Mills and Elizabeth Shown Mills, *The Forgotten People: Cane River's Creoles of Color*, rev. ed. (Baton Rouge, La.: Louisiana State University Press, 2013).

1801 Church Census

3 June	(x)	RACHAL with LABERI, widow of MARTINEAU, on whom I did not place the veil.
11 August		BREVEL with DERBANE
10 September	(x)	PEROT with GAGNÉ, on whom I did not place the veil since she was the widow of Louis DAVION

Editor's note:
All of these marriages are more fully recorded in the marriage registers of St. François Church, now held by its successor, Immaculate Conception Church, Natchitoches. Translated abstracts of all relevant detail have been published in Elizabeth Shown Mills, *Natchitoches, 1729–1803: Abstracts of the Catholic Church Registers of the French and Spanish Post of St. Jean Baptiste des Natchitoches in Louisiana* (New Orleans: Polyanthos, 1977), nos. 3445–3454.

1802 Church Census
24 February 1803

Statistical count of inhabitants, parish of St. François des Natchitoches. .

Category	Age Group	Total No.
White males	Aged 1 to 15	203
	Aged 15 and above	220
Free Negro & Mulatto males	Aged 1 to 15	9
	Aged 15 and above	11
Male Negro & Mulatto slaves		512
Total males		(1,025)
White females	Aged 1 to 15	166
	Aged 15 and above	203
Free Negro & Mulatto females	Aged 1 to 15	7
	Aged 15 and above	11
Female Negro & Mulatto slaves		436
Total females		(823)
Total general population		1,848

Clerical notes:

The population has increased by 60 persons. I have not had the satisfaction I wish for the Easter duty. The church does not have a fee schedule. The administration has received no funds. In faith of which I have signed at Natchitoches, the 24th of February 1803.

P. PAVIE, Pastor
Church of St. François

Records of the Diocese of Louisiana and the Floridas, 12.

Appendix A
Name Conversion Table

Showing French, Spanish and English equivalents of baptismal names most frequently used at Natchitoches.

French	Spanish	English
Antoine	Antonio	Anthony
Athanase	Athanasio	–
Baptiste	Bautista	Baptist
Barthélemy	Bartolo, Bartolomeo	Bartholomew
Césaire	Cezerio	Caesar
Charles	Carlos	Charles
Chrisostomé	Crisostomo	–
Christophe	Cristobal	Christopher
Claude	Claudio	Claude
Dominique	Domingo	Dominick
Edouard	Eduardo	Edward
Elisabeth	Isabelle	Elizabeth
Étienne	Estevan	Stephen
François (male)	Francisco	Francis
Françoise (female)	Francisca	Frances
Gasparite	Gasparito	–
Guillaume	Guillermo	William
Henri	Enrique/Henrique	Henry
Honoré	Honorato	–
Ignace	Ignacio	–
Jacques	Iago/Santiago/Sn Iago	James
Jean (male)	Juan	John
Jeanne (female)	Juana	Jean
Jorge	Jorge	George
Julien	Julian	Julian
Louis (male)	Luis	Lewis
Louise (female)	Luisa	Louise
Laurent, Laurence	Lorenzo	Lawrence
Marie	Maria	Mary
Marin	Mariano	–
Mathieu	Matheo	Matthew
Michel	Miguel	Michael

Appendix A: Name Conversion Table

French	Spanish	English
Narcisse	Narciso	—
Paul	Pablo	Paul
Pierre	Pedro	Peter
Remy	Remigio	—
Remond	Ramon	Raymond
Thérèse	Teresa	Theresa or Therese
Ursulle	Ursula	Ursula
Victoire	Victoria	Victoria

Appendix B
Nicknames & *Dit* Names in Colonial Natchitoches

Nickname/Dit name*	Baptismal Name or Meaning
Belle fleur	Beautiful flower
Blondin	A fair-headed child, or light-complexioned
Bontemps	Good times
Bourbon	Bourbon (the drink) or one attached to the French House of Bourbon, by kin or service
Bourguignon	Native of the French province of Burgundy
Brim d'amour	Full of love
Cadet	The younger
Champagne	Native of the French province of Champagne
Coco	Short for *Dominique*; also "chap" or "fellow"
Coincoin	African name used by the freed woman Marie Thérèse
Dauphinois	Native of the French province of Dauphin
De Rosiers	From the rose bushes
Doclas	African name used by the freedman Nicolas
Duffresne	From the ash trees
Du Sable	From the sand
Fify	Dear little thing, ducky
Fanchon :	
Fanchonette:	Françoise
Frambois(e)	Strawberry; also an alcohol fermented with strawberries
Gasparite	Gaspard
Goupillon	A holy-water sprinkler
Grenoble	Native of Grenoble, France
Jacquot	Jacques (French) or Jacob (German)
Jeannot	Jean
La Bonte	The good one, goodness
La Croix	The cross
La Douceur	Sweetness, mildness

---

*See the discussion that prefaces the index for an explanation of *dit* names and the context in which they were used at Natchitoches.

Appendix B: Nicknames & *Dit* Names of Colonial Natchitoches

Nickname/Dit name*	Baptismal Name or Meaning
La Forest	The forest
La France	The Frenchman
La Guerre	The warrior
La Jeunesse	The younger
La Joye	The happy one
La Lime	The lime, the file
La Rivière	The river
La Rose	The rose
La Tulippe	The tulip
La Verdule	Foliage, forest scenery
La Vigne	The vine, the vineyard
Le Brun	The dark one
Le Gros	The fat one
Le Maigre	The lean one
Le Petit	The smaller, the younger
Le Suisse	The Swiss, the porter, church officer
Le Veille	The old one
Lionnois	From Lyon
Lise (French) :	
Lisette (French) :	Louise, Luisa, or Elisabeth
Luisetta (Spanish):	
Manette	Marie or Marianne
Manuel	Emanuel
Mariotte	Marie
Marly	A decorative band or gauze trimming
Melite	Carmelite
Meunier	Miller
Navarre	From Navarre
Noël	Emanuel
Picard	From Picardie
Piedferme	Firm footing
Pierrite	Pierre
Poupon	Chubby-cheeked child
Pret a boire	Ready to drink
Printemps	Springtime
Provençal	Native of the French province of Provence
Rat	The Rat
Sans chagrin	Without grief or peevishness

Appendix B: Nicknames & *Dit* Names of Colonial Natchitoches

Nickname/Dit name*	Baptismal Name or Meaning
Sans Façon	Without style or affectation
Sans Quartier	Without quarter or mercy
Sans Regret	Without regret
Sauterelle	Grasshopper
Suzette	Susanne
Tonnant	The thunderer
Tourangeau	Native of the French Touraine
Versailles	From Versailes
Ville Franche	French town
Zité	Osite, Ausite

Document Sources

France
Ministère des Colonies. Séries C, G. Archives Nationales d'Outre Mer. Aix-en-Provence, France.

Mexico
Ramo de Historia and Ramo de Provincias Internas. Archivo General y Público. Mexico City. Manuscript volumes microfilmed as 479 rolls for University of California, 1951.

Spain
Audencia de Santo Domingo. Archivo General de Indias. Seville, Spain.
Papeles Procedentes de Cuba. Archivo General de Indias. Seville.

United States
Colonial Notarial Records. Office of the Clerk of Court, Natchitoches.
Colonial Records Collection. Center for Louisiana Studies. University of Louisiana at Lafayette.
Jack D. L. Holmes Collection. Northwestern State University Archives. Natchitoches. Microfilmed documents from Papeles Procedentes de Cuba, Archivo General de Indias, Seville.
Louisiana Miscellany Collection, 1724–1837. Manuscripts Division. Library of Congress. Washington, D.C.
Melrose Collection. Cammie G. Henry Research Center. Northwestern State University Archives. Natchitoches. Documents removed from the Natchitoches Parish courthouse in the early twentieth century.
Natchitoches Parish Records Collection. Department of Archives. Hill Memorial Library. Louisiana State University. Baton Rouge. Documents removed from the Natchitoches Parish courthoues in the early twentieth century.
Records of the Diocese of Louisiana and the Floridas, 1576–1803. Microfilm, 12 rolls. Notre Dame, Indiana: University of Notre Dame Archives, 1967. Primarily records of the office of the first bishop installed in Louisiana, 1796–1803.
Vaudreuil Papers. The Huntington Library. San Marino, California.

Further Study
(Other Mills works on Colonial Natchitoches and its people)

Books

Mills, Elizabeth Shown. *Isle of Canes.* Provo, Utah: Ancestry.com, 2004.

———. *Natchitoches, 1729–1803: Abstracts of the Catholic Church Registers of the French and Spanish Post of St. Jean Baptiste des Natchitoches in Louisiana.* New Orleans: Polyanthos, 1977. Revised edition for Kindle, 2016.

———. *Natchitoches, 1800–1826: Translated Abstracts of Register Number Five of the Catholic Church Parish of St. François des Natchitoches in Louisiana.* New Orleans: Polyanthos, 1980. Revised edition for Kindle, 2016.

———. *Natchitoches Church Marriages, 1818–1850: Translated Abstracts from the Registers of St. François des Natchitoches, Louisiana.* 1985. Reprint, Bowie, Md.: Willow Bend Books, 2004. Revised Kindle edition, 2017.

——— and Gary B. Mills. *Tales of Old Natchitoches.* Natchitoches, La.: Association for the Preservation of Historic Natchitoches, 1978. Reprint, Berwyn Heights, Md.: Heritage Books, 2015. Kindle edition, 2017.

Mills, Gary B. and Elizabeth Shown Mills. *The Forgotten People: Cane River's Creoles of Color.* Revised edition. Baton Rouge: Louisiana State University, 2013.

Book Chapters

Mills, Elizabeth Shown. "Marie Thérèse Coincoin (1742–1816): Cane River Slave, Slave Owner, and Paradox." In Janet Allured and Judith F. Gentry, editors. *Louisiana Women: Their Lives and Times.* Athens: University of Georgia Press, 2009. Pages 10–29.*

——— and Gary B. Mills. "Missionaries Compromised: Early Evangelization of Slaves and Free People of Color in North Louisiana." In Glenn R. Conrad, editor. *Cross, Crozier, and Crucible: A Volume Celebrating the Bicentennial of a Catholic Diocese in Louisiana.* New Orleans: Archdiocese of New Orleans, 1993. Pages 30–47.*

Mills, Gary B. "The Faith of Their Fathers." In Charles E. Nolan, editor. *Religion in Louisiana.* Lafayette: Center for Louisiana Studies, 2004. Pages 176–91.

---

* All items marked with an asterisk are archived online at Elizabeth Shown Mills, *Historic Pathways* (https://historicpathways.com) under the "Articles" tab.

———. "*Liberté, Fraternité*, and Everything but *Egalité*: Cane River's *Citoyens de Couleur*." In B. H. Gilley, editor. *North Louisiana*: vol. 1, *To 1865: Essays on the Region and Its History*. Ruston, La.: McGinty Trust Fund Publications, Louisiana Tech University, 1984. Pages 93–122.

———. "Piety and Prejudice: A Colored Catholic Community in the Antebellum South." In Jon L. Wakelyn and Randall M. Miller, editors. *Catholics in the Old South: Essays on Church and Culture*. Macon, Ga.: Mercer University Press, 1983. Pages 171–94.

Articles (Peer-reviewed)

Mills, Elizabeth Shown. "Deliberate Fraud and Mangled Evidence: The Search for the Fictional Family of Anne Marie Philippe of Natchitoches, Louisiana." *The American Genealogist* 72 (July–October 1997): 353–68.*

———. "(de) Mézières-Trichel-Grappe: A Study of a Tri-Caste Lineage in the Old South." *The Genealogist*. Ser. 1, vol. 6 (Spring 1985): 4–84.*

———. "Demythicizing History: Marie Thérèse Coincoin, Tourism, and the National Historical Landmarks Program." *Louisiana History* 53 (Fall 2012): 402–37.*

———. "Documenting a Slave's Birth, Parentage, and Origins (Marie Thérèse Coincoin, 1742–1816): A Test of Oral History." *National Genealogical Society Quarterly* 96 (December 2008): 245–66.*

———. "Identifying Jean Baptise Derbanne of Louisiana's Natchitoches Militia, 1780–82: Participant in the Gálvez Campaigns of the American Revolutionary War Era," *The American Genealogist* 68 (January 1993): 33–45.

———. "*Isle of Canes* and Issues of Conscience: Master-Slave Sexual Dynamics and Slaveholding by Free People of Color." *Between Two Worlds: Free People of Color in Southern Cultural History*; a special issue of the *Southern Quarterly* 43 (Winter 2006): 158–75.*

———. "Quintanilla's Crusade, 1775–1783: 'Moral Reform' and Its Consequences on the Natchitoches Frontier." *Louisiana History* 42 (Summer 2001): 277–302.*

———. "Social and Family Patterns on the Colonial Louisiana Frontier." *Sociological Spectrum* 2 (July–December 1982): 233–48.*

———. "Which Marie Louise Is 'Mariotte'? Sorting Slaves with Common Names." *National Genealogical Society Quarterly* 94 (September 2006): 183–204.*

——— and Gary B. Mills "Louise Marguerite: St. Denis' *Other* Daughter." *Southern Studies* 16 (Fall 1977): 321–28.*

———. "Slaves and Masters: The Louisiana Metoyers." *National Genealogical Society Quarterly* 70 (September 1982): 164–89.*

---

* All items marked with an asterisk are archived online at Elizabeth Shown Mills, *Historic Pathways* (https://historicpathways.com) under the "Articles" tab.

Mills, Gary B. "A Portrait of Achievement: Nicolas Augustin Metoyer, f.m.c." *Red River Valley Historical Review* 2 (Fall 1975): 332–48.

———. "Coincoin: An Eighteenth-Century 'Liberated' Woman." *Journal of Southern History* 42 (May 1976): 203–22.

———. "Monet-Rachal: Backtracking a Cross-Racial Heritage in the Eighteenth and Nineteenth Centuries." *The American Genealogist* 65 (July 1990): 129–42.

Articles (Other)

Mills, Elizabeth Shown. "Breathing Life into Shadowy Women from the Past: Marie Thérèse Coincoin." *Solander: The Magazine of the Historical Novel Society* 9 (November 2005): 21–24.*

———. "European Origins of the Early French Families of Natchitoches, Louisiana." In Sharon Sholars Brown, editor. *Papers of the Sixth Grand Reunion of the Descendants of the Founders of Natchitoches.* Natchitoches: Founders of Natchitoches, 1986. Pages 27–45.

———. "François (Guyon) Dion Despres Derbanne: *Premier Citoyen*, Poste St. Jean Baptiste des Natchitoches." *Natchitoches Genealogist* 6 (October 1981): 1–9.

———. "From Chez Bienvenu to Cane River: Four Generations of the Pierre Brosset Family." *Natchitoches Genealogist*, serialized, vols. 11–14 (1986–89).

———. "Jeannot Mulon *dit* La Brun, f.m.c., Colonial Natchitoches, Louisiana." "Work Samples," *Board for Certification of Genealogists.* http://www.bcg-certification.org/skillbuilders/extended report.pdf.

———. "Marie Therese, the Metoyers, and Melrose." In *Proceedings of the Seventeenth Annual Institute of the Louisiana Genealogical and Historical Society*, 13–25. Baton Rouge: The Society, 1974.

———. "Marie Thereze *dit* Coincoin: A Cultural Transfer Agent." In *Four Women of Cane River: Their Contributions to the Cultural Life of the Area*, 1–18. Natchitoches, La.: Natchitoches Parish Library, ca. 1980.

———. "Natchitoches Baptisms, 1724–1776: A Supplement." *Natchitoches Genealogist* 7 (April 1983): 6–11.

———. "Parallel Lives: Philipe de la Renaudière and Philipe (de) Renault, Directors of the Mines, Company of the Indies. *Natchitoches Genealogist* 22 (April 1998): 3–18.*

———. "Speculation, Hypothesis & Proof." *Evidence Explained: Historical Analysis, Citation and Source Usage* (https://www.evidenceexplained.com/content/quicklesson-16-speculation-hypothesis-interpretation-proof : posted 21 March 2013). A case study in the identification and reconstructed life of an enslaved child sold from Natchitoches to Texas in 1771.

---

* All items marked with an asterisk are archived online at Elizabeth Shown Mills, *Historic Pathways* (https://historicpathways.com) under the "Articles" tab.

———— and Elizabeth Shown Mills. "Marie Thérèse and the Founding of Melrose: A Study of Facts and Fallacies." *Natchitoches Times*, July 29, August 5, 12, 19, 1973.

Encyclopedia Essays
Mills, Elizabeth Shown. "Antonio Emanuel de Soto y Bermudes." In Glenn R. Conrad, ed., *Dictionary of Louisiana Biography*, 2 vols. Lafayette: Louisiana Historical Association, 1988. 2:755–56.
————. "Jean Delvaux." In Glenn R. Conrad, editor. *Dictionary of Louisiana Biography*. 1:63–64.
————. "Louis de Quintanilla." In Glenn R. Conrad, editor. *Dictionary of Louisiana Biography*. 1:187–88.
————. "Marie des Neiges Juchereau de St-Denis." In Glenn R. Conrad, ed., *Dictionary of Louisiana Biography*. 1:449–50.
"Marie Thérèse Coincoin (1742–1816)." In Louisiana Endowment for the Humanities, David Johnson, editor, *Knowla: The Digital Encyclopedia of Louisiana and Home of Louisiana Cultural Vistas*. http://www.know louisiana.org/entry/marie-therese-coincoin : posted 14 March 2011
Mills, Gary B. "Augustin Metoyer" and "Louis Metoyer." In Glenn R. Conrad, editor. *Dictionary of Louisiana Biography*. 1:565.
————. "Coincoin (1742–1816)." In Darlene Clark Hine, editor. *Black Women in United States History*, 2 vols. Brooklyn: Carlson Publishing, 1990. Pages 1:258–60.
————. "Claude Thomas Pierre Metoyer." In Carl A. Brasseaux and James D. Wilson Jr. *A Dictionary of Louisiana Biography: Ten-Year Supplement, 1988–1998*. Lafayette: Louisiana Historical Association, 1999. Pages 154–56.

Thesis
————. "Family and Social Patterns of the Colonial Louisiana Frontier: A Quantitative Analysis, 1714–1803." New College honors' thesis, University of Alabama, 1981.*

Index

This index covers personal names, place names, and cultural and economic symbols such as crops, firearms, and livestock. With regard to personal names, several issues complicate both identifications of people and the use of indexes to colonial records such as those in this volume.

- **African names.** Newly enslaved Africans and their offspring at this outpost were typically baptized in the Catholic church and given a Catholic saint's name at baptism. Natchitoches custom also allowed enslaved Africans to use African names if they chose. The records covered by this volume include several first- and second-generation Louisianians of African extraction who did use African names. This index treats those names as surnames (e.g., Marie Thérèse *Coincoin* and Nicolas *Doclas*) because these men and women identified themselves in this fashion when they created legal records.
- *Dits* **and nicknames.** *Dits* (nicknames used in place of surnames) exist primarily for men and typically originated as a soldier's *nom de guerre*. The document transcriptions in this volume differentiate between surnames and *dits* by placing surnames in a small-caps font. Here in this index, the primary listing for individuals who used a *dit* appears under the surname to which the *dit* is added. The *dit* name is also indexed, with a cross-reference to the primary entry under the surname. Following standard conventions for nicknames that are used in place of given names, this index places those dimunitives in quotation marks immediately after the given name—as in Sebastien "Bastien" Prud'homme and Dominique "Coco" Rachal.
- **Duplication of names.** French colonial Louisiana was a society in which infants were commonly named by and for their godparents. As a consequence—and in contrast to naming patterns in other societies—two living siblings might carry the same exact name. Sometimes this occurred because the same-sex godparent of both of them carried the same given name(s). Sometimes it occurred because an older brother was a godparent to a younger brother and bestowed his name upon the infant. When these duplications occurred, scribes would typically differentiate them as, say, François Rouquier, *elder brother*, and François Rouquier, *younger brother*. Because family members often stood as godparents for each other, the same names are also found repeated in

different branches of the same family—as with the Rachal family that included Barthelemy, son of Barthelemy; Barthelemy, son of Louis; Louis, son of Louis; Louis Barthelemy, son of Louis; and Louis Barthelemey, son of Barthelemy. To assist users of this source book, this index separates same-name individuals into separate listing—drawing identifications not only from the documents in this volume but also from other colonial and church records that these individuals created.

- **Erratic spellings.** Standardized spellings did not exist in this society. Literate men and women typically adopted a single mode of spelling their names; but the scribes who created documents about them—and about the predominantly illiterate population—were likely to spell names phonetically. (As an example, the settler Claude Thomas Pierre Metoyer self-identified as "Pierre Metoyer" and consistently wrote his surname as *Metoyer*. However, the scribes who created the records in this volume wrote his name variously as *Metoyé*, *Métoyé*, and *Mettoyer*.) When the records herein use different surname spellings for a person or for members of the same family, this index consolidates the variant spellings into one surname entry with all the variants shown in parentheses. Non-related individuals who carried the same surname will not appear within that family grouping.
- **Gender endings.** Many researchers new to French and Spanish records are confused by variant spellings of what appears to be the same given name—for example, *Bernard* and *Bernarde*, *François* and *Françoise*, *Joseph* and *Josephe*. These are not alternative spellings of the same name. These variations reflect gender, with the final "e" used for female names. One other source of gender confusion that researchers should be familiar with is the use of the name *Marie* by males. This holiest of all Christian names is best known as a female name; but it was often used for males in elite families, and the combination *Joseph Marie* was used for males even among those of humble origins—as with the Indio-Spanish José María Torres, whose name Anglo scribes would currupt as Joseph Maritaurus.
- **Particles.** Many French and Spanish surnames were prefaced by particles such as *de, de la, du, la,* and *le*. Sometimes, yesteryear's scribes used the particles and sometimes they ignored them. When they included particles, the scribes may have left a space between the particle and the name, or they may have written the two as a single word (example: *Le Comte* and *Lecomte*). Historically, scribes who created alphabetized rolls usually alphabetized individuals under the main portion of the name, not the particles (for example: *Soto*, not *De Soto*, as shown on the 1794 public-works roster at p. 171). Modern indexing practices will typically index names under the particle. However,

standard practice today (used also by database algorithms) will create one grouping for names that carry a space after the particle (*La Berry, La Cour, La Malathy, Le Court,* etc.) and a separate grouping for names in which the particle is run into the surname (*Laberry, Lacour, Lamalathy, Lecourt,* etc.). Because spelling was erratic in the colonial era, and entries for the same person will be written both with and without the space, this index arranges all surnames into one alphabetic sequence, regardless of capitalization or whether a space appears after the particle. As when searching any French records, if your person of interest seems not to appear in the index, you should try adding or deleting particles.

- **Racial or ethnic designations.** Both the document transcripts and this index retain the precise terminology recorded by the colonial scribes. Users should note the distinctions between *free negro* (f.n.) and *free man of color* (f.m.c.) or *free woman of color* (f.w.c.). The first term designates individuals who are known to be (or appear to be) of full African heritage, while the latter pair denotes those of known or apparent multiracial heritage—typically African heritage, but sometimes Native American. These designations help researchers distinguish between individuals—as with "Pierre, free Negro" vs. the multiracial "Pierre, f.m.c." who sometimes was accorded the surname *de Blanc.*

- **Translated names.** Colonial Natchitoches was a fusion of cultures whose residents included Africans, Canadians, English, French, Germans, Irish, Italians, Mexicans, and Spanish, as well as Native Americans. Their names were often, but not consistently, translated or transliterated into the official language at the time: i.e., French or Spanish. (The British-born James Young, for example, appears variously in records as Jaque Jeuin, Gimes Joung, Gimes Irelanday, and Gime Lengles.) This index notes all surname variants, but renders the given name in the standard spelling for that person's culture. Thus, Jacques de Mézières is indexed as *Jacques* de Mézières, although in some records his given name appears as "Diego" or "Sⁿ Iago" (both short for *Santiago,* the Spanish equivalent of Jacques). Appendix A provides a name-conversion table that shows the French, Spanish, and English variants of the names that were translated or transliterated in these records.

No surname
Andre (bachelor 1766) 52–53
André (b. ca. 1780) 114
Augustin, enslaved by Rouquié (d. 1801) 194
Baptiste (b. ca. 1752) 119

Capitaine, Indian (1795) 176
Diego (itinerant 1794) 167
Jacques, orphan (b. ca. 1777) 117, 148, 162, 168, 173
Marie Antoinette (b. ca. 1771) 104
Michel, enslaved by Trichel 194

Pierre, enslaved by Rouquié (d. 1801) 185
Pierre, f.n. 111
Sylvie (b. ca. 1774) 117

A
Accaux, Sieur 16
Adaïs (Adaÿes; N'Adais), tribe 44, 68, 84
Adlé (Adelay, Adelet, Adlay, Adlet, Aldelt)
  François 116
  Jean I 81, 86, 91, 94, 116, 128, 138, 152, 162
  Jean I, wife of 116
  Jean Baptiste 116, 153, 165
  Pierre 116
  Thimothée 116
  Valentine 116
Ailhaud (Ailhaut) Ste. Anne, Jean Baptiste 81, 87, 91, 94, 99, 120, 122, 128, 130, 132, 142, 144, 150, 152, 159, 165, 177, 180
Aimond, itinerant 165
Alemand (Alomand, Lalemand), Pedro 147, 155, 165, 185
Alemand. *See also* L'Allemand
Alorge (Allorge)
  Pierre I, *dit* St. Pierre 16, 19, 22, 28, 32, 34, 35
  Pierre I, widow of 50–51, 60–61
  Pierre II 60–61, 66, 115, 137, 147, 157, 165
Anty (Hantt)
  Ignace 48–49, 60–61
  Jean Baptiste I 67, 81, 87, 95, 112, 123, 126, 133, 144, 149, 158, 165, 178
  Jean Baptiste II 112
  Louis 81, 87, 91, 94, 106, 120, 128, 136, 142, 151, 160, 165
  Louis, wife of 106
  Louis Cesaire 106
  Valery 112
Apalaches, nation 62
Ardouin, François 165

Arizaval, Vent^a 125
Armant (Armand)
  Adelaïde 102
  Athanase 102
  Doctrouve 102
  Emilie 102
  Jean Baptiste (older brother) 81, 87, 92, 153, 165
  Jean Baptiste (younger brother) 102
  Joseph Marie 102, 147, 156, 165, 178, 185
  Joseph Marie, wife of 102
  Louis 74–75, 82, 88, 133
  Valery 102
Arnould, Louis 165
Artaud. *See* d'Artaud
Audebrande, Antoinette 15
Auret, Beltran 68

B
bacon 78
Badin
  Pierre 48–49, 56–57, 72–73, 77, 103, 137, 157, 165, 178, 185
  Pierre, wife of 103
Baillio (Bailliot, Baillo, Baillou, Bailoux, Balloux)
  Augustin 109
  Helenne 109
  Jean Louis 109
  Pelagie 104
  Pierre I 50–51, 56–57, 72–73, 77
  Pierre I, widow of 109, 159, 177
  Pierre II 131
Bailly, Paul 110
Ballé, ensign 19
Balloche, B^d 109
Barbaroux (Barbarroux, Barberouse, Barberousse, Barberoux, Barberraux),
  Guillaume 81, 86, 91, 94, 114, 120, 128, 137, 142, 152, 156, 165
  Guillaume, wife of 114
Barbier, François, *dit* Marechal 17
Barbot, Guillaume 16
Bardon,

Catherine 119
Widow 119
Barker (Bargare, Barkar), Jean Baptiste
   101, 133, 155, 166, 185
Barr (Barre), William 153
Barranco. *See* Varangue
Bâton, Jean Christophe 25
Baudoin. *See* Beaudoin, French family;
   and Bodin, Spanish family
Baulieu. *See* Beaulieu
Bayonne ("Baiony"), France 68, 69
Bayou Brevelle 175, 177
Bayou Jean de Jean 180
Bayou Pierre (Bayou aux Pierre) 118
Bayou Plat 173
Bayou Portage 177
beans 47, 49, 51, 53
bear oil 78
Beaudoin (Baudoin, Baudouin),
   French family
   Marie Jeanne 113
   Nicolas 113, 133, 146, 151, 161, 164,
      166, 176
   Pierre 96, 113, 121, 128, 133, 143,
      151, 161, 166, 176, 181
   Thérèse 113
Beaulieu (Baulieu), Pierre 146, 151,
   161, 164, 166, 175
Beautemps, François 22, 25, 28, 30, 33,
   34
Bellanger (Belanjer), Pierre 87, 92
Belle Avance, Ignace 102
Belle Fleur. *See* Mouton *dit* Belle Fleur
Bellerose. See D'Ardenne *dit* Bellerose
Beltran. See Bertrand
Benoist, Marianne (Mme. Pierre
   Rachal) 14
Benoist. *See also* de Benoist
Berardinis, Robert D. 22, 28, 32, 36, 42
Berger. *See* Verger
Bergeron (Bergeon, Berjon), Antoine
   146, 151, 161, 164, 166, 176
Bernabane. *See* Derbanne
Bernard
   Elie (Ellie, Hely) 81, 86, 91, 94, 102,
      120, 128, 138, 142, 152, 157, 166

Elie, wife of 102
Marie Josephe 102
Pierre Elie 102, 138, 153, 157, 166
Bernarde, Marie, f.n. 104
Bernardin, Pierre, *dit* La Boute 19
Berrier, Jacques Daniel 104
Berry, François 14
Berry. *See also* La Berry
Bertrand (Beltran)
   Claude, *dit* Dauphine 16, 19, 22, 28
   Hyacinthe 115
   Louis 68, 79, 82, 88, 97, 115, 124,
      127, 138, 144, 149, 157, 165
   Louis, wife of 115
   Marie Louise 115
   Pierre 115
Besson (Beson)
   Jean Baptiste 116
   Julien 67, 82, 88, 90, 97, 115, 124,
      127, 138, 144, 148, 162, 166, 173,
      173, 179
   Julien, wife of 115
   Pierre 68
Bibo, Jean Baptiste, *dit* La Joye 19, 23,
   29, 30, 31, 33, 37, 39
Bidaïs (Bydaye), Indian village 85
Black Lake. *See* Lac Noir
Blan, Franc⁰ 60
Blard. *See* St. Louis *dit* Blard
Blondin. *See* Rachal *dit* Blondin
bluffs. *See* écores *and* Monet's Bluff
Bodin (Beaudoin), Spanish family
   Gaspard, orphan 109, 130, 135, 143,
      153
   Geneviève, orphan 109
   Jean Laurent 131, 153, 176
   Jean Pierre 153, 166
   Nicolas Martin 146, 151, 161, 164,
      166, 176
   Pierre 115, 148, 162, 173
Bodin. *See also* Beaudoin, French
   family
Boeuf, Boeufs. *See* Le Boeuf
Boissot, Maturin 143
Bonnafons, physician 54–55
Bonneaux, Jacques 23, 29, 33, 37, 38

Bonnet
　Jean 60, 151, 159, 166
　Martine (Mme. Pierre Dupin *dit* Riortaur) 17
Boquet, [Jean Baptiste?] 17
Bordelon (Bourdelon)
　Antoine 147, 152, 158, 166, 177
　Hypolite 179
Bordon. *See* Bourdon
Borme
　Clemence 119, 166
　Jean Louis 46-47, 54-55, 66, 70-71, 76, 80, 86, 90, 93, 94
　Jean Louis, widow of 100
　Louis 119, 166
Borranger
　André 60-61
　Pierre 60-61
Bosque, Sieur 56-57
Bossier (Bossaur, Bossie, Bossié)
　Eulalie 106
　François 67, 110, 128, 135, 141, 142, 158, 165, 180
　Guillaume I, *dit* LeBrun 17
　Ildebert 106
　Jean François 106
　Paul François 93, 94, 106
　Paul François, wife of 106
　Placide 135, 151, 158, 166
　Silvestre 106, 130, 135, 141, 143, 150, 158, 165, 175, 181, 182
　Soulange 106, 130, 136, 143, 150, 158, 164, 166, 175
　syndic 146, 148, 174, 176, 177
Bossier. *See also* Le Brun
Bouché, François 111
Boulet (Boulé)
　Jean Baptiste, *dit* Brindamour 23, 29, 33, 43
　Joseph 67
Bourbon. *See* Maigros *dit* Bourbon
Bourdelle
　Paul, dit St. Nicolas 23, 29, 33, 37, 43, 45
　Widow 50-51, 58-59
Bourdelon. *See* Bordelon

Bourdon (Bordon), Antoine 153, 161, 166
Bouset. *See* Brosset.
Boutière, Jean Baptiste, *dit* La Rose 21, 23, 29, 31, 33, 34
Bouvié (Bouvier), Pierre 135
Bragnard, Nicolas 43
Brevel (Brevelle)
　Baltasar 139, 147, 149, 163, 166?
　Jean Baptiste II 46-47, 56-57, 68, 72-73, 77, 139, 141, 147, 163, 166, 179
　Jean Baptiste III 163, 166?, 195
Brevelle Bayou 175, 177
Brindamour. *See* Boulet *dit* Brindamour
Broquedis, Pierre 81, 83, 86, 91
Brosset (Bouset), Pierre 67, 81, 86, 134, 151, 161, 165, 181
Brumeaux, Sieur 56-57
Buard (Bouard, Buar, Buare, Buart)
　Auguste, *fils* Louis 104
　Augustin, *fils* Gabriel 87, 92, 95, 105, 121, 129, 136, 143, 149, 158, 166, 180
　Denis 105, 136, 158, 166, 178
　Eugenie 104
　Françoise 105
　Gabriel 48-49, 56-57
　Gabriel, widow of 72-73, 77, 105, 136
　Jean Baptiste, *fils* Gabriel 82, 88, 89, 97, 105, 123, 126, 136, 144, 149, 158, 165, 180
　Jean Baptiste, *fils* Louis 104
　Jean Denis 130, 143, 153
　Jean Louis, *fils* Louis 104
　Louis 66, 72-73, 77, 82, 88, 89, 104, 123, 126, 136, 144, 157, 165, 180
　Louis, wife of 104
　Marianne 105, 136, 158, 165
　Marie Jeanne 105
　Sylvestre 104
buffalo skins 78
Bunel, Jacques, *dit* Normand 41, 43, 44

Burcareli, Texas 79
Burgundy ("Bortguio"), France 67, 68, 69
Bydaye. *See* Bidaïs

C

Cadet. *See* Fiol *dit* Cadet
Caddo (Cadoe Dakiou), Grand, nation 62, 85
Caddo (Cados Dakiou), Petite, nation 62, 85
Cajau. *See* Caseau *dit* Faulevent
Calinan, François 131
Callé (Callay, Calle), François 93, 96, 100, 128, 132, 142
Callere, Joseph 153
Calvenne, Laurent 60-61
Campti (Cameté, Camté) 138, 179
Canada 66, 67
Capot, chief of Bidaïs 85
Capuran (Capurand, Capurant)
   Joseph 94, 100, 120, 136, 141, 156, 166, 178, 185
   Joseph, wife of 100
Carles
   François 48-49, 58-59
   Ollivier 58-59
   Pierre "Pierrite" 117, 122, 130, 138, 145, 148, 149, 162, 166, 173
Carnes, Denis 153
carts, oxen 63
Caseau (Cajau, Cazeau)
   Pierre, *dit* Faulevent (Fauleven, Faulevant) 113, 133, 161, 167, 176
   Pierre, wife of 113
Castel. *See* Varangue *dit* Castel
Castlevie, Jean 110
Castro
   Francisco 58-59
   Joseph 58-59
cattle 14-18, 47, 49, 51, 53, 55, 57, 59, 61, 99-120
Cavalier, Louis 115
Cazeau. *See* Caseau
Chabert. *See* de Chabert
Chabus, François 102

Chagnau (Chaignau, Chaigneau, Chaigneaut, Chagnaux, Chaniau Chaniot, Chegnau), 16
   François 52-53, 58-59
   François, widow of 102
   Jean 52-53, 67
   Michel 82, 87, 92, 95, 102, 121, 128, 133, 145, 149, 156, 166, 173
   Thomas 67
Chaler (Chalair, Chalaire, Chalere)
   Pierre, *dit* Versailles 105, 121, 128, 134, 143, 151, 160, 166, 181
   Pierre, wife of 105
Chamart (Chamard)
   André 119
   Louis 119, 130, 143, 153, 155, 166
   Louis, wife of 119
   Marie 119
   Melite 119
   Michel 119
Champagne. *See* Jambert *dit* Champagne
Chaniau. *See* Chagnau
Charbonau, Joseph 67
Charbonnet, Antoine "and brother" 50-51, 54-55, 70-71, 76
Chardon, Sieur 17
Charly, Pierre 23, 29, 33, 37, 39
Charpentier
   Pierre 96, 112, 128, 162, 164, 167
   Pierre, wife of 112
Charroye (Charoye, Charrois), Claude 35, 36, 38
Chauvin, Pierre 60
Chavois, Chavoye. *See* de Chavoye
Chedhomme, Jean 56-57
Chekaniches, nation 62
Chegnau. *See* Chagnau
Cheletre (Chelatre, Chelayte Chelettre)
   Barnabé 81, 87, 91, 94, 108, 120, 128, 135, 142, 150, 159, 167, 180
   Barnabé, wife of 108
   Fanchon 108
   François 96, 121, 128, 143, 151
   Jean Pierre 109

Josette 108
Marie Pelagie 109
Michel, widow of 108, 135, 159,
   166, 177
Paul François 108, 135, 159, 166
Pierre 87, 92, 95, 109, 121, 128, 135,
   142, 151, 159, 166, 180
Pierre, wife of 109
Rosalie 109
Chevert (Chever)
   Guillaume, *dit* Duffresne 19, 23, 24,
      29, 33, 37, 43, 52-53, 60-61,
   Guillaume, *fils* 67, 82, 83, 88, 89, 97,
      103, 123, 127, 137, 152, 157, 166,
      178
   Guillaume, wife of 103
Chime. *See* Sims
Chiq, f.n. 83
Christy (Christil, Christill, Clisty,
   Cristil, Cristy)
   François 118
   Jacques I 81, 76, 92, 118, 139, 148,
      163, 166, 174
   Jacques I, wife of 118
   Jacques II 118
   Magdelaine 118
Claussen, Lt. 14
Clavier. *See* Leconte
Clisty. *See* Christy
Closeau (Clausaut, Clausaux,
   Clauseaux, Clauso, Claussseau,
   Closo, Clozeau)
   François 58-59
   Gilbert 82, 88, 90, 97, 103, 123, 127,
      144, 149, 157, 166
   Louis 98, 103, 121, 128, 137, 143,
      149, 157, 166
   Thérèse 103
Cloutier
   Alexis 96, 112, 121, 128, 133, 143,
      151, 162, 166, 180
   Marguerite 112
   Jean Pierre "Fifi" 151, 162, 164, 167
Cocaille, chief of Yatasse 84
Coincoin, Marie Thérèse, f.n. 100, 135,
   159, 171, 180

Coindé, Antoine 131, 133, 143, 151,
   162, 167
Colmanne (Colma), Nicolas 153, 166,
   167
Combas, Louis 105
Conand (Connand), Joseph 159, 166,
   177, 179, 180
Conechin, Conelty. *See* Quinelty
corn 47, 49, 51, 53
Côte Joyeuse, aka Grande Côte 134-
   36, 180, 185
Côte Tulin 178
Cotolleau, Pierre *dit* Duplessis 14, 17
Coupiere, Andres 79
Couvie, Pierre 109
Coutant (Coutin), Pierre 87, 93, 95,
   112, 121, 146, 151, 162, 164, 167, 176
Couty (Coutie), Jean Paul 110, 151,
   160, 166
Crespes, Charles 56-57
Cristy. *See* Christy
Cromir, Sieur 17
Cureau, Jacques 74-75
Cusson, Sieur 17

D

Danis. *See* Denis
Darbanne. *See* Derbanne
D'Ardenne, Charles, *dit* Bellerose 20
D'Arrazola, Capt. 27, 30, 31, 32, 36
D'Artaud (Dartaud), Capt. 35, 36, 38,
   40, 42, 43
Dartigaux (Dartigo, Dartigeaux)
   Jean Baptiste 90, 94, 100, 120, 128,
      148, 149, 150, 159, 167, 177, 180,
      182
   Pierre 68, 70-71, 76, 100, 111, 142,
      148
   Pierre, wife/widow of 100, 133,
      148, 159, 167
Daublin, Noel 87
Dauclas. *See* Doclas
Dauphine. *See* Bertrand *dit* Dauphine
D'Autrives, Capt. 31, 32, 33, 36, 37,
   42, 43

David
- André 81, 104
- Baptiste Mathurin 100
- Elisabeth 110
- Jean Baptiste 133, 143, 148, 153, 155, 167, 173
- Jean Jacques 82, 88, 89
- Louis 131, 138, 143, 131, 138, 147, 152, 162, 167, 173
- Marie [*fille*] Mathurin 100
- Mathurin I 46–47, 56–57, 67
- Mathurin II 130
- orphan, 116

Davion (Daviont) 194
- Charles, *dit* St. Prix 16
- Dominique, *dit* St. Prix (St. Primo, Sempry) 79, 82, 88, 90, 97, 115, 123, 127, 138, 145, 149, 157, 167, 179
- Emanuel "Manuel" 145, 149, 180
- François 133, 162, 167
- Jean Baptiste I, *dit* St. Prix 20, 50–51, 58–59, 72–73, 77
- Jean Baptiste II, *dit* St. Prix (St. Prie) 82, 88, 89, 97, 115, 122, 123, 126, 130, 138, 145, 149, 153, 157, 179
- Jean Baptiste, "the younger" *dit* Fify 143 147 157, 179
- Jean Baptiste, "orphan" 117
- Joachim "Joacinthe" 162, 167, 176
- Julien *dit* L'Eveille, 20
- Louis, *dit* St. Prix (Sempry) 87, 92, 95, 115, 121, 137, 144, 149, 157, 167, 179
- Louis, wife of 115
- Manuel 97, 107, 124, 127

de Arze, Maximillien 117
de Benoist, Capt. 22, 29, 32, 37, 43
De Blanc
- Celeste Mathilde 99
- Cesaire, *fils* Louis Charles 99
- César, Commandant 30, 34, 38, 44
- Jean Baptiste d'Espagnet 99
- Jean Baptiste Dorsinaux 99
- Joseph Marie Charles 99
- Louis Marie Cezerio 149
- Louis Charles 35, 36, 40, 42, 70–71, 82, 88, 89, 90, 96, 99, 122, 124, 126, 127, 144, 145, 148, 149, 150, 178
- Louis Chevalier 99
- Marie Louise Marthe 99
- Pierre "Pierrot," f.m.c. 83, 111

de Chabert, Capt. 31, 32, 33, 36, 37, 42, 43
de Champignole, Sgt. 15
de Chavoye (Chavois, Savoye), Capt. 19, 22, 23, 25, 29, 33, 37, 43
de Cour. *See* Le Court de Presle
deer skins 78
de Gourdon, Capt. 26, 30, 35, 36, 42
de Grandmaison, Lt. 22, 28, 36, 42
de Grandpré (Grandpres), Capt. 39, 40, 42, 43
de la Barriere, Sieur 50–51
de la Chaise de St. Denis, Jacques 70–71, 76
de la Est, Jean 138
de La Gautrie, Capt. 45
de La Gauvray, Capt. 21, 22
de la Haye, Jean 99
de la Houssaye, Lt. 19, 25, 29, 33, 37
de la Mazilliere (de Mazillier), Capt. 21, 23, 26, 29, 37, 39, 43
de la Peña, Joseph 69, 119, 125
de la Perrier, Commandant 46–47, 54–55
de la Renaudière (La Renaudière, Larenodiere, Larnaudière, Larrenaudiere)
- Charles 50–51, 60–61
- Jean Baptiste 82, 88, 89, 97, 100, 123, 126, 138, 144
- Jean Baptiste, wife of 100
- Pierre 79, 82, 88, 90, 98, 108, 124, 127, 134, 145, 161, 168, 175, 181
- Pierre, wife of 108
- Poupone 108
- Severin 108

de la Ronde, Chevalier 22, 26, 28, 32, 35
de Larré, Capt. 23
de La Tour, Capt. 23, 29, 33, 36, 37. 42

de l'Isle, Marie Jeanne Elizabeth "Lisette." *See* Lisette
Delouche (Deslouches)
    Jean Baptiste 96, 110, 122, 128, 134, 151, 164, 167, 175, 181
    Jean Baptiste, wife of 110, 143
    Jean Louis 110, 161
de Macarty, Capt. 26, 28, 30, 32, 33, 36, 40, 42, 43
de Magny, Cesar 25, 26
de Marentine (Marantine), Capt. 28, 32, 36, 42
de Mazilliere. *See* de la Mazilliere
De Mézières (De Messieres)
    Antoine Marie 79
    Athanase I 22, 25, 28, 32, 36, 42, 46–47, 54–55, 68, 69, 79
    Athanase I, wife of 70–71
    Athanase II 32, 35, 36, 40, 42, 119, 132, 155, 169, 179
    Athanase II, children of 104
    Cesaire Marie 39, 40, 42, 132
    Jacques 125, 132, 155
    Marie Felicité 119
    Marie Josephe 119
de Monberault (Monverault), Capt. 23, 29, 33, 37, 43
de Moncharveaux, Capt. 21, 23, 29, 33, 37, 43
de Mortier, Pierre 23, 25, 29, 31
de Mouy, Maurice 79, 88, 89, 96, 100, 122, 126, 144, 149, 185
de Murat, Capt. 23, 25, 26, 28, 29, 30, 32, 33, 36, 37, 42, 43
Denis (Danis, Denys)
    Charles 133
    François 104
    Jean Baptiste I 81, 87, 92, 94, 113, 121
    Jean Baptiste I, wife of 113
    Jean Baptiste II 113, 133, 161, 176
Denoir, Jouachin 151
de Noyon, Capt. 21, 23, 29, 33, 36, 37, 43
de Pontalba, Capt. 23, 29, 33, 37
de Putre, Marie Catherine 15

Derbanne (Bernabane, Darbanne, Darbonne, Derban, D'erbanne, Dervan, Dervanne, d'Herbanne)
    Cyprienne 106
    Emanuel 106, 136, 158, 167, 177
    François Guyon *dit* Dion Despres d'Herbanne 14, 15, 17
    Gaspard I 48–49, 58–59, 72–73, 77, 88
    Gaspard II "Gasparite" 66, 82, 88, 89, 97, 117, 123, 126, 135, 144, 148, 153, 163, 167, 174
    Gaspard II, wife of 117
    Jean Baptiste, *fils* Gaspard 67, 79, 82, 83, 88, 89, 97, 123, 126, 139, 144, 149, 163, 179
    Joseph, fils Pierre 87, 92, 95, 106, 121, 128, 136, 143, 147, 151, 158, 167, 177
    Louis Pierre "Niny" 87, 92, 95, 106, 121, 128, 136, 143, 149, 158, 167, 177
    Marie 117
    Marie de l'Incarnacion (Mme. Joseph Dupré I; Mme. Jean Varangue) 181
    Manuel. See Emanuel
    Melanie (Mme. J. B. Brevel III) 195
    Pierre I 50–51, 58–59, 72–73, 77, 106, 136, 158, 167, 177, 180
    Pierre I, wife of 106
    Pierre II, "Pierrite" 68, 69, 79, 82, 88, 90, 97, 106, 124, 127, 136, 145, 146, 149, 158, 167, 177, 180
    Pierre II, wife of 106
    Pierre III 106
de Reclot, Lt. 14
de Reggio (Regio), Capt. 21, 23, 29, 33, 37, 40, 43, 45
Derneville
    Capt. 23, 25, 28, 29, 32, 33, 36, 37, 43, 45
    Elisabeth Pompone (Mme. Louis De Blanc) 99
de Rosiers. *See* Renaud *dit* de Rosiers

Dervan, Dervane, Dervanne. See Derbanne
DeSance, Jean 17
de Saulles (Dessoles), Jean 92, 103
desertions 26, 34, 39, 40, 45
des Noyer, Joseph 82
de Sommes (Desommes), Capt. 26, 28, 30, 32, 33, 34, 37, 43
de Soto
   Antonio Manuel Bermudes y 48-49, 58-59
   Antonio Manuel, wife of 70-71. *See also* Juchereau de St. Denis, Maria
   Marcel 152, 156, 171, 179, 182
Despres (Desprez), Antoine, *dit* Pretaboire 23, 29, 31, 33, 37, 39, 48-49
Dessaule, Jean 174
de St. Denis. *See* Juchereau de St. Denis
de Taillefer. *See* Taillefer
de Trant, Capt. 36, 39, 41, 42, 43
de Varennes (des Varennes), Capt. 21, 23, 29, 33, 39, 42, 45
de Vaugine, Capt. 81, 83, 85, 87, 88, 90, 93, 105, 120
de Villemont, Capt. 31, 32, 36
de Villiers
   Balthazard 70-71, 75
   Capt. 26, 29, 33, 37, 43
   Monsieur & chevalier 70-71
d'Hazeur, Capt. 23, 29, 33, 37, 43
d'Herbanne. *See* Derbanne
Diard, [Louis] 102
Diron, Sieur 15
Doclas (Dauclas, Docla, Docras), Nicolas, f.n. 134, 160, 170, 177, 180
Dolé (Dore, Dolet)
   Dulino 118
   Pierre I, *dit* Sans Quartier (Sans Cartier) 19, 21, 23, 29, 31, 33, 34, 37, 43
   Pierre I, widow of 48-49
   Pierre II 82, 88, 89, 97, 118, 123, 126
   Pierre II, wife of 118
   Pierre III 118

donkeys 63
Dore *dit* Sans Quartier. *See* Dolé
Dorgon, Capt. 38, 40, 43
D'Ortoland (D'Ortoland, D'Ortolant, Dortholand, Dortolan)
   Athanase 114
   Bernard 79, 82, 88, 96, 114, 122, 126, 132, 144, 152, 154, 156, 170
   Bernard, wife of 114
   Chevalier 114
   François 114
Dorval, Antoine 60
Doucet, François, *dit* ___rgon, *dit* St. Eustache 20, 23, 24, 29, 32, 37, 43, 60
Drouillon, Sieur 17
Du Boïs (Dubois)
   Antoine 95, 121, 128, 138, 143, 147, 152, 156, 167, 185
   François 89, 97, 116, 123, 126, 138, 144, 147, 149, 157, 167
   François, wife of 116, 185
   Henry, *dit* Jolyboïs 23, 29, 33, 37, 43
   Jean Baptiste I 46-47, 56-57, 72-73, 77
   Jean Baptiste II 82, 83, 88, 89, 97, 102, 109, 123, 126, 135, 145, 149
   Pierre, *dit* St. Pierre 14, 17, 44, 45
du Coder, Ensign 19
Duc. *See* Le Duc
Dudoigt, Pierre François 60
Duffresne. *See* Chevert *dit* Duffresne
Duguet (Duguet, Duguette, Goguet), Étienne 87, 92, 148, 163, 173
Duhamel, Jean Baptiste 153, 167
Dujardin, Manuel 167
Dumont, Charles 14, 16
Dupain, Pierre Emanüel Victor 25, 28, 32, 36, 38, 42, 46-47, 66, 70-71, 76
Du Pain. *See also* Dupin *and* Pain
Dupart, Jean, *dit* Le Maigre 23, 29, 33, 39
Dupin, Pierre, *dit* Riortaur 17
Duplessis. *See* Cotolleau *dit* Duplessis
Du Pont. *See* Pont

Dupré (Dupre, Dupree, Dupres, Duprest)
- Athanase 111, 146, 149, 160, 164, 167, 175
- Cécile 107
- David 111
- Jean Baptiste I 46–47, 56–57, 66, 72–73, 77
- Jean Baptiste, *fils* Joseph 111
- Joseph I 46–47, 56–57, 72–73, 77, 79, 181
- Joseph II 82, 88, 89
- Joseph II, widow of 112
- Joseph III 112
- Marie 111
- Marie Louise 111
- Pierre 96, 111, 121, 128, 134, 143, 151, 160, 167, 181
- Robert 48–49, 56–57

Dupuy
- Ensign 14
- Pierre *dit* Goupillon 15

Durand
- Étienne Vincent 102
- Louis I, *dit* Vigé 81, 91, 94, 117
- Louis II, *dit* Vigé (Viger) 102, 120, 147, 158, 185
- Louis II, wife of 102

Duret, Charles 122, 137, 140, 141, 143, 153, 156, 167, 185

du Tillet (Dutillet), Capt. 22, 23, 24, 28, 29, 32, 33, 37, 38, 42, 43

Duverger, Claude, *dit* Joly Coeur 23, 29, 33, 37, 39

Duvivier, Jean 60

Duvivier. *See also* Vivier

E

écores. *See* Grande Écore, Petite Écore and Monet's Bluff

Egard, Jean Baptiste 39, 43

Ernandes. *See* Hernandes

Englishmen 56, 87, 93, 139, 166

Errie. *See* Herrié

Ettie, François 153

Ettredge (Etreisen), William 153

F

Fabre
- Honoré 60
- Jean 143, 153

Faulevent. *See* Caseau *dit* Faulevent

Faupied, Jean 23, 29, 33, 37, 39

Faure, Jacques 159, 167

Fausse, Pierre 14

Fausse Rivière 139

Fayard, site near Campti 179

Fayard (Frillard), *dit* La Lancette 20

Fazende
- Jacques, "the younger" 39, 40, 42, 46–47, 54–55, 74–75, 77
- Sieur, "the elder" 26, 28, 30, 32, 34, 36, 42, 46–47, 54–55

Febles, Francisco 125

Fifi. *See* Davion *dit* Fifi. Also Derbanne, Louis "Fifi"

Filibert, Gaspart

Fiol (Fiole, Fiolle),
- Gaspard I 56–57, 68, 79, 82, 88, 90, 97, 100, 133, 143, 146, 147, 155
- Gaspard I, wife/widow 100, 179, 185
- Gaspard II, *dit* Cadet 95, 100, 128, 153, 168

firearms 18, 47, 49, 51, 53, 55, 57, 59, 61

Fitzpatrick(?), John. *See* Philispatric

Flamier, François 40, 43, 44

Florio, François 168

Fonteneau (Fontenau, Fontenaut),
- Louis 87, 91, 94, 116, 120, 128, 138, 141, 142, 148, 152, 162, 168, 173, 179
- Louis, wife of 116
- Modeste 116

Fort
- Fanchonette 110
- Jacques 81, 87, 91, 94, 109, 120, 135, 177, 180, 193
- Jacques, wife of 109
- Marie Louise 110
- Marie Marthe 109

Fortin,
- Louis, *dit* Le Gros 81, 87, 91, 94, 102, 128, 142, 153
- Louis, *dit* Le Petit 87, 91, 94, 120, 128, 142, 152, 156, 168, 185

Fournier, Nicolas 79

Frederic (Frederiq, Frederique, Phrederiq)
- André, *fils* Philipe II 109, 135, 151, 156, 159, 167
- André Philippe 81, 86, 91, 94, 109, 120, 128, 142, 159
- François 102, 135, 159, 168
- François, wife/widow of 102, 133, 147, 156, 185
- Jean Baptiste 109
- Jean François, *fils* Philipe 109
- Marie Barbe 109
- Marie Catherine 109
- Marie Jeanne 102
- Marie Pelagie, *fille* Philipe II 109
- Pelagie, *fille* Philipe I 109
- Philipe I 109, 135, 159, 167, 177
- Philipe I, wife/widow of 109, 161
- Philipe II 81, 87, 91, 94, 109, 120, 128, 135, 142, 151, 159, 167, 180
- Philipe II, wife of 109
- Rosalie 109

Frenière, Antoine 81, 87

Fredieu, Augustin 151, 161, 164, 168, 181

Frillard *dit* La Lancette. *See* Fayard

G

Gagné (Gagñe, Gagnez, Gagnier, Gaigné, Gaiñe, Gañier, Gannié),
- Basile 115, 153, 157, 168
- Étienne 67, 70-71, 76, 115, 138, 157, 168
- Étienne, wife of 115
- Henriette 103
- Jean Baptiste 103
- Joseph 103, 157, 168
- Josephe 137
- Marie Josephe (Mme. Louis Davion; Mme. Remy Perot) 103, 195
- Pelagie 115
- Pierre I, *dit* Grand 66, 70-71, 81, 86, 91, 94, 103, 137, 141, 147, 157, 168, 178, 185
- Pierre II 124, 128, 130, 137, 143, 153, 157, 168, 179, 194
- Pierre II, wife of 103
- Susanne 103
- Ursule 115

Gagnon (Gaignon)
- Marie Louise 103
- Pierre 96, 103, 120, 128
- Pierre, wife of 103

Gallando, Andres 125

Gallien (Galien)
- Joseph 122
- Marie Jeanne Euphrosine (Mme. Jacques Therin Vercher) 194
- Nicolas 81, 87, 92, 113, 130, 133, 143, 151, 161, 164, 168, 181
- Nicolas, wife of 113
- Pierre Noël, widow of 112

Gascony, France 67

Gautier (Gotier), René, *dit* La Fleur 20, 23, 29, 33, 37, 39

Gerard. *See* Girard

Gillot, Louise Françoise (Mme. Charles Davion *dit* St. Prix; Mme. Étienne Le Roy) 14

Girard (Gerard)
- Antoine, *dit* Printems 40, 43, 56
- Pierre, *dit* Leveille 74-75

goats 18, 63

Goguet. *See* Duguet

Goie. *See* Gouelle

Gonin (Gonain, Gonnin)
- François 108, 131, 135, 143, 151, 159, 168
- Jean Baptiste 58-59, 67

Gonzalez, Manuel 125

Gouelle (Gouel, Gouille, Goy), Simon 110, 133, 151, 162, 168

Goupillon. *See* Dupuy

Gotier. *See* Gautier *and* Goutière

Goutière (Goutierrez, Gutierrez)
  Pierre   52–53, 56–57
  Silvie   117
Grandchamp, Capt.   23, 29
Grande Côte (Cotte) aka Côte Joyeuse   134–36, 180, 185
Grande Écore   113, 137–38, 179
Grandes Caddo (Cadox)   62
Grandmaison. *See* de Grandmaison
Grandpres. *See* de Grandpré
Grappe (Grape)
  Alexis, *dit* La Verdure, *dit* St. Alexis   19, 22, 28, 31, 32, 34, 35, 36, 42, 52–53, 58–59, 70–71, 76
  Alexis, widow of   117, 138, 147, 162, 168, 173
  François, *dit* Toulin   82, 88, 89, 97, 115, 123, 126, 138, 144, 147, 162, 168, 173, 179
  Françoise   117
  Jean Baptiste   81, 88, 89, 97, 117, 123, 126, 138, 144, 147, 149, 162, 168, 173, 179
Green, Edward   130
Grenot, Jeanne   15
Grillet (Grillte)
  Antoine   105, 153, 158, 168
  Jean Baptiste   105
  Magdelaine   105
  Marie Barbe   105
  Marin, *dit* Sauterelle (Sautrelle)   23, 24, 33, 37, 43, 46–47, 56–57, 66, 72–73, 77, 105, 158, 168, 178
  Marin, wife of   105
Guedon, Jacques, *dit* Nantais   17
Guerbois, Louis   168
Guichard, Antoine   96, 104
Guillot. *See* Gillot
Guinchard (Guischard), Étienne   26, 37, 43
Guinoche. *See* Totin *dit* Guinoche
guns. *See* firearms
Gutierrez. *See also* Gautier *and* Goutière
Guyon. *See* Derbanne
Gypsies   83

H
Hantt. *See* Anty
Haraud (Herault), Pierre   19, 22, 28, 31, 32, 36, 42
Hazeur. *See* d'Hazeur
Hernandes (Ernandes, Hernandez)
  Antonio   125
  Michel   110, 131, 135, 143, 151, 160, 169, 180
  Michel, wife of   110
Herrié (Errié), Jacques   153, 194
Hervé, François   20
Hidalgo, Gaspard   81
Himel (Himelle, Hymel)
  Antoine I   96, 110, 135, 139
  Antoine I, wife/widow of   110, 159, 168, 177, 180
  Antoine II   110
  Eleonore   110
  François I   96
  François II   110
hogs, pigs   18, 47, 49, 51, 53, 55, 57, 59, 61, 63
Hoppok (Obhor, Opocque),
  Jean Jacob   118, 130
  Michel   118
  Widow   180
Horé, Jean   19, 22, 25
Horn, John (Jean Horne, Hornie, Hornne)   134, 141, 150, 161, 164, 168, 176, 181
horses   14–18, 47, 49, 51, 53, 55, 57, 59, 61, 63, 78, 99–120
Houssaye. *See* de la Houssaye
Hubert, Jacques   74–75
Hugues (Hughes, Hugue)
  François *dit* Tonnan (Tonant)   79, 112, 133, 146, 151, 161, 164, 176
  François, wife of   112
Hymel. *See* Himel

I
indigo   78
Ingram (Ingrand, Ingrum), Joseph   168, 174

Isle à Brevel (Ille à Brevel, Isle Brevelle) 134, 176, 180, 181, 189
Isle à Vaches 84
Illinois 21, 40
Indian slaves 14–18, 47, 49, 51, 53, 78
Ingle, Pierre 87, 92
Irishmen 95
Isquierdo (Izcuerdo, Izguierdo, Ysquierdo), Gil 131, 143, 151, 161, 168, 175

J
Jallot, Sr. 14, 15
Jambert (Jambart), Jean, *dit* Champagne 40, 43
Jan Rich. *See* Ris
Jarnac, Jean 81, 87, 91
Jaubard. *See* Lamalathie *dit* Jobard
Jeannot, f.m.c. *See* Mulon
Jeanris. *See* Ris
Jeanson (Jamson, Janson), Joseph 81, 87, 91, 94, 100, 128, 142
Jeune, Jeuin. *See* Young
Joannis, Sieur 77
Jobard, Jobare, Jobart. *See* Lamalathie *dit* Jobart
Joly Cöuer. *See* Duverger *dit* Joly Coeur *and* Raison *dit* Joly Cöuer
Jolyboïs, Jolyboïs. *See* DuBoïs *dit* Jolyboïs; LeVasseur *dit* Joliboïs
Jonca (Jonka), Crisosthomé 96, 118
Jonnau, Jean 69
Jougny (Jurinny), Sieur 56–57
Joung. *See* Young
Jovar. *See* Lamalathie *dit* Jobart
Juchereau de St. Denis (Sⁿ Denis)
  Louis I, commandant 14, 16
  Louis Antoine 22, 26, 28, 32, 36, 42, 46–47, 54–55, 70–71, 76
  Louis Antoine, widow of [Marie Louise Marguerite Derbanne]104, 136, 158, 167, 185
  Maria, wife of de Soto 76
  Pierre Antoine, Chevalier 19, 26, 28, 32, 36, 42, 46–47, 54–55
Jurinny. See Jougny

Jussiau, Sieur, cadet 19

K
Kankaguayes, nation 62
Kaunion, nation 62
Kelly, John 63
Kidesingues (Quy de Singes), nation 62, 85
Kuakanas, nation 62
Kuayaches, nation 62
Kyaava-douche, chief of Nadaques 84

L
La Berry
  Jean Baptiste I 48–49, 58–59, 72–73, 77, 108, 135, 159, 169
  Jean Baptiste I, wife of 108
  Magdelaine (Mme. Jean J. Martineau, Mme. Simeon Rachal) 108, 195
Laborde (La Borde), Mathieu 81, 87, 92, 95
La Boucherie, Sieur 17
La Boute. *See* Bernardin *dit* La Boute
Labrie, Pierre 81, 87, 91
La Casse (Lacase, Lacasse), Jacques 130, 134, 143, 151, 161, 169, 175, 181
Lacaze (La Caze), François 102, 132, 141, 155, 168, 178, 185
Lac Noir 96, 117, 139, 173, 179
Lacoste, Pierre 67, 69
Lacour (Lacourt, Lecour)
  Gaspard "Gasparite" 106, 130, 136, 143, 151, 160, 169
  Pierre I 67, 80, 86, 91, 106, 136, 160, 169, 176
  Pierre I, wife of 106
  Pierre II 96, 106, 121, 128, 136, 143, 151, 160, 169
Lacour. *See* also Le Court
La Croix. *See* Thomas *dit* La Croix
La Douceur. *See* Prud'homme *dit* La Douceur
La Fleur. *See* Gautier *dit* La Fleur
Lafitte (LaFita)
  Baptiste 118
  Bouëtte, *fils* 131

Denege 118
Marie 118
Paul Bouëte 67, 72-73, 77, 81, 86, 91, 118
Paul Bouëte, wife of 118
Pierre 118
La Fontaine, Sieur 17
La Forest, François 87
La Forest. *See* Launay *dit* La Forest
Laforet, Louis 119
La France. *See* Turpeaux *dit* La France
Lagé. *See* Leger
La Grenade, Antoine 93
La Guerre. *See* Perron (Peron) *dit* La Guerre
La Houssaye. *See* de la Houssaye
Laignon (Lagnon), Nicolas 60, 101
Laitanos, nation 62
La Jeunesse. *See* Prud'homme *dit* La Jeunesse
La Joye. *See* Bibo *dit* La Joye
La Lancette. *See* Fayard (Frillard) *dit* La Lancette
La Lande
  Jean 52-53, 60, 96, 117, 139, 162, 169
  Jean, wife/widow of 117, 173, 179
  Jean Pierre 117, 122, 129, 139, 144, 148, 149, 163, 169, 173, 179
  Marie Jeanne 117, 194
L'allemand (Lallemand) Nicolas 87, 92
L'allemand. *See also* Alemand, Risse *dit* L'Allemand
La Lime
  Mr. 69
  Widow 106
La Lime. *See also* Le Maître
Lamalatie (La Malathie, Lamalathy, Lamalty)
  Louis I, *dit* Jobart (Jaubard, Jobar, Jobard, Jobare, Jobart) 50-51, 58-59
  Louis II 69, 72-73, 77, 81, 87, 92, 116, 138, 131, 138, 147, 162, 169, 173, 179, 182
  Pierre, *dit* Jobar 104

La Mazilliere. *See* de la Mazilliere
Lambre (L'ambre)
  Antoine 104, 131, 135, 143, 151, 158, 168
  Jacob (Jacques) 50-51, 58-59, 66, 72-73, 77
  Jacob (Jacques), widow of 104, 136, 160, 169, 175
  Jean 48-49, 58-59, 66, 70, 77, 81, 86, 91
  Joseph 104, 158, 169, 180
  Louis 97, 104, 124, 127, 134, 144, 146, 151, 162, 164, 169, 176, 180
  Louis Joseph 136
  Marie, *fille* Jacob 104
  Marie, orphan 106, 136
  Remy 82, 88, 90, 97, 104, 123, 126, 132, 144, 152, 160, 168, 175, 180, 181, 182
L'Anglais. *See* Langlois *and* Young land 16-17, 55, 57, 59, 61, 99-120, 155, 156, 158, 159, 176, 185
Langlois (El Angloz, Lingleise)
  Auguste 160, 169, 175
  François I, *dit* Sans Regret 22, 25, 27, 29, 33, 43, 45, 48-49, 58-59, 66
  François I, widow of 147, 155, 185
  François II 131
  Joseph 107
La Poule, Claude François 23, 24
La Renaudière. *See* de la Renaudière
La Rivière. *See* Roubelet *dit* La Rivière
La Roche, Jacque 67
La Rochelle ("Rochela"), France 66, 67, 68
La Rose. *See* Boutière *dit* La Rose
La Tour. *See* de La Tour
Lattier (Latie)
  François 135, 151, 161, 169
  Françoise 109
  Jean Baptiste 96, 109, 121, 128, 135, 143, 151, 161, 169, 181
  Joseph I 56-57, 96, 109, 135, 161
  Joseph II 109, 121, 128, 151
La Tulipe, Sieur 17
La Tulipe. *See also* Rachal *dit* La Tulipe

Launay (Launnay), Charles, *dit* La
    Forest 23, 29, 33, 43
Laurent
    Jean Pierre, *dit* Prevostiere 16
    Joseph 60-61
Lauve
    Nicolas 96
    "the younger" 181
La Verdure. *See* Grappe *dit* La
    Verdure
La Vergne, Sieur 16
Lavespère (La Vespere)
    François 106, 130, 136, 143, 147,
        150, 158, 169, 177
    François, wife of 106
La Vigne
    Jean Baptiste 131, 134, 143, 151, 161,
        169
    Joseph 126
    orphan 116
    Pierre 131, 143, 151
La Vigne. *See also* Tessier *dit* LaVigne
Lebaseur. *See* Le Vasseur
Le Boeuf (Beuf, Boeufs, Leboeuf,
    Lebough)
    Andres 82, 88
    Louis 67, 88, 90
Lebreton, Sieur 111
Le Brun
    André 131
    Anete 111
    Elisabeth 111
    Guillaume II 83, 111, 134, 161, 164,
        169, 176, 181
Le Brun. *See also* Bossier *dit* LeBrun
Le Clerc (Le Clair, Le Cler)
    George 72-73, 77
    Louis 50-51, 58-59
Le Comte (LeCompt, Le Compte,
    Lecomte, Leconte)
    Ambroise 82, 88, 90, 97, 112, 123,
        127, 133, 145, 149, 162, 168, 180
    Ambroise, wife of 112
    Jacques 112
    Jean Baptiste I 24, 30, 33, 37, 39, 42,
        45, 48-49, 56-57, 72-73, 77

    Jean Baptise I, widow of 112, 133,
        161, 168, 180
    Jean Baptiste II 112
    Marguerite 112
    Marguerite, f.n. 146, 161, 164, 176
    Thérèse (Mme. Louis Metoyer) 194
Leconte (Lecomte, Lecompte)
    Eleonore 108
    François Clavier, *dit* Saideck 81, 87,
        91, 108, 135, 153, 159
    François, wife of 108
    Marie Louise 108
    Pierre 108
    Reine Barbe 108
    Rosalie 108
Lecour, Jacques, "frater" 45
Le Court des Presle (de Cour, Lecourt,
    Prelle)
    Athanase 96, 112, 121, 128, 133, 143,
        149, 161, 164, 169, 181
    Barthelemy 96, 112, 126, 133, 145,
        146, 149, 161, 164, 168, 176
    Cécile 112
    Fanchonette 112
    Louis Matthias, Lt. 19, 22, 26, 29,
        30, 32, 36, 42, 46-47, 54-55, 72-73,
        77
    Pelagie (Mme. Antoine Joseph
        Metoyer) 112, 194
Le Doux
    Madame 70-71, 76
    Sieur, cadet 45
Le Duc
    Jean Baptiste, *dit* Ville Franche 66,
        79, 87, 93, 100, 185
    Joseph, *dit* Ville Franche 19
    Joseph, widow of 48-49, 56-57
Lefevre, Antoine 80
Le Gros. *See* Fortin *dit* Le Gros
Le Jeune. *See* Young
Le Jeunesse. *See* Prud'homme *dit* Le
    Jeunesse
Le Maigre. *See* Dupart *dit* Le Maigre
Le Maître
    Baptiste 101
    Euphrosine 101

François, *dit* La Lime 101, 133, 155, 169
François, *fils* 101, 185
François, wife of 101
Victoire 101
Leger
    Jean Baptiste, *dit* Piedferme 17, 68, 116, 138, 148, 162, 168, 170, 173
    Jean Baptiste, wife of 116
Le Moine (Lemoine, Le Moinne)
    Antoine 96, 98, 111, 124, 127, 134, 145, 149, 160, 169
    Charles I 46-47, 56-57, 111, 134, 160, 169
    Charles II 87, 92, 95, 111, 121, 129, 134, 143, 151, 160, 168, 176
    François 14
    Jean Baptiste 95, 111, 121, 128, 135, 143, 151, 161, 169
Lengles. *See* Young
Le Noir (Lenoir)
    Antoine, *dit* Liston 79, 82, 88, 97, 114, 124, 127, 138, 152, 156, 168, 179
    Antoine, wife of 114
Le Petit. *See* Fortin *dit* Le Petit
L'Epine (Lepine), Jacques 151, 169
Leon, Ives 14
Le Roy, Étienne, *dit* Framboise 14, 19
Lestage
    Agate 108
    Barnabé 108
    Barthelemy 108
    François 108
    Geneviève 108
    Guillaume 68, 80, 86, 91, 108, 135, 159, 168, 180
    Guillaume, wife of 108
    Jean Baptiste 108
Le Vasseur (Lebaseur, Levasseur)
    Emanuel "Manuel" 113
    François 50-51, 58-59, 72-73, 77, 113, 136, 156, 169, 178
    François, wife of 113
    Françoise 113
    Geneviève 113
    Jacques I *dit* Jolibois 17, 67, 111, 160, 168, 175, 181
    Jacques I, wife of 111
    Jacques II 113, 121, 134, 142?, 150
    Jean François, "the son" 95, 113, 129, 136, 143, 153, 156, 169
    Louis 113, 153
    Simeon 194
    Victorin 111
L'Eveille. *See* Davion *dit* L'Eveille
Leveille. *See* Girard *dit* Leveille
L'Huissier, Antoine 151, 169
Lingleise. *See* Langlois
Liston. *See* Le Noir *dit* Liston
Lionnois. *See* Samüel *dit* Lionnois
Lisette, freed Indian (Marie Jeanne Elisabeth "Lisette" de l'Isle) 58-59
Lissilour (Lissilourd, Lissivour), Yves 130, 132, 143, 151, 160, 169, 175, 181
Loisel (Loiset), Jean Baptiste 111, 134
Longueville, Jeanne (Mme. Pierre Pichon) 15
Los Adaïs, capital of Texas. *See* Nuestra Señora del Pilar de los Adaïs
Luisetta, freed Indian. *See* Lisette
Luña, Joseph 105
Lunau, Pedro 68
Luret, Charles 130
Lussié, Antoine 137, 163
Lyonais. *See* Samüel *dit* Lionnois

M

Macarty, Guillaume 170
Macarty. *See also* de Macarty
Maës (Maies)
    Pierre Joseph 95, 101, 121, 128, 135, 143, 146, 163, 164, 180
    Pierre Joseph, wife of 101
Magny, Jean, *dit* St. Jean 23, 26, 29, 30, 33, 43
Magny. *See also* de Magny
Maigre. *See* Mercier *dit* Maigre
Maigros, Antoine, *dit* Bourbon 22, 26, 28, 31, 33, 43

Mailloux (Maillioux, Malloux, Mayou)
- Anastasie "Lestasie" 114, 194
- Cécile 114
- Ignace 81, 86, 91, 94, 113, 120, 128, 137, 140, 147, 156, 182
- Ignace, wife of 113
- Laurent 131, 137, 143, 153, 156, 169
- Pierre 114, 153, 156, 170
- Thérèse 114

Malbert
- Jean Baptiste, *dit* Sans Façon 23, 29, 31, 33, 37, 43, 48-49, 60-61
- Widow 161

Malige
- Angelique 101
- Eulalie 101
- Joseph 101, 130, 143, 153, 158, 170, 178, 185
- Joseph, wife of 101
- Josette 101
- Manette 101
- Roseline 101

Manguin (Monguin), Simon 23, 26, 29, 33

Marantin. *See* de Marentin

Marchand, Jean Marc 153

Marcollay (Marcolay), Paul 80, 91, 94, 100, 120, 128, 132, 142, 150, 155, 170

Marechal. *See* Barbier *dit* Marechal

Mariano, Joseph 105, 113, 143

Marionneau (Marion), Pierre 15, 16

Mariotte (Mariote), Marie Louise, f.n. 146, 161, 164, 176

Marmillion, Sieur 70-71

Marmillon, Jacques Daniel, *dit* St. Mailae 20

Martin
- Joseph 81, 83, 87, 92, 95, 96, 102, 104, 128, 130, 138, 142, 153, 157, 170
- Zakarie 131

Martinau (Martineau)
- Jean Joseph 130, 135, 141, 142, 150, 195
- Joseph 129

Marly. *See* Sorel *dit* Marly

Massip (Masip, Massipe)
- Dorothée 108
- Elisabeth 108
- Étienne 108
- Jean 68, 81, 87, 91, 94, 108, 120, 128, 135, 142, 151, 161, 164, 169, 175, 181
- Jean, wife of 108
- Pierre 108

Matchass, Antoine, f.n. 170, 175

Maubeuge, Sieur 17

Maurin (Morain, Moreyn, Morin), Jean Baptiste 52-53, 58-59, 67, 72-73, 81, 86, 91, 94, 102, 120, 128, 132, 133, 139, 141, 170

Mayou. *See* Mailloux

Mazola. *See* d'Arrazola

McDaniel, John (Magdanel, Jean) 153

meat, salted and dried 78

Melmies, Sieur 56-57

Mercier
- Claude de, Dr. 69, 72-73, 76
- Felicité 115
- François 131, 143, 147, 153, 156, 170, 185
- Marie Josephe Adelaïde "Josete" (Mme. Simeon Le Vasseur) 115, 194
- Louis 96, 115, 121, 128, 138, 143, 147, 153, 156, 170
- Louis, wife of 115
- Nicolas 115, 131, 153, 156, 170
- Pierre *dit* Navarre, *dit* Maigre 23, 26, 29, 33, 43

Mesnard, Mr. 50-51, 54-55

Metoyer (Metoyé, Métoyé, Mettoyer)
- Antoine Joseph 100, 194
- Augustin, 165
- François, 100
- Louis 194
- Pierre I 66, 77, 82, 87, 92, 100, 132, 139, 140, 141, 142, 148, 159, 169, 180, 182
- Pierre II 159, 170
- Pierre Toussaint 100

Meunier, Sieur 17
Meunier. *See also* Totain *dit* Meunier
Michel. *See* Zarichi
Millet, Jean 68
Missouri post 21
Monbrun, François 129, 143, 151
Moncharveaux. *See* de Moncharveaux
Monet's Bluff 180
Monet (Monette)
   Louis 79, 82, 88, 89, 97, 107, 123,
      126, 135, 144, 149, 169, 176, 180
   Louis, wife of 107
Mongin, Sieur 22, 27, 28, 30, 31, 32, 36
Monginaut (Monginot), François 136,
   141, 169, 178, 185
Monpierre, Bartolo 79
Montanary (Monthanary), Benoist
   100, 130, 138, 143, 147, 153, 162,
   169, 173, 179
Monteche, Dominique, *dit* St.
   Dominique 20, 48-49, 54-55, 72-
   73, 77
Monverault. *See* de Monberault
Morin
   Jean 105
   Jean, wife of 105
Morin. *See also* Maurin
Morino, Gil 81
Morphy. *See* Murphy
Morron (Morin? Morrow?), Nicolas
   151
Mortier. *See* de Mortier
Morvan (Morvant)
   Antoine François 87, 92, 143
   François 74-75, 81, 87, 91, 119
Motar, Sieur 56-57
Mouton, Philippe, *dit* Belle Fleur 24,
   25, 30, 33, 37, 43
Muler, Sieur 16
mules, donkeys 63, 78
Mulon, Jeannot, f.m.c. 46-47, 58-59,
   83
Murat. *See* de Murat
Murphy (Morphille, Murfphy),
   Edward 93, 95, 105, 121, 128, 136,
   143, 153, 158, 169, 178, 179, 182, 185

N
Nacogdoches, nation (Pequenos
   Nakodoches) 62
Nadaque (Nadacos), nation 62, 84
Naigle
   François 100, 133, 170
   Jacques 50-51
   Jacques, widow of 60-61
Nantais. *See* Guedon *dit* Nantais
Natchez post, Mississippi 21
Natchitoches Indian village 62, 84
Natchitoches, town 119, 133, 185, 186
Navarre, bachelor 52-53
Navarre. *See also* Mercier *dit* Navarre
Necesite, François 153
Negle. *See* Naigle
Nesates, nation 62
Neveu, François 35, 38, 43
New Orleans 9, 25, 30, 31, 40, 69, 122,
   123
Nicotaque-Nanan, chief of
   Kidesingues nation 85
Normand, Louis 170
Normand. *See also* Bunel *dit* Normand
Normandin, cavalryman 153
Normandy, France 68
Nuestra Señora del Pilar de los Adaës
   10
Nugent, Eduardo 63

O
Obhor. *See* Hoppok
Obreville, Pierre, *dit* Rencontre 19
O'Connor, Jim (Oconome, Gim) 118
Olivier, Hugues, Sieur 31, 32, 36, 39
Opocque, Opok. *See* Hoppock
Ortolant. *See* d'Ortoland
Ouachita (l'Uachitas), nation 62
Ouyas village 21
ox carts 63
oxen 63

P
Pacheque, rifleman 81
Padilla, Juan Manuel 79
Paillet, Mathieu 96

Pain
  Daniel 23, 30, 34, 38, 44, 46-47, 54-55
  François Daniel 39, 40, 43, 44, 45, 54-55
  Louis 43, 44
Pain. *See also* Dupain, Dupin
Palvado (Palvadeau, Palvadot), Jean 148, 153, 162, 170, 173
Papa (Poyra?), Jean 81
Paul, Nicolas 113
Pavie (Pavia)
  Étienne I 50-51, 54-55, 68, 81
  Étienne I, widow of 99
  Étienne II 99
  Helene 99
  Joseph 67, 80, 86, 90
  Pierre, Rev. 184, 188, 190, 191, 192, 196
Peoria village 21
Pequenos Caddo (Cadox), nation 62
Pequenos Nadacos, nation. *See also* Nadaque 62
Pequenos Nakodoches, nation 62
Peres, Conception 112
Perot (Perau, Perault, Peraux, Pereault, Pero, Perrau, Perrault, Perraut, Perreault), a *dit* of the Canadian Vildec family
  Chrisostomé. See Jean Chrisostomé
  Faustin 117
  Felicité 117
  François 67, 68, 117, 139, 148, 170, 179
  François, wife of 117, 163
  Jean Chrisostomé 79, 82, 88, 89, 97, 117, 118, 123, 126, 139, 144, 149, 163, 170, 179, 179
  Jean Chrisostomé, wife of 117
  Joseph 60-61
  Pierre Vildec (Villedeque) *dit* Perot 61
  Magdeleine 117
  Remy 87, 92, 95, 117, 123, 127, 139, 144, 148, 149, 163, 170, 173, 195
Perrier, Capt. 22, 23, 29

Perrier. *See also* Pierrier
Perron (Peron), Gabriel, *dit* Sans Chagrin, *dit* La Guerre 27, 28, 30, 31, 32, 34, 35, 36, 42, 45
Petite Cados Dakiou, nation 84
Petite Écore, on Côte Joyeuse 180
Philbert, Gaspard 110
Philippe. *See* Frederic
Philispatri (Fitzpatrick?), Jean, Irishman 96
Picard. *See* Roüence *dit* Picard
Picquery, Nicolas, f.m.c. 101, 170
Piedferme. *See* Leger *dit* Piedferme
Pierrier, Widow 15
Pierrier. *See also* Perrier
pigs. *See* hogs
Pipes (Pipe), Bernard 81, 87, 91
Piseros (Pissarau), Sieur 54-55, 70-71, 76
Plaisance (Plasance)
  Bertrand 103, 137, 147, 157, 170, 185
  Jean Baptiste 103
  Louis 103, 146, 147, 157, 170
  Mathieu 60-61, 68, 80, 86, 91
Plauché (Plaucher, Plauchet, Ploché)
  Antoine 87, 114, 137, 141, 157, 170
  Antoine, wife of 114
  Étienne 114
  Marie 114
Poeÿfarre (Poëlferré), Sieur 56-57, 74-75
Poirier, Vincent 56-57
Poissot (Poasso, Poisau, Poisot, Poisseau)
  Agnes, f.w.c. 111
  Antoine Remy 95, 97, 104, 121, 131, 139, 141, 148, 170, 174
  Athanase I 68, 72-73, 77, 82, 118, 136, 141, 149, 158, 170, 178, 185
  Athanase I, wife of 118
  Athanase II 118, 158, 170
  Marie 105
  Modeste 105
  Paul 105
  Pierre 67
  Remy I 46-47, 54-55, 66, 70-71, 76

Remy II 46–47, 56–57, 67, 72–73, 77,
    82, 88, 90, 105, 134, 160, 170, 175,
    181
Remy II, wife of 105
Silvestre 118
Victoire 105
Pomier (Pommier)
    Jean 81, 87, 92, 95, 107, 121, 128,
        134, 142, 150, 161, 170, 181
    Jean, wife of 107
Pont (du Pont, Pent, Pon, Pons),
    Nicolas, f.m.c. 79, 88, 90, 97, 123,
    127, 133, 170
Pontalba. *See de* Pontalba
Populus, Capt. 22, 36, 42
Poulido, François 110
Pousset, Sieur 17
Pretaboire. *See* Despres *dit* Pretaboire
Prevau, Jean 52–53
Prevost, Nicolas 17
Prevostiere. *See* Laurent *dit*
    Prevostiere
Printemps. *See* Gerard *dit* Printemps
Provençal (Provensal), François 60
Provence, France 66, 67
Prud'homme (Prudhomme)
    Anette 99
    Antoine 87, 92, 95, 99, 122, 128, 137,
        139, 143, 151, 160, 170, 175
    Bastien. *See* Sebastien
    Catherine 103
    Cezaire 115
    Deneige 115
    Dominique 95, 98, 99, 124, 127, 136,
        144, 149, 155, 170, 178, 185
    Emanuel "Manuel" 82, 87, 92, 95,
        104, 128, 136, 143, 150, 160, 170,
        175, 181
    Emanuel, wife of 104
    François 66, 81, 87, 92, 95, 114, 137,
        147, 156, 170
    François, wife of 114
    Jacques Bastien 96, 103, 122, 128,
        137, 144, 149, 158, 170, 185

Jean Baptiste I, *dit* La Jeunesse 20,
    23, 29, 33, 35, 36, 42, 54–55, 70–71,
    76
Jean Baptiste I, widow of 99
Jean Baptiste, *fils* Emanuel 104
Jean Baptiste Bastien 87, 92, 95, 103,
    121, 128, 143, 153, 160, 170
[Jean Pierre Philipe] 16
Manuel. *See* Emanuel
Marie Louise 103
Pierre Sebastien, *dit* La Douceur 23,
    24, 29, 33, 37, 43, 52–53, 60–61,
    72–73
Pierre Sebastien, widow of 102
Pierre, *dit* Sanspeur 20, 52–53
Sebastien II "Bastien" and
    "Bastienitte" 82, 88, 89, 97, 103,
    123, 126, 137, 140, 144, 149, 163,
    170
Susette 99
witness 182

Q
Quensy, chief of the Adaïs 84
Quinelty (Conechin, Conelty), John
    119
Quy de Singes, nation. *See*
    Kidesingues

R
Rabalais (Rabalay, Rabalet)
    Joseph 111, 131, 134, 143, 151, 160,
        171
    Joseph, wife of 111
    Marie Jeanne 111
Rachal (Rachale)
    Antoine, *fils* Louis I 95, 111, 121,
        128, 134, 143, 148, 151, 160, 171,
        180
    Antoine, *fils* Louis I, wife of 111
    Antoine, *fils* Barthelemy I 106, 151
    Barthelemy I, *dit* La Tulipe 21, 23,
        25, 29, 33, 37, 43, 48–49, 57, 68, 69,
        72–73, 77
    Barthelemy I, widow of 106, 136,
        158, 171, 177, 180

Barthelemy II, *fils* Barthelemy I 96, 106, 122, 128, 134, 143, 151, 160, 171
Barthelemy *fils* Louis I, 79, 82, 88, 90, 98, 107, 123, 127, 134, 145, 149, 159, 171, 176
Barthelemy, *fils* Louis, wife of 107
Dominique "Coco" 111, 134, 160, 171
Emanuel "Noel," *fils* Barthelemy I 106, 136, 151, 158, 171, 177
Étienne, *fils* Barthelemy I 106, 136
Étienne, *fils* Jacques 105, 161, 171
Felicité 107
Isabelle 107
Jacques (var. Jacob), *dit* St. Denis 48–49, 57, 67, 81, 86, 91
Jacques Dominique 95, 121, 128
Jean, *dit* St. Denis 19, 35, 38, 39
Jean Baptiste Barthelemy 95, 111, 124, 127, 134, 145, 149, 151, 160, 171, 175
Jean Baptiste Louis 107, 159, 171
Julien I 81, 87, 92, 95, 107, 121, 129, 134, 143, 151, 161, 171, 175, 181
Julien I, wife of 107
Julien II 107
Louis I, *dit* Blondin, *dit* St. Denis, *dit* Rat 20, 23, 29, 33, 37, 43, 48–49, 56–57, 72–73, 77, 107, 134, 141, 159, 164, 176
Louis I, wife of 107
Louis, *fils* Barthelemy 82, 88
Louis II, *fils* Louis 81, 90, 97, 107, 123, 127, 134, 145, 159, 171, 180
Louis II, wife of 107
Louis Barthelemy, *fils* Louis I, *dit* Rat 88, 90, 97, 123, 127, 145, 149, 171
Louis Barthelemy, *fils* Barthelemy I 110, 134, 160, 171, 177, 180
Louis Barthelemy, *fils* Barthelemy I, wife of 110
Marie, *fille* Louis I 107
Marie Françoise 106
Marie Jacob 111
Marie Louise, *fille* Barthelemy I 106
Marie Louise, *fille* Louis Barthelemy 110
Melanie 107
Pierre, *dit* St. Denis 16, 19, 21, 29, 31
Simeon 107, 130, 134, 141, 143, 146, 161, 164, 171, 176, 195
Raimond[?], André 114
Raison (Rasson), Jean, *dit* Joly Cöuer 25, 29, 30, 33, 37, 40
Rambin (Rambint)
  Adelaïde 101
  André I 50–51, 60–61
  André I, widow of 101, 156
  André, *fils* André Antoine 101
  André Antoine 66, 80, 101, 133, 156, 171, 178, 185
  André Antoine, wife of 101
  François 68, 80, 86, 91, 94, 101, 120, 128, 133, 142, 185
  François, widow of 173
  Jean Baptiste, *fils* François 101
  Jean Baptiste François, *fils* André I 156
  Jean Baptiste François, widow of 156
  Marie Louise Euphrasie 101
  Michel 87, 92, 95, 114, 121, 128, 133, 143, 153, 156, 171
  Ozite "Zité" 101
Rameau, Diegue 137
Ramis (Ramise, Ramiz), Pedro 125, 147, 155, 171, 179, 185
Rat. *See* Rachal *dit* Rat
Raymond, Zacharie 83, 87, 91
Rebeqiy, Lorenzo 66
Remont, François 74–75
Renaud
  Jean Baptiste, *dit* de Rosiers, (Derosiers) 23, 25, 26, 28, 31, 32, 36, 42
  Sieur 56–57
Renaudière. *See* de la Renaudière
Renoul, Louis 150
Rencontre. *See* Obreville *dit* Rencontre
Riche, Antoine 67

Ride, Jacques 74–75
Rigeur, Giles 109
Riortaur. *See* Dupin *dit* Riortaur
Ris (Jan Rich, Jean Ris, Jeanris)
  Geneviève 102
  Jean, *dit* L'Allemand 23, 24, 29, 33, 34, 37, 43, 48–49, 68
  Joseph 81, 83, 87, 92, 95, 102, 121, 128, 137, 142, 153, 156, 168
  Marie 102
  Rivière aux Cannes 85, 87, 95, 112, 121, 133, 140, 175, 176, 190
Robin
  Anne 112
  Manuel 112
  Michel 56–57, 112
  Michel, wife of 112
Robinson [?], François 153
Robleau (Roblo, Roblot)
  Pierre 153, 156, 171
  Widow 147, 156
Robzean. *See* Robinson
Rolland, Sieur 16
Rondin (Rondain)
  Julien 67, 79
  Louis 50–51, 60–61, 68
  Widow 50–51, 60–61
Rosseau (Rosau), Jacob 67
Roubelet (Roublet), Jean, *dit* La Rivière 23, 24, 29, 33, 36, 38, 39, 40, 42, 44
Roüence (Roüenle), Claude, *dit* Picard 23, 24, 29, 33, 37, 43
Rougot (Roujot), Jean Baptiste 70–71, 76
Rouquier
  Aimée 99
  François I (older brother) 87, 92, 99, 132, 147, 155, 171, 178, 185, 193, 194
  François I, wife of 99
  François II (younger brother) 155, 171, 178, 185
  Joseph Marie 99
  Tonton 99
Rousillon, Pierre 153
Rousseau
  Nicolas 104, 126
  Nicolas, wife of 104
  Pierre 98
Roy, Joseph 153, 157, 171

S

St. Aigne, Pierre 40, 43
St. André (Botien de St. André)
  André 131, 134, 143, 146, 151, 162, 164, 165, 176
  Jacques 151
St. Denis (Saint Denis), Antoine, rifleman 79, 82, 88
St. Denis. *See also* Juchereau de St. Denis; Rachal *dit* St. Denis
St. Dominique. *See* Monteche *dit* St. Dominique
St. Eustache. *See* Doucet *dit* St. Eustache
St. François, Sieur 16
St. Germain, François 151
St. Jean. *See* Magny *dit* St. Jean
St. Louis *dit* Blard, Sieur 17
St. Mailae. *See* Marmillon *dit* St. Mailae
St. Nicolas. *See* Bourdelle *dit* St. Nicolas
St. Pierre (Saint Pierre), Joseph 81, 87, 92
St. Pierre. *See also* Alorge *dit* St. Pierre; Davion *dit* St. Pierre; *and* DuBoïs *dit* St. Pierre
St. Prix. *See* Davion
Ste. Anne, Antoine 80, 86, 90
Ste. Anne. *See also* Ailhaud Ste. Anne
Saintalette, Mr. 50–51, 54–55
Saintes, Saintonge, France 69
Saintonge (Xaintonge), France 69
Salvant (Salvan)
  Catherine 118
  Marie 104
Samüel, Jean Baptiste, *dit* Lionnois (Lyonais) 23, 24, 29, 33, 35, 37, 43, 52–53, 58–59, 74–75, 81
San Antonio de Bexar, Texas 79, 122

Sanchez (Senche), Michel 81, 87
Sans Chagrin. *See* Perron *dit* Sans Chagrin
Sans Façon. *See* Malbert *dit* Sans Façon
Sans Quartier. *See* Dolet *and* Doré *dit* Sans Quartier
Sans Regret. *See* Langlois *dit* Sans Regret
Sansom. *See* Jeanson
Sanspeur. *See* Prudhomme *dit* Sanspeur
Saurelle. *See* Sorel
Sauterelle (Sautrelle). *See* Grillet *dit* Sauterelle
Sauvage, Joseph 81, 87
Saverulle (Savouelle). *See* Savoyelle
Savio, Jean Baptiste 171
Savoye, Capt. *See* Chavoye
Savoyelle (Saverulle, Savouelle, Savoye), Jean Baptiste 131, 143, 153
Saydeck. *See* Leconte *dit* Saydeck
Schnauday, Scnoday. *See* Snoddy
Segonvau, Saintonge, France 69
Sempry. *See* Davion *dit* St. Prix
sheep 18, 47, 49, 51, 53, 55, 57, 59, 61, 63
Sims (Chime), Richard 131, 133, 143, 151
Snoddy (Schnaudy, Schnoday, Snodey), William Sr. 148, 153, 163, 171, 173
Sorel (Saurelle, Sorelle)
  Dominique 101, 132, 153, 155, 170
  François, *dit* Marly 81, 91, 132
  Luc, *dit* Marly 95, 101, 121, 128, 132, 143, 153, 155, 169, 178
  Marie Géneviève 101, 169, 178
  Marie Jeanne 101
  Pierre I 50-51, 58-59, 68, 70-71, 76
  Pierre II, *dit* Marly 82, 88, 89, 101
Sorage, Nicolas 153
Stanislas, Rev. 48-49, 54-55, 69, 70-71
Stil, Thomas 153
Stimat, Jorge 87

Superville, Pierre 110, 135, 151, 160, 171
Surriray, Sieur 50-51

T
Taillefer, Lt. de 19
tallow 78
Taures. *See* Torres
Tautin. *See* Toutin
Tauzin, Joseph 148, 156, 171, 178, 182, 185
Teal (Thil, Till)
  Cristophe 153, 163, 185
  Edward 185
Ternier (Teurnie, Thernier)
  Étienne, widow of 157
  Pierre *dit* Grenoble 131, 143, 152, 157, 171, 179
Tessier (Tessie, Tessié)
  Jean, *dit* LaVigne 87
  Joseph, *dit* LaVigne 92, 95, 168?
  Pierre 138, 172
Tessier. *See also* LaVigne
Thernier. *See* Ternier
Thibault, Nicolas C. 74-75, 81
Thomas, René, *dit* La Croix 24, 26, 30, 31
Thomassino (Thomasine, Thomassine, Tomassino)
  Catherine 110
  Louis I 110, 135, 160, 172, 177, 180
  Louis I, wife of 110, 140
  Louis II 110
Thonin. *See* Tonin
Tobacco 47, 49, 51, 53, 78
Tomassino. *See* Thomassino
Tonin (Thonin), Jean Baptiste 153, 171
Tonnan. *See* Hugues *dit* Tonnan
Torres (Taures, Tores, Torre)
  Conception 113
  Dolores 113
  Gabriel 151, 176
  Joseph 113, 131, 133, 146, 162, 164, 171, 176
  Joseph, wife of 113
  Joseph Marie 113, 151

Marcello 113, 143
Marie l'Assumption (Mme. J. B. Valeri) 194
Toutin (Tautin, Totain, Totaine, Toten, Totin, Toutant)
  Charles, *dit* Villeneuve 17, 20
  François, *dit* Guinoche 82, 83, 88, 89, 97, 123, 126, 144, 146, 149, 159, 171, 177
  Louis I 68, 88, 90, 97, 151, 159, 171, 181
  Pierre 133
  Ramon 68
  Remy 79, 82, 88, 97, 119, 123, 126, 137, 144, 148, 149, 157, 171, 185
  Remy, wife/widow of 119, 178
  Sieur, 17
Trant. See de Trant.
Trichel (Trich, Trichele, Trichelle, Trichle, Trichll)
  Alexis 116
  Athanase 116
  church warden 54–55
  Étienne 103
  Fanchonette 103
  Françoise 103
  Henri I 50–51, 70–71, 76
  Henry II 116, 138, 145, 147, 149, 162, 171, 173, 179
  Jean Baptiste I 66, 72–73, 76
  Jean Baptiste I, widow of 103, 137, 157, 171, 178
  Jean Baptiste II 103, 137, 157, 171
  Joseph I 79, 88, 131, 138, 147, 153, 162, 173
  Joseph II 116
  Joseph, *fils* Manuel 172
  Manuel I 67, 70–71, 76, 116, 138, 141, 147, 162, 179
  Manuel I, wife/widow of 116, 147, 162, 171, 173
  Manuel II, *fils* Emanuel I 116
  Manuel III, *fils* Jean Baptiste I 103
  Marie Josephe "Josette" 103, 137, 157, 171

Thérèse 116
Sieur 194
Tristant, Pierre 58–59
trucks, game 78
Trudau (Trudeau), Pierre 60
Trudel, Francisco 66
Tuacanas, nation 68
Tulipe. See Rachal *dit* Tulipe
Tunica village 21
Turgeon (Tujon, Turjon), Pascal 81, 87, 92, 95, 117, 128, 142, 147
Turpeaux, Jacques, *dit* La France 23, 29, 33, 37, 43
Tynikouan, chief of Grand Caddo 85

V
Vacocû. See Vascocu
Valentine (Valantine)
  André 103, 143
  François 56–57
  Pierre 48–49, 72–73, 77
Valeri, Jean Baptiste 194
Varangue (Barranco, Varrangue)
  Jean, *dit* Castel, *dit* Marchand 83, 88, 89, 97, 111, 123, 126, 134, 145, 149, 160, 172, 175
  Jean, wife of 111, 181
  Jean Baptiste 111
  Widow (Cécile Christophe, widow Joseph Sarde Barranco *dit* Varangue) 56–57
Vardet. See Warden
Vasseur. See Le Vasseur
Vascocu (Vacocû, Vascocu, Vascocue, Vast-cocu, Vastcocu, Vastcoque)
  André 82, 88, 90, 97, 114, 124, 127, 137, 149, 156, 172
  André, wife of 114
  Antoine I 39, 43, 52–53, 60–61, 133, 137, 143, 156, 172
  Antoine II 82–83, 87, 92, 95, 114, 121, 128, 153, 157, 185
  Eulalie 114
  François 114, 130, 137, 143, 153, 157, 172
  Louis 98, 124, 127, 145, 149, 156, 172

Verchaire (Vachere, Verchair, Vercher, Verchere, Verchêre)
  Adelaïde 110
  Jacques 110, 147,
  Jean Louis 110, 134, 137, 151, 160, 172
  Jean Pierre 110
  Joseph 110
  Louis 66, 81, 86, 91, 94, 110, 120, 128, 134, 142, 150, 160, 172, 180
  Louis, wife of 110
  Rosalie 110
Verchaire. *See also* Vercher
Verdalay (Verdelay), Jean André 100, 143, 153, 172
Verger (Berger, Verge, Vergé. Verjer)
  Celeste 105
  Étienne I 48–49, 60, 66, 82, 87, 89, 92, 97, 123, 126, 136, 144, 161, 172, 181, 193
  Étienne I, wife of 105
  Étienne II 105
  Joseph I 17
  Joseph II. 48–49, 60, 68
  Louis 66, 70
Verger. *See also* Vercher
Versailles, Jean 96
Versailles. *See also* Chaler *dit* Versailles
Vigé (Viger). *See* Durand *dit* Vigé
Villard (Vilar), Jean Pierre 67, 70–71, 76

Ville Franche. *See* Le Duc *dit* Ville Franche
Villedeque. *See* Perot
Villemont. *See* de Villemont
Villeneuve. *See* Toutin *dit* Villeneuve
Vincent (Vincent, Vinsant), Michel 138, 141, 148, 153, 163, 172
Vivier, Honoré 67

W
Wallace (Wales, Wallis),
  Mr. 118
  "the son" 131
Warden (Vardet, Warder, Wardet)
  William 68, 104, 137, 141, 158
  William, wife/widow of 104, 158
Werdlay, André 130

X
Xaintes (Saintes), France 60
Xaintonge (Saintonge), France 69

Y
Yamoh, chief of Natchitoches tribe 84
Yatasse (Yatazees), nation 62, 84
Young, James "Jim" (Gimes Ingles, Gime Juene, Le Jeune) 87, 93, 95, 128, 139, 141, 143, 185
Ysquierdo. *See* Izquierdo

Z
Zarichi, Pierre Michel 105, 135

www.ingramcontent.com/pod-product-compliance
Lightning Source LLC
Chambersburg PA
CBHW070250230426
43664CB00014B/2480